STATE FAILURE AND VIOLENT ORDER

Islamist Extremism and Power Politics in Afghanistan

STATE FAILURE AND VIOLENT ORDER

Islamist Extremism and Power Politics in Afghanistan

Timor Shah Bushar

PENTAGON PRESS LLP

First published in 2026 by
PENTAGON PRESS LLP
206, Peacock Lane, Shahpur Jat
New Delhi-110049, India
Contact: 011-26490600

Typeset in AGaramond, 11.5 Point
Printed at
PRINTS 24X7, Quiinkit Infotech Pvt. Ltd., Gurugram

ISBN 978-81-997728-3-0

www.pentagonpress.in

CONTENTS

PREFACE

Afghanistan remains one of the most consequential theatres in contemporary international politics. Far from being a peripheral conflict zone, it has evolved into a strategic nexus where Islamist extremism, regional rivalries, and global power competition intersect with profound implications for international security. This book examines Afghanistan not merely as a site of ideological militancy but as a geopolitical arena shaped by state and non-state actors pursuing strategic advantage.

A central argument of this book is that the failure of state-building in Afghanistan was not accidental but structurally produced. Efforts to construct a stable political order after 2001 were undermined by the instrumentalization of Afghanistan's institutions by external powers, the exclusionary nature of elite politics, and the persistent entanglement of Islamist extremism with regional and global strategic agendas. Militant groups were alternately confronted, tolerated, or leveraged by competing actors, while regional and global powers pursued short-term security and geopolitical objectives at the expense of institutional legitimacy and political sovereignty. As a result, Afghanistan's state-building project remained externally dependent, internally fragmented, and vulnerable to collapse, culminating in the reassertion of extremist forces and the breakdown of republican governance.

The resurgence of Islamist extremist groups following the withdrawal of Western forces has altered the regional balance of power and reintroduced Afghanistan as a focal point of contestation among neighbouring states and global powers alike. Pakistan, China, Russia, Iran, and the Central Asian republics now engage Afghanistan through competing security, economic, and ideological lenses. At the same time, global actors recalibrate their strategies in response to shifting realities on the ground.

This study adopts a policy-centric approach, analysing extremist networks alongside state strategies, regional security dilemmas, and the broader architecture of global power politics. It seeks to move beyond binary narratives of terrorism and counter-terrorism, instead situating Islamist extremism within the structural dynamics of regional competition and international order.

Designed for policymakers, scholars, defence professionals, and strategic analysts, this book aims to inform decision-making by offering grounded assessments, historical context, and forward-looking insights. Understanding Afghanistan today is essential not only for regional stability but for anticipating future challenges to global security in an increasingly multipolar world.

December 2025

Timor Shah Bushar
Goa University
Goa, India

ACKNOWLEDGEMENTS

This book is the culmination of sustained research, reflection, and engagement with the evolving strategic dynamics of Afghanistan and its broader regional and global implications. I am deeply indebted to the scholars, analysts, and practitioners whose work in international relations, security studies, and political Islam has informed and shaped the analytical framework of this study.

I wish to acknowledge the invaluable insights drawn from academic literature, policy papers, official reports, and archival sources, which provided both historical depth and a contemporary perspective. My sincere appreciation goes to colleagues and peers who offered constructive feedback at various stages of the manuscript, helping refine arguments and enhance analytical clarity.

I am grateful to the publisher and editorial team for their professionalism, patience, and commitment to academic excellence, and for guiding this work from conception to publication. Their support ensured that the manuscript met the highest scholarly standards.

I also acknowledge the institutions, libraries, and research centres whose resources significantly facilitated this study. Finally, I extend my heartfelt gratitude to Dr. Bibhu Prasad Routray, the late Prof. Aparajita Gangopadhyay, Prof. Dattesh D. Parulekar, Prof. Rahul Tripathi, and Prof. Ganesha Somayaji for their invaluable guidance and scholarly support. I am deeply grateful to my late father, my mother, my elder brother Abdul Wakeel Walizada, and my wife, Ms. Anjila Bushar, for their constant encouragement, patience, and understanding throughout this demanding intellectual journey.

ABBREVIATIONS

A.D.	Anno Domini, Iin the year of our Lord
A.H.	Anno Hegirae, In the year of Hijra
ANSC	Afghanistan National Security Council
BICC	Bonn International Centre for Conversion
BRI	Belt and Road Initiative
CASA 1000	Central Asia-South Asia Power Project (Kyrgyzstan and Tajikistan to Afghanistan and Pakistan)
CE	Common Era
CIA	Central Intelligence Agency
DRA	Democratic Republic of Afghanistan
FBI	Federal Bureau of Investigation
GME	Greater Middle East
HPC	High Peace Council
HQN	Haqqani Network
ISAF	International Security Assistance Forces
ISI	Inter-Services Intelligence
ISIS	Islamic State of Iraq and Syria
ISKP	Islamic State of Khorasan Province
MAK	Maktab al-Khadamat
MOAB	Mother of All Bombs
NATO	North Atlantic Treaty Organization
OHCHR	Office of the High Commissioner for Human Rights

PDPA	People's Democratic Party of Afghanistan
PBUH	Peace Be Upon Him
SAARC	South Asian Association for Regional Cooperation
SCO	Shanghai Cooperation Organization
SMT	Social Movements Theory
TAPI	Turkmenistan-Afghanistan-Pakistan-India Pipeline
UN	United Nations
UNAMA	United Nations Assistance Mission in Afghanistan
USSR	Union of Soviet Socialist Republics

LIST OF FIGURES, MAPS AND TABLES

Chapter 1

Afghanistan, Islam and Political Islam: A Critical Internal Overview

1.1 INTRODUCTION

This Chapter will deal with Afghanistan, Islam, and political Islam. In fact, it seeks to explore what is Islam as a religion and political Islam as an approach and how the practice of both affects Afghanistan. This chapter has three parts. The first part deals with Islam and political Islam, the second part explains the roots of Islamists extremism in Afghanistan. I will try to trace the beginning of Islamic extremism in Afghanistan and how it evolved over time and finally, part three answers the question of how different political regimes had dealt with Islamic extremism?

1.2 ISLAM

The review and discussion about the principles and sub-principles, rules, and history of Islam are not in the scope of this chapter. But it tries very briefly to discuss what concerns *Islam* as a religion and *political Islam* as an approach. Islam, like many other religions, has various jurisprudential and theological sects within it, which I will not discuss here. Rather, I am trying to clarify the true Islam up to what is being introduced today by various groups.

Islam arose in the seventh century in the form in which we recognise it today is a relatively young religion, which originated in Mecca in the Arabian Peninsula through Prophet Muhammad (b. 570 CE) Peace be Upon Him (PBUH),[1] Muslims believe that Islam is a universal religion. They believe it started with the first human and continued through time under various names, the constant element being the message that God is one (oneness). (Hussain & Alami 2005: 1)

Muslims believe that Islam is a religion for all people from whatever race or background they might be. That is why Islamic civilization is based on a unity which stands completely against any racial or ethnic discrimination. Such major racial and ethnic groups as the Arabs, Persians, Turks, Africans, Indians, Chinese and Malays in addition to numerous smaller units embraced Islam and contributed to the building of Islamic civilization. Moreover, Islam was not opposed to learning from earlier civilizations and incorporating their science, learning, and culture into its own world view as long as they did not clashed with the principles of Islam. Each ethnic and racial group which embraced Islam made its contribution to the one Islamic civilization to which everyone belonged. The sense of brotherhood and sisterhood was so heavily emphasized that it overcame all local attachments to a particular tribe, race, or language—all of which became subservient to the universal brotherhood and sisterhood of Islam. (Haghnavaz 2013: 213)

The word 'Islam' comes from the Arabic and means 'submission' or 'surrender' of one's will to the only true God, known in Arabic as 'Allah'. One who submits his will to God is termed in Arabic as a 'Muslim'. All the Prophets or Messengers mentioned in the *Taurat* (Torah) and the *Injil* (Bible) are recognized and distinguished in Islam; in fact, Islam is a culmination of the monotheistic religions that came before it. There are many similarities between Islamic practices and the moral practices of other major religions before Islam at the time of Prophet Muhammad. (Salleh 2015) This word comes from the same root as the Arabic word 'salaam', which means 'peace'. As such, the religion of Islam teaches that in order to achieve true peace of mind and purity of heart, one must submit to Allah and live according to his divinely revealed Law. The most important truth that Allah revealed to mankind is that there is nothing divine or worthy of being worshipped except for Almighty Allah; thus all human beings should submit to Him. (Haghnavaz 2013: 213).

Prophet Muhammad was selected as a prophet at the age of 40 in AD 610 while he was worshipping in the cave of Hira,[2] and the first revelation from Almighty Allah was revealed to him by Gabriel. Most Islamic scholars agree that the first verse of the Qur'an that was revealed to the Prophet of Islam was *Iqra,* recitation, which means to read or recite unlike most Islamic groups that are strongly opposed to reading and studying. Due to the political and social conditions of Mecca, Prophet Muhammad secretly invited people for three years, after which he publicly and openly invited the people of Mecca and other Arab tribes to Islam for another ten years. According to narrations of history, the Prophet of Islam and the Muslims in Mecca did not have a good and appropriate political and social situation and always faced the opposition of the Quraysh elders and other ruling Arab tribes in Mecca and its environs. The political, social, cultural and economic situation of Mecca was complex and was based on primitive principles that could not be described in the available historical sources.

At the time of the rise of Islam, political power in Mecca was divided between several Arab tribes, most of whom had long-standing animosities. Mecca was also the centre of trade and economy of the Arabian Peninsula at the time, when different people from all over Mecca came and traded in different seasons. Culturally, Mecca was the gathering place of the Arabs during Hajj, when people from different parts of the peninsula gathered at a certain season and everyone worshipped according to their religion.

1.3 QU'RAN REVELATION

The Qur'an was revealed to the Prophet of Islam on two different times and at two different places. First, in Mecca in the first thirteen years of prophecy and second, in Medina in the second ten years of prophecy. The verses he received from Allah during the thirteen years in Mecca were mostly about the call to monotheism, and in some cases were about the biographies of past nations. According to most Islamic historians, the Arabian Peninsula was in a state of ideological decline at the time, and most pre-Islamic religions were repeatedly distorted. According to these historians, all humanity, in general and the inhabitants of Mecca and the Arabian Peninsula in particular needed the unity of religious beliefs. Hence, the greater focus of Islam and the Prophet in the early days was on the unity of belief, which was a call to monotheism and the worship of one God (Allah). This approach did not suit the temperament of most Arab tribes, and they considered this invitation a heresy and stood up to oppose it. They narrowed the space for the Prophet of Islam and other Muslims in Mecca and persecuted them. Therefore, the Prophet of Islam allowed the migration of Muslims from Mecca to the city of Medina; he too migrated.

The emigration of the Prophet of Islam and the Muslims to the city of Medina is a turning point in the history of Islam, and the Muslims were politically, socially, and economically in a much better position than they were in Mecca. In fact, the emigration of the Prophet of Islam to Medina meant the creation of the first Islamic state and, on the other hand, the verses revealed by Allah to the Prophet of Islam by Gabriel in Medina are all verses of the rulings that are the source of all Islamic law. The Muslims were able to take advantage of successive victories and the spread of Islam. Prophet Mohammad (PBUH) preached and spread Islam in Medina for another ten years; he received the last message from Allah that "*This day have I perfected your religion for you, completed My favour upon you, and have chosen for you Islam as your religion*". (Qur'an 5:3) I am sure most analysts and scholars on Islamic issues agree with me that the start of the problems within Islam was the demise of the Prophet. After that, discord among Muslims emerged in the three parts—politically, socially, and ideologically—and they are issues that are a matter of discussion.

The first political and social problem was the issue of the successor of the Prophet of Islam, a dispute arose among the Muslims over who could be a good successor. Eventually everyone agreed on Abu Bakr al-Siddiq[3] as the caliph of Islam. Political disputes over who can be a good representative of Islam have been going on for centuries and will continue to do so, of which the current rivalry between Iran and Saudi Arabia is a good example. In the social and cultural dimensions, different groups were formed with different beliefs, which faced strong reaction from the Muslim Caliph, Abu Bakr Siddiq. These problems continued until the fourth caliph of the Muslims, Imam Ali. As I mentioned at the beginning, a detailed discussion about the events of early Islam is not within the scope of this chapter, but I want to explore how Islamic extremism originated today, how modern Islamic extremism has gone through history, which is more the focus of this chapter with issues of jurisprudential and beliefs and rules.

According to most scholars, the periods of jurisprudence can be divided into two important periods: 1. The period of legislation or issuance of rulings; and 2. The period of extraction and inference of rulings. Twenty-three years of the life of the Prophet of Islam have been a period of legislation. During this period, Muslims used to go to the Prophet on any religious issue, and if the Prophet had received a verse from the Qur'an in that regard, he would read it out to them in answering their questions. If no verse had been received, he would follow his own judgement (His speech, actions, and narration) and solve the problem. The period of the Companions[4] begins with the death of the Prophet of Islam and ends in the first Islamic century. At that time, Muslims learnt the rules of jurisprudence and religious teachings from a number of prominent companions of the Prophet of Islam such as Imam Ali, Umar ibn al-Khattab, Mu'adh ibn Jabal, Zayd ibn Thabit, Abdullah ibn Mas'ud, Abu Musa al-Ash'ari, Abdullah ibn Abbas and many others who had learnt them from the Prophet.

After the time of the Companions, seven famous sub-companions[5] took over the jurisprudential leadership of the Muslims. They lived in Medina. In addition to these seven sub-companions, a few more of the jurisprudent also issued *fatwas* in cities in Islamic lands such as Mecca, Yemen, Syria, Egypt, Kufa, and Basra. The Sunnis initially followed these seven before Imam Abu Hanifa,[6] and later on the Abu Hanifa sect of jurisprudence (Hanafi), the Malik Ibn Anas (b. 179 AH) sect of jurisprudence (Maliki), the Muhammad ibn Idris Shafi'i (b. 204 AH) sect of jurisprudence (Shafi'i) and the Ahmad ibn Hanbal (b. 241 AH) of the Maliki sect of jurisprudence became the authorities of the Sunnis.

1.4 Sources of Islamic Law

Hence, I think it is necessary to mention the sources of inference of Islamic jurisprudential rules among the Sunni jurisprudential sects. Four important sources among most Sunni schools of jurisprudence are sources of inference of Islamic rules, including the Qur'an and Sunnah that all schools agree on as the main sources. The other two sources, which are called sub-sources, are consensus and analogy, to which, except for the Hanbali sect, all the other sects accepted them. A total of four sources (Quran, Sunnah, consensus, and analogy) are the sources of inference of Islamic jurisprudential rules among the Sunnis.

Most scholars of Islamic sciences divide the Sunni jurisprudential schools into two major schools:

1.4.1 The Textualist School

In its interpretations and inferences of jurisprudential rulings, it paid more attention to the appearance of the texts of the Qur'an and hadiths, and their rulings were based on them. This jurisprudential method originated from Hejaz (Medina) and jurists such as Malik ibn Anas, Muhammad Idris Shafi'i, Sufyan al-Thawri, and Imam Ahmad ibn Hanbal adhered to this jurisprudential method. At the same time, some scholars consider this school to be anti-rational. In my opinion, giving generality to all followers of the textual school is not an academic and fair judgment. It is true that a number of followers of this school, such as Imam Ahmad ibn Hanbal, were in conflict with wisdom and reason regarding the rules of Islamic jurisprudence, but extending it to people like Imam Shafi'i is not fair.

1.4.2 Rationalist School

This school paid attention to wisdom, opinion, and analogy in deriving religious rules. The most prominent member of this school is Imam Abu Hanifa whose origin was in Iraq. Imam Abu Hanifa, in addition to the main Islamic sources (Qur'an and Sunnah), used secondary sources such as consensus, analogy, and merit in deriving Islamic rules.

The Iraqi school was formed in a land whose people had a long history of civilization and urbanization, and urban and cultural life existed before the conquest of Iraq by Arab Muslims. Therefore, the early Islamic Shari'a rules did not meet the needs of these civilized societies, and they had to resort to other means in accordance with the Qur'an and Sunnah, such as consensus and analogy, to meet the jurisprudential needs of Muslims. But the issues raised in Medina were few because jurisprudential issues and problems are a function of civilization and Medina was very simple and far from the complexities of civilization.

Also, before entering into the main topics of the present study, which are the topics of political Islam, radical Islam, and Islamic fundamentalism, I find it necessary to examine the issue from another dimension; the relationship between reason and faith in the realm of religion in order to identify correctly contemporary Islamist extremism.

Considering that, on one hand, the issue of reason and faith is one of the most fundamental topics in the theology and philosophy of religion on the other, it links it to issues such as 'science and religion', 'reason and revelation', 'textualism and rationalism' This leads us to answer whether we can get the side of reason (wisdom) or faith when confronted with religious propositions? And what is the validity of each? What is the definition of faith and reason? Why should we get the side of faith or reason (wisdom) in religious matters? These questions require comprehensive research and philosophical work that cannot be addressed in the scope of this work, but for the sake of clarity on the topic, I will focus on some of them.

Most religions address their followers and ask them to worship; the followers love worshipping more than explanation and intellection. It seems that the path of religion is not walkable without achieving a level of submission. By paying close attention to religious propositions, they can be divided into propositions that agree with wisdom and disagree with reason. The second type (propositions that do not agree with reason) can be divided into irrational propositions and anti-rational propositions. The existence of these last two types of religious propositions has led the followers of the religions to face the question by relying on reason (wisdom) to reject irrational and anti-rational propositions; in other words, to rationalize the religious propositions or vice versa. In fact, here is the question of choosing between reason (wisdom) and faith, which, if we substitute R for reason and F for faith, the logical expression of the proposition could be: R vs. F. In contrast, some believed in R and chose F, and some believed in violation of F and chose R.

Some scholars identified six different roles for reason in relation to religion of which two of them are at odds.

1. Understanding the meaning of religious propositions
2. Inference of religious propositions from texts (main source)
3. Arrangement of propositions
4. Teaching of religious propositions
5. Proof of religious propositions
6. Defending religious propositions

The position of understanding the meaning, inferring, and teaching the propositions of religion is agreed upon by proponents and opponents of reason in religion. The third work is not so controversial, because even the adherents of faith and worship and the textualists do not accept an incoherent set of religious propositions. Internal coherence between a set of religious propositions is the least condition for its acceptance in the system. Of course, adherents of faith and worship acknowledge the existence of contradictions in their set of beliefs, but in their view, the contradiction of religious beliefs with non-religious beliefs does not harm faith.

In the fifth and sixth roles, that is, proving and defending religious propositions, the difference is whether religious propositions should be proved and defended rationally with the help of reason (wisdom). In other words, should religious propositions be rationalized to determine their validity? And how can we choose one among different religious belief systems? The difference is upon the role of faith and reason in this position. In this situation, several cases are conceivable. First, to choose reason and reject faith. Second, to become a believer and reject reason altogether. Third, to accept both reason and faith, which can be conceived in two ways: first, to base faith on reason and to give preference to reason and finally to base faith on reason, and give preference and honour over faith.

All these situations are conceivable, but in the real world, among the various theories and solutions offered, several theories are more important. They are: 1. Extreme faith; 2. Moderate faith; 3. Maximum rationalism; and 4. Critical or moderate rationalism.

1.4.3 Extreme Faith

This theory mocks those who dig into religious truth objectively and with the help of evidence state that without risk, there is no faith. It is precisely the contradiction between the infinite passion of the individual soul and objective uncertainty. According to this theory, if one is able to know God objectively, one no longer has faith; but precisely because he is unable to do so, he must believe. Scholars of this theory believe that religion is not the realm of reason, but is the realm of love, the realm of the game of faith, and the realm of risk. They believe that if we could conclusively prove the existence of God, it would be impossible to believe because then we have knowledge, not faith.

1.4.4 Moderate Faith

Scholars of this theory believe that not all religious beliefs and teachings can be rationally proven, and faith is a category of worship that does not fall in the hands of reason. They believe that one should not only adhere to sensory and empirical knowledge, but should recognize all areas of human existence, that other dimensions of human existence have laws other than scientific and experimental laws, and should not apply the rules and regulations of one game to another.

When a person enters the realm of religion, he should not expect to apply the rules of the game of science to it but should obtain instruction in the field of religion and practice religion according to it. Criticism of religious practices and beliefs also cannot be done from the base of the game of science or philosophy. Hence, religion and faith are irrational, the only criticism that can be levelled against the actions and opinions of religious people is internal criticism, not external. The irrationality of religion and its language does not mean that they are opposed to reason, but it does mean that the realm of religious issues is subjectively beyond rational evaluation. People have the right to accept or reject religion but it cannot make it the subject of scientific and philosophical evaluation. Religion can be decided, but no logical or empirical argument can be made.

1.4.5 Maximum Rationalism

According to this view, in order for the system of religious beliefs to be true and rationally acceptable, it must be possible to prove it, and only a theorem can be accepted rationally that could be proved true for all sages at all times and places. Therefore, every accepted theorem is either so improvised that all rational people accept it, or it must be proved to all rationally with the help of the preliminaries of the obvious truth and the rules of inference, which are also the obvious truth.

1.4.6 Moderate Rationalism

This theory believes that the system of religious beliefs can and should be evaluated based on rational criteria. However, it is not possible to prove them conclusively and one cannot expect that these beliefs will be proven so conclusively and firmly that everyone will be convinced against them. Adherents of this theory have a meek and limited vision towards reason. They believe that we should not claim rational certainty for what is really available to us. Moderate rationalism is based on conventional rationality or commonsense.

Therefore, most Islamic extremist groups such as the Taliban, al-Qaeda, and ISIS have an extremist faith approach to Islamic religious issues. Their approach to the issue of reason in religious matters is hostile. In the view of these extremist Islamic groups, the realm of religion and religious practice is not the realm of reason. According to them, religion is divine and human intellect is not able to understand most of the religious issues that are divine. They believe that behind every divine commandment lies wisdom that the human intellect is incapable of understanding. In addition, these extremist groups are mostly followers of the schools of jurisprudence in Medina and have a textual approach to religious rulings and religious practice.

1.5 Political Islam

Islamism is a sign that has been used, among other signs and symbols, for the Islamic political thought movement. Terms such as Islamic fundamentalism, Islamic awakening, Islamic radicalism, and political Islam, and other topics are among the words that have many uses. Scholars of Islamic movements have used different interpretations to express this phenomenon. In general, it seems that among the existing words, signs such as *Islamism* and *Political Islam*[7] are more appropriate words to describe and name the macro of contemporary Islamic movements.

Political Islam is a new term and belongs to the modern world. Before the domination of Western modernism and the doctrine of secularism, such a term had not been used. As Robbert A.F.L. Woltering believes, generally Islamism is defined more or less as an ideology of protest. Its discourse is usually rigid and simplistic, and rarely worked out beyond the level of slogan chanting. (Woltering 2002: 1135) They claim 'authenticity' of conduct on all accounts: social, economic, religious and political. This authenticity is juxtaposed with elements which have entered society from abroad and retain a 'foreign' identity. Most of these elements are, as a product of past colonisation and current world domination, originally Western elements. (Woltering 2002: 1135)

Some other scholars have an extremist belief that Islamism (that is, radical or militant Islam) is an ideology based on the view that Allah requires that the entire world become Muslim and be governed by Muslim law. This view says that Islam commands Muslims to deny the legitimacy of 'infidel' governments and be permanently at war- in some way against all non- Muslim governments.

The USA and all democracies are permanent enemies, regardless of what they do. (Singer 2018: 9)

In the Islamic world, according to the traditional view, Islam was considered a comprehensive religion and included political issues, and therefore there is no need to redefine and restrict Islam to political constraints. With the West's all-out invasion of the Islamic world and the formation of Islamic resistance against it and the rejection of the teachings of Western modernism and the efforts of Muslim revivalists to revive Islamic civilization and return Islam to the realm of political life, Westerners do show it as abnormal and reactionary. (Behrozlak 2021) The use of the term 'political Islam' has also been the product of such an effort. From the point of view of Western modernism, religion was separate from politics, and as a result, any presence and interference of religion in the political arena were considered abnormal, negative, and reactionary while Muslims believe that religion is not separate from politics and politics is not considered apart from religion. And this is the conflict and contention point between the West and its teachings with Islam. Islam is in many ways the most political religion among the world's great religions. Islam's response to political challenges and its readiness to defend itself against theoretical political challenges reflect this fact. Although some elements of Christianity also have the potential to be politicized as the Jews created Zionism but Islam has had a leadership almost from the beginning, which was not just that of a religious leader but a leadership that formed the government, which was almost the first government in Saudi Arabia.

'Fundamentalism' is a vague and inaccurate word. The word has its roots in Western Christianity. American Evangelical Protestants first used the term voluntarily in the 1920s with the publication of pamphlets titled *Fundamentals* and in opposition to the principles of modernism considered a return to Christian principles that were considered strict and fanatical from the point of view of the modern Western world and they could have raised it. (Behrozlak 2021) The use of violence, anti-Western values and liberal thought, dogmatism, returnism, and authoritarianism are the characteristics of fundamentalism.

Because of the early application of fundamentalism by Evangelical Protestants in the USA, the modern Western world, in the face of the contemporary Islamic movement, also used these terms for Islamists regardless of the differences between evangelical Protestants and Muslims. In the first application of fundamentalism to the Islamic world, it encompasses all Islamists and calls for the whole Islamic movement to oppose fundamentalist Westernism. Some scholars believe that Islamism is particularly different from fundamentalism because it does not separate the realm of religion from the world (politics) but refuses to sacrifice values to achieve the goal. Islamism considers illegal the use of any political conspiracy to use completely anti-Islamic sources to gain power in the name of Islam. (Mostaqeemi & Ebrahimi 2010: 339)

Such an application of fundamentalism lies largely in the Western view of existing Islamists. The main conflict between this current and Western modernism is in its focus on religion and religious teachings. Accordingly, in the West, any movement that speaks of the return of religion to the political arena is considered fundamentalist. Woltering in his article titled 'The Roots of Islamist Popularity; has stated that, for all their diversity, what all Islamist groups have in common is the desire to 'Islamise' society: their desire is to change the very basics of the social fabric. It is the belief of Islamists that today there is no society in the world that lives according to the principles of Islam, and that this is a bad thing. So, they state their goal in religious terms: there should be more Islam in society. As regards the political aspect of their desire, all Islamists have in common the conviction that sooner or later the realm of politics will have to be altered fundamentally. (Woltering 2002: 1136)

Islamisation may start at the bottom, or it may be implemented from above, but it is clear that any Islamisation of society cannot be complete until the existing political system of the country in question is replaced with a usually undefined Islamic one. Ideally, such a replacement would result in an 'Islamic state'. Although this desired result is rarely satisfactorily defined, and the proposed road towards it varies with each separate Islamist group, the implementation of Shari'a is an almost constant factor in the advocated goal of Islamisation.

1.6 Afghanistan and Political Islam: Roots of Islamist Extremism

Afghanistan is a country in which about 99 per cent of its population are Muslims. Different sources indicate different percentages for the two large groups within Afghanistan: some state that 84 per cent are Sunnis and 15 per cent are Shiites (*Hawza News Agency* 2011); other sources say that 80 per cent are Sunnis and 19 per cent are Shiites, while some others state that 74 per cent are Sunnis and 25 per cent are Shiites. (*BBC* 2009) But Afghanistan's Shiites believe that they constitute about 30 per cent of Afghanistan's Muslim population. (Afghanistan Information Network 2020) However, due to lack of accurate, transparent and unbiased census in Afghanistan, precise statistics cannot give the exact breakup between the two communities. Religious compatibility and peaceful coexistence has been a long-term multi-religious attribute of Afghanistan society that is rooted in the religious teachings of the Afghanistan people.

Unfortunately, this convention has been around for more than half a century, no longer practised by the people of Afghanistan, and has undergone regional and global competition. Different countries have provided various narrations of Islam based on their interests and position at international levels and have used it as a tool of their foreign policy. One of the most important narratives of Islam in the 19th century is Islamist extremism with a Salafism (Wahhabism) approach, which affected both Islamic and non-Islamic states. Of course, it is noteworthy that in the rise, survival, and expansion of Wahhabism in Afghanistan and other countries in the region and around the world, the USA, Pakistan, Saudi Arabia and Qatar have played a major role; they have supported Islamist extremism strategically. The birthplace of Islamist extremism in the contemporary era is Afghanistan and its existence had coincided with the occupation of Afghanistan by the Soviet Union.

Islamic extremism has existed in Afghanistan for a long time. At that time, it had more political burden, and the rulers of Afghanistan from time to time resorted to religion to suppress their political rivals. Islamic extremism in Afghanistan has caused a deep rift between the two major Islamic sects in Afghanistan (Shia and Sunni), and this phenomenon has led to an early religious conflict between the Sunnis and the Shiites of Afghanistan, which was politically motivated. But at the same time, with the Soviet invasion of Afghanistan, religious conflicts took on a wider religious dimension and went beyond the two sects. Now, in Afghanistan, Islamic extremism, which has led to religious conflicts, has taken the form of a triangle with the Shiites of Afghanistan on one side, the followers of the indigenous Hanafi school on the other, and the Salafi extremists forming the third.

1.6.1 Afghanistan's Extremists

Extremism is one of the phenomena that has spread in Islamic countries. This phenomenon is not new and innovative and it has been affecting Islamic and non-Islamic states for decades. This phenomenon has also threatened international security, stability, and order. In recent decades, it has greatly influenced the interaction of the West with Islamic countries. The presence of the USA and its allies in Afghanistan has been to suppress religious extremism of the Islamic type. Russia's presence in Syria is also due to the suppression of ISIS and other Islamist extremist groups. Despite the pivot of extremism in the West's interaction with Islamic countries, however, religious extremism has not only weakened, but extremism has become an important indicator of Islamic societies. This phenomenon has affected the people of Afghanistan more than any other Islamic country. Afghanistan has been an important centre of activity for various extremist groups.

The issue of religious extremism in Afghanistan has been around for a long time and has had its ups and downs throughout history. A clear example of this was the extremist religious reaction to the Amani reforms in 1919-1929, in which a number of Afghanistani clerics rejected any reform of the Afghanistan institutional system and took up arms against it under the leadership of Amir Habibullah Kalkani, which led to the fall of the Amani government. Other external and internal factors also played a role in the fall of the Amani government, but the most important factor was the use of Islamist extremism, which was used as a tool for the fall. The trend of extremism has existed at all times since the fall of Amanullah Khan. Various political individuals and groups with Islamic suffixes were formed in Afghanistan; their main task was to spread religious extremism.

The Soviet Union's invasion of Afghanistan caused the process of religious extremism to grow significantly in the form of a well-written established ideology in Afghanistan, which led to the formation of extremist parties and movements and more than 15 political parties. Among these political parties, not all of them were extremists, but those parties and movements that were politically and economically dependent on Saudi Arabia, Pakistan and the USA at the time of the jihad for various reasons and were somehow supported by Saudi Arabia, slowly led to the spread of Islamist extremism in Afghanistan in the form of a codified ideology for years to come. There are al-Qaeda and sectarian groups, the Taliban, ISIS, Hizb ul-Tahrir, and hundreds of other anonymous and gray groups active in the growth and nucleation of Islamic extremism, all rooted in the 1980s during the Soviet invasion of Afghanistan.

1.6.2 The spread of Islamist Extremism in Afghanistan

The issue of the spread of Salafism can be considered one of the most important challenges of international security, especially in the last decade It has played a prominent role in destabilizing the regional and global space. Two major issues have played a role in reinforcing the violence of Salafi movements. The first goes back to the *takfiri* (excommunicator) worldview of these groups, which stems from the other anti-Semitic ideas of Imam Ahamad Ibn Hanbal, Ibn Taymiyyah and Mohammad Ibn Abdul Wahab Najdi and his followers. The second factor must also be sought in the accelerating and increasing mobility and dynamism of these movements, which themselves are nourished by claimed values such as jihad and anti-polytheism.

1.6.3 History of Islamist Extremism in Afghanistan

The acquaintance of the Afghanistan's people with Salafi-Wahhabi thought has a history of about one hundred years and dates back to AD 1912. Sheikh Mohammad Shaareh who has been moved from Medina to Ferghana[8] Valley and has invited people to Wahabism found supporters who later spread this ideology in the tribal areas of Badakhshan, Kunar, Khost, and Nuristan of Afghanistan, which due to its proximity to the Indian subcontinent were the site of disputes between the rulers of Afghanistan and Britain and brought a situation that created a power vacuum in the shadow of these conflicts.

The promotion of Salafi-Wahhabi ideology in these areas by supporters of Sheikh Shaareh was not only unsuccessful due to intra-tribal rivalry in these areas, but also intensified the rivalry between the pro and anti tribes.

In this way, the Afghanistan tribes in the mountainous regions that faced the benignity of the political power vacuum, became familiar with Salafi-Wahhabi thought in the form of guidance-propaganda but never reached a level where it was possible to could spread these thoughts and ideas to other parts of Afghanistan. The occupation of Afghanistan by the former Soviet Union paved the way for the influence of Salafi-Wahhabi thought in these areas and so those small tribes embraced Salafi-Wahhabi thought and implemented Islamic rules and values in accordance with the Wahhabi interpretation of Islam.

Thus, in the 1950s, only three tribes in three regions of Afghanistan were mentioned that had Salafi-Wahhabi tendencies. However, because these regions were mountainous and far from large cities, they had little impact on the current developments in Afghanistan. After the Soviet occupation of Afghanistan and the introduction of the Western-backed 'jihad' and the entry of Wahhabi-leaning Arab jihadist volunteers into the battlefield, these small tribes were absorbed by the dominant Salafi-Takfiri[9] movement and left no trace.

There is a different view among most of the Afghanistan people, who believe that the origins of Islamist extremist movements in Afghanistan is the product of the Islamic teachings of the Deoband School in the Indian subcontinent. This claim is based on the fact that in the past most Afghanistani religious scholars have a long historical connection with Deobandi schools in the Indian subcontinent. Before the partition of India and the emergence of Pakistan in 1947, most Afghanistani Sunni students went to Deobandi schools in India to continue their higher education. They learnt Islamic teachings from Deoband based on the Hanafi jurisprudence school. There are narrations that Shah Waliullah Dehlavi, the founder of the Deoband School at the time of Mohammad Ibn Abdul Wahab Najdi, was the founder of Wahhabism. they are believed to have met during the Hajj. Subsequently, Shah Waliullah Dehlavi was influenced by the thoughts of Ibn Abdul Wahab and he based the Islamic teachings of the Deoband School on the thoughts and ideas of Wahabism.

Deobandiyya of the Indian subcontinent and Wahhabism of the Arabian Peninsula are two important schools of thought and belief of the Sunnis whose tendency towards Salaf[10] and Ahl al-Hadith is the most important common point among them, with the fundamental difference that the definition of Wahhabism refers to the Salaf in the extreme while Deobandiyya accepted Salafism moderately. Deobandiyya also pays much attention to Sufism and rationalism unlike Wahabism. For this reason, much of their behaviour and beliefs have been criticized by Wahabism. Wahhabism has excommunicated Deobandiyya, just as Deobandiyya rejected the extremist interpretation of

Wahhabism from Islamic teachings and their stubbornness in apparently adhering to verses and hadiths and the oppressive behaviour of Wahhabis.

The differences between the two schools of thought intensified to the point that even Wahhabism in the current situation has called the claim of some Deobandis deceptive as there is no fundamental difference from Wahhabism and has, therefore, not accepted it. Many books and articles have been written by Wahhabism against Deobandiyya and several sites are working against them. In most of them, Deobandiyya has been mentioned as grave-worshipper and heretic and accordingly have been excommunicated.

Islamic extremism in Afghanistan culminated in the Soviet military invasion and later in the civil war in Afghanistan and the formation of a new government after the fall of the Taliban. This phenomenon increased in Afghanistan from 2001 to 2019. Based on the findings of the present study, it has become clear that extremism in Afghanistan exists both among the followers of the Sunnis and among the followers of the Shiites, in which case the Sunni scholars of Afghanistan are divided into two parts. The first part is the native and indigenous Hanafi scholars who are influenced by the thoughts and teachings of the Deobandi scholars of India and the second part is the scholars and those who are influenced by the extremist thoughts and ideas of the Arabs of Egypt and Saudi Arabia and the Deobandi of Pakistan during the Afghanistan jihad. The religious disputes between these two classes of Afghanistani Sunni scholars are mostly jurisprudential. Based on this, it can be generally said that a triangle has been formed on the issue of Islamic extremism in Afghanistan; on one side are Sunni extremist scholars from Afghanistan who are influenced by Arabs extremists and on the other two sides is a triangle of indigenous Hanafi scholars (Deobandiyya of India) and Shiites of Afghanistan. Based on the above issues, I strongly reject the role of the Deobandi School of India in religious conflicts in Afghanistan, because the indigenous Hanafi scholars of Deobandi India have never issued a fatwa on the excommunication and murder of other Muslims, neither in Afghanistan nor elsewhere.

It follows from the above that the role of the Deoband School in Islamic extremism in Afghanistan can be examined in two stages:

1. In the process of establishing the Deoband School in India, which in terms of time between 1867 to 1947;
2. In the stage of separation of Pakistan from India in terms of the time from 1947 to 2019 (Deobandi Pakistan).

In the first stage, the Indian Deoband School, for political and social reasons, and especially considering the situation of Muslims, not only in Afghanistan but even in India itself, have not paid any attention to issues that would cause a division among Muslims. This is because the leaders and decision-makers of the Indian Deoband School have believed that smoothing out jurisprudential and doctrinal disputes weakens Muslims in India and other Islamic countries and that the enemies of Islam use that weakness against Muslims. At this stage, more attention and investment were paid to the Deoband School itself, which strengthened its position in India and among Muslims. Those who were eager to acquire religious higher education and could not go to Al-Azhar in Egypt or Medina found a suitable alternative in India's Deoband School, from which most of the current Hanafi indigenous scholars in Afghanistan are directly or indirectly influenced. Of course, the current Hanafi indigenous scholars are opposed to the scholars influenced by the extremist ideas of Muhammad ibn Abd al-Wahab and other contemporary extremists.

The second stage is after the separation of India and Pakistan. In this stage, more than anything else, it is important to understand a fundamental issue that the Deoband School of India is completely different from the Deoband School of Pakistan. This difference includes the attitudes and approaches of both schools to the situation of the Muslims of the world, their scientific status, their way of working, and their claims This is because the Pakistan Deoband School fell into the hands of the governments of Pakistan and Saudi Arabia after partition. Following its weakening and financial situation, the school failed to maintain the independence that had been established at the Deoband School in India. The shift in the Deoband School of Pakistan has led to dire religious consequences in both Pakistan and Afghanistan.

Pakistan's Deobandi School is the representative of the 'official religion' in present-day Pakistan, and its followers are predominantly Sunni Muslims. The number of Deobandis in Pakistan has always been increasing, especially in the last two decades; this increase has been accelerated due to the spread of Islamic extremists in the region and large Saudi Arabian investments. The most prominent groups affiliated with the Deobandi School in Pakistan are the Jamiat Ulema-e-Islam, the Lashkar Tayyaba, and the Ahl al-Hadith. These three groups have the same beliefs, slogans, and external support. The only difference between them is that the Jamiat Ulema-e-Islam, led by Fazlur Rehman and Samiul Haq, has become the political scene in Pakistan, while the Lashkar Tayyaba and the Ahl al-Hadith are involved in military and cultural activities, respectively. The internal coordination of these three groups against their opponents has been very impressive. The Taliban movement in Afghanistan is closely linked to all three groups and has enjoyed the spiritual, material, and even human support of all of them over the years. Such links with the 'Jamiat Ulema-e-Islam,' due to cultural, linguistic, and racial factors as well as political experience, have been and are in practice more than the other two groups. Both Maulana Fazlur Rehman and Samiul Haq are of Pashtun descent and wield considerable influence in Baluchistan, the main home of Pakistani Pashtuns and the border provinces.

After Pakistan's independence, most of Afghanistan's Sunni scholars have shifted from India to Pakistan's north-western border state, and most of Afghanistan's southern and eastern states with schools along the Pakistani border and schools in north-western and south-western states. They have created a link with Pakistan's Baluchistan, and the cultural influence of Pakistani religious schools in Afghanistan has been palpable ever since. The works of the great Deobandi scholars of Pakistan have been translated from Arabic into Pashto and published in Afghanistan.

1.7 Factors in the Emergence of Islamic Extremism in Afghanistan

Given the historical experiences and scientific studies that have been done on extremism and how to fight it, it can be said that a set of political, social, cultural, historical, and economic factors in society work together in a network to collude and collaborate with each other to facilitate extremism. Extremists use religious ideologies and specific interpretations of Islamic texts and values as the greatest tool to create, promote, and institutionalize extremist thought by linking arbitrary religious readings to political, social, and cultural variables appropriate to the circumstances of societies. For example, the political life of countries like Pakistan lies in 'political Islam' and the export of special manifestations of political Islam to other countries. Political Islam has become the dominant ideology of Pakistan. Throughout Pakistan's history, religious institutions in the form of political parties and tendencies have used a variety of non-Islamic activities to achieve political goals and defend the country's identity borders. Unless this fundamental dilemma is addressed, extremist thought will be presented to the world on a larger scale and systematically in a politico-religious framework supported by governments. However in the case of Afghanistan, the causes of extremism can be examined in two dimensions—internal and external.

1.7.1 Internal Dimension

Some areas in Afghanistan, in terms of structure and social context, are such that they have the potential to become extremists. Usually, such areas are geographically remote areas of Afghanistan that have little or no knowledge of contemporary modern science. Whether this is natural or intentional is another matter. The inhabitants of these areas are mostly tribal and Bedouin; they behave according to the laws and customs of their tribes and do not believe in or follow the current laws of Afghanistan.

Second, Afghanistan is a multi-ethnic country where, according to unofficial statistics, more than twenty different ethnic groups live. But political power and resources in Afghanistan have never been evenly or equitably distributed among its ethnic groups. Historical and social deprivation of ethnic groups in socio-political structures and unfair distribution of wealth and material and cultural assets of a nation, lack of equal economic opportunities, discrimination and prejudice, ethnic, linguistic, religious, and ethnic supremacy and monopolization of political power by one ethnic group are the main factors and grounds for the maturation of extremist ideas and incentives.

For more than two hundred years, the Pashtun people have had a legacy of political power in Afghanistan, with the exception of two, and have never been willing to share it equally and fairly with other ethnic groups in Afghanistan. This does not mean that other ethnic groups are Islamic extremists, but that most Islamic extremists in Afghanistan are Pashtuns like the Taliban. Rather, it means that Pashtunism has given rise to Islamic extremism. Whenever the Pashtuns of Afghanistan have fallen short in politics and civil struggles, they have simultaneously resorted to Islamic extremism. For example, from 2001 to 2021, look at the political regime in Afghanistan, Pashtuns were in power (president) and during this period other ethnic groups increased their internal capacities, and very soon they have been able to gain Afghanistan's political power in civilian ways. But Ashraf Ghani Ahmadzai, despite the existence of an institution called the High Peace Council within the Afghanistan government and a lot of work done, concluded a shameful and secret deal and surrendered political power to the Taliban. Over 250,000 Afghanistan's armed forces were annihilated and government institutions and 21 years of achievements were destroyed.

Third, the curriculum of educational institutions and universities is a major factor in extremism. In the curriculum, topics are not presented scientifically and coherently; the lack of sequence and adaptation of religious concepts to the realities and needs of the new world in the curriculum of religious centres has clearly generated extremist thinking. This has been an invitation for the spread of radicalization in educational institutions and is considered a serious threat against the national security of and development of Afghanistan. Research by the Afghanistan Institute for Strategic Studies shows that there is extremist activity in Afghanistan universities and research centres. ISIS and Taliban flags have been raised many times in universities. (Zaman & Mohammadi 2024: 23)

Fourth, the roots and main causes of Islamist extremism in Afghanistan relate to poverty, injustice, and social grievances. These have been the main causes of growing opposition to the Afghanistan government and extremist activities, and if these factors are considered a fundamental solution, the number of extremists will fall to an extremely low level.

1.7.2 External Dimension

1.7.2.1 Regional and Global Power Rivalries

An important turning point in the mobilization and operational activism of Islamist extremist movements in Afghanistan was the Soviet Union's occupation of the country. Salafist volunteer entities, also referred to as *Afghan Arabs*, were recruited for military service all around the Middle East after the incident. For this reason, the services office (Maktab al-Khidamat, or MAK) was founded in Pakistan in 1984 with assistance from the USA, Pakistan, and Saudi Arabia.

The goal was to assemble Salafist volunteer armies globally and arm, train, and equip the Arab mujahedeen to fight the former Soviet Union.

The gathering of intelligence information and military and political backing from several Western powers, including the USA, Saudi Arabia, the United Arab Emirates, Pakistan, China, and Iran, as well as several sovereign actors was a significant factor in the movement of jihadist extremists. It resulted in the Islamic extremist groups receiving significant reinforcements. The Carter administration in the late 1970s and early 1980s began providing military and financial aid to the Afghan mujahideen to counter the Soviet invasion and military presence in Afghanistan. This aid, which was part of the US foreign policy to contain Soviet influence in the region, included supplying weapons, military training, and financial support. The program to support the mujahideen, conducted in collaboration with the CIA and other allied intelligence agencies, had a significant impact on weakening Soviet forces and ultimately led to their withdrawal from Afghanistan. (Brzezinski 1983; Gates 1996:146; Coll 2004)

In order to support volunteer extremists and deploy them in Afghanistan, the CIA also initiated one of the most extensive and costly programs in its history following the Soviet occupation. Osama bin Laden and other militant groups received financial backing, military equipment, and training from the US intelligence agency during the 'Hurricane' campaign. The average annual aid amount climbed from $ 20–30 million in 1979 to $ 630 million in 1987. (Prakash 2003: 5)

Arab volunteers from all over the globe were coordinated and sent to Afghanistan by the CIA and Saudi Arabia. For instance, several of the Egyptian Islamic jihad movement's leaders, including Ayman al-Zawahiri, who had been imprisoned following Anwar Sadat's murder, were released from Egyptian jails after US intervention so that they could face the Soviet army and join the Afghanistan jihad.

In any event, the MAK was able to train and equip thousands of fighters from many nations in order to defeat the Soviet Union in Afghanistan within 10 years with the help of the CIA, which was a direct ally of Pakistan, Saudi Arabia, and China. An efficient and cohesive network of jihadists had resulted in jihad in Afghanistan. In the process, it has created a culture of movement and mobility among radical Islamist organizations across the area.

Furthermore, China, a significant regional force and the Soviet Union's principal rival, took advantage of the situation and joined forces with the opposition. The Chinese government was concerned about two main issues: first, that the Soviet Union, which was present in Wakhan-Badakhshan in the Northern Province of Afghanistan, would support extreme Islamist minority and separatist groups in Xinjiang. Second, China stated that the USSR had long intended to invade Afghanistan militarily in order to get access to the Indian Ocean and sea routes as well as to occupy regions rich in oil. Consequently, China secretly supplied the Afghan resistance with military supplies through Pakistan. (Imran & Xiaochuan 2016: 143)

1.8 Political Regime Types of Afghanistan versus Islamic Extremism

In the last two centuries, Afghanistan has experienced different political regimes such as absolute monarchy, constitutional monarchy, republic, democratic republic, Islamic state, Islamic Emirate of Taliban and Islamic republic with Marxist teachings and methods, moderate and extremist Islam, and liberal democracy. The fact of the matter is that none of these regimes has created stability, prosperity, comfort, and security for the people of Afghanistan. If we examine the contemporary history of Afghanistan carefully, we will conclude that these regimes in Afghanistan have all failed. This does not mean that all these regimes are bad and have not had any good application worldwide, but it does mean that the way each of these political regimes operated in Afghanistan was wrong. I do not want to discuss the political regimes in Afghanistan here. I will discuss Afghanistan's political regimes in detail in later chapters. The subject I want to examine here is how these regimes interacted and dealt with Islamic extremism in the course of Afghanistan's contemporary history. Therefore, we need to evaluate each of these regimes independently.

In the history of Afghanistan, Islam has been the only good tool for achieving political power, wealth and suppressing the opposition. In the past, if the government and regime in Afghanistan were in financial trouble, they would use Islam as a pretext and expand the territory of Islam mobilizing their people under the guise of jihad and attack neighbouring countries. In some cases, the element of religion and religious beliefs may not be completely ignored in these attacks; nevertheless, religion and religious beliefs have always been used as tools.

Jawaharlal Nehru in his book '*Glimpses of World History*', mentions the attacks of Sultan Mahmud of Ghazni, Sultan Shahab al-Din Ghori, and Ahmad Shah Abdali. Nehru's account of these attacks is highly critical, but at the same time reveals a fact, which is the difference between Muslim behaviour and the true teachings of Islam. In other words, the behaviour of Muslims does not reflect the principle of religion; the religion of Islam is one thing, and the use of religion by its followers is another. "*While Islam brought an element of progress to India, the Muslim Afghans brought an element of barbarism. Many people mix up the two, but they should be distinguished.*" (Nehru 2004: 232) It remains a religious angle that some have tried to justify these campaigns from a religious perspective. The fact is that Islam invaded India, including Pakistan and Bangladesh today, not through war but through Islamic trade and mysticism, and later Mahmoud Ghaznavi's campaigns led to its spread. However, in the time of Ahmad Shah Abdali, the rule of the vast land of India was in the hands of the Muslims. Historians believe that these campaigns weakened the rule of the Muslim Mongols in India and paved the way for the conquest of India by British colonists. (Husseini 2019) War is not praiseworthy in any religion unless you are attacked. If war is sacred, it is for the defenders, not the invaders.

1.8.1 Independence of Afghanistan and the Reign of King Amanullah Khan (1919-1929)

Amanullah Khan became King of Afghanistan in 1919 after the assassination of his father, Amir Habibullah. In the first act, he called on the people to wage jihad against the British occupation under the guise of religion, declaring that British colonialism must end and Afghanistan must gain its independence as a country. Afghanistan gained independence in May 1919, and King Amanullah Khan was nicknamed Ghazi.[11] It is a good and praiseworthy action by the people of Afghanistan. Ghazi Aman Khan, after gaining independence, started a series of reforms in various sectors. Historians call this period the period of modernization of Afghanistan. During Amanullah Khan's term, the constitution of Afghanistan was formed, education was obligated for everyone, more funds were allocated to the Afghanistan education system, and large numbers of Afghanistani girls were sent abroad to study. In 1927, Amanullah Khan travelled to Turkey, Egypt, Iran, India, Italy, France, Germany, Britain, and Russia for six months to learn from the experience of other countries and practise it in Afghanistan to bring about reforms and modernization. However, as soon as he returned to Afghanistan, he was angry with the people. During his absence, the reactionaries who opposed him came forward. Conspiracies were hatched and rumours were spread against him. Apparently, a lot of money was spent on propaganda against Amanullah Khan, and no one knew where the money came from. It seemed that many mullahs and clerics had been paid large sums for this purpose, and they declared Amanullah Khan an 'infidel' and an enemy of religion throughout the country. Inappropriate photos of Queen Suraya in a European evening dress or a dress were printed in thousands of copies and distributed in the villages of Afghanistan to show people how she dressed inappropriately. (Nehru 2004: 783) There are some historical narrations that behind all this was British intelligence in order to disturb the rural people to revolt against the reign of Amanullah Khan.

According to some historians, the first uprising took place in the village of Shinwari in south eastern Afghanistan against King Aman Khan; the protestors wanted King Amanullah Khan to divorce his wife. (Akhaliq 2015) Subsequently, Habibullah Khan Kalkani from northern Afghanistan mobilized the people against Amanullah Khan. Each of the insurgents claimed that King Amanullah Khan, in the name of reforms and modernization, was weakening the religion of Islam and leading the people astray. Therefore, rebellion against such a king is legally legitimate. In 1929, Habibullah Kalkani became victorious and proclaimed himself King of Afghanistan.

Here I want to recall the main topic of this section once again. As noted above, Amanullah Khan called on the Afghanistan people, under the guise of religion to wage jihad against British colonialism, and succeeded in Afghanistan's independence and extending his life as a vassal. But at the same time, by this element of religion, he was ousted from power and lost his kingship. Those who sided with Amanullah Khan in the jihad against British colonialism turned against him. I state that whoever or whichever group in Afghanistan seizes political power, they have resorted to religion and used it as a weapon of victory. Of course, this is an objective fact of Afghanistan society, and what other factors besides the element of religion can play is a separate issue. I cannot generalize whether religion has such a state in other Islamic countries or not.

1.8.2 The end of the Monarchy and the Beginning of the Republic (1933-1973)

In 1973, Zahir Shah, the King of Afghanistan (1933-1973), was on an official visit out of Afghanistan when Daud Khan, prime minister who was also the king's cousin, seized power in a coup, ending Afghanistan's monarchy for ever and declaring Afghanistan a republic. Dawood Khan had communist ideas and came to power with the support of the Soviet and the People's Democratic Party of Afghanistan. During Daud Khan's presidency, the first seeds of the Islamic movement were formed at Kabul University, and there were frequent disputes between Islamist and communist-minded students at the student association of Kabul University. Slowly, the Islamic Movement infiltrated and strengthened among the university students and the people in the cities and villages, but they were not strong enough to overthrow Daoud Khan which led a communist-leaning republic. At that time, President Daud Khan ordered the arrest of the leaders of the Islamic Movement, as a result of which several of its leaders were arrested and some escaped. In 1978, Daoud Khan, the founder of the republican system in Afghanistan, was assassinated in a bloody coup, and the fully communist-leaning People's Democratic Party of Afghanistan came to power and declared the political system of Afghanistan on 30 April 1978 as the Government of the Democratic Republic of Afghanistan. (Mehrin 2012)

1.8.3 Democratic Republic of Afghanistan (1978-1992)

The Democratic Republic of Afghanistan (1978-1992), which had direct Soviet financial and military support, ruled Afghanistan for 14 years. Various persons, including Noor Mohammad Taraki, Hafizullah Amin, Babrak Karmal, and Najibullah from the People's Democratic Party of Afghanistan (PDPA), became the President of the Government of the Democratic Republic of Afghanistan. In general, they went in opposite directions from the beginning, and finally tried to impose socialist and Marxist doctrines on the people by force, and succeeded. The press, which was tightly controlled by the government, promised the people freedom from all forms of oppression, but in practice, in their daily lives, they were executed and sent to torture chambers, forcing the people to revolt. The party that sought to consolidate its position by seizing power through coups did not recognize the manifestations of the timing of the other political components of society and forced others to obey it. It was certain that it used violence and bloodshed. Available sources show that hundreds of political dissidents (Islamic and non-Islamic) and innocent people were killed every day. During communist rule, the Islamists were severely repressed, but at the same time, internal, regional, and global conditions shifted in the Islamists' favour. Accordingly, with the financial and military support of the USA, Saudi Arabia, and Pakistan, the Mujahideen established the Islamic government of Afghanistan.

1.8.4 Islamic State of the Mujaheddin (1992-1994)

The Mujaheddin seized political power in Afghanistan in 1992 and fought against the Soviet Union and the government of the People's Democratic Republic of Afghanistan, which had the financial and military support of the Soviet Union, and finally defeated the communist government. These 14 years of war and jihad are turning points in the emergence and spread of Islamic extremism in Afghanistan, which must be carefully examined. One thing must be clear here that 1992 is the year of the victory of the Afghanistan Mujahideen over the Soviet Union and its communist government in Afghanistan, not the year of the victory of Islamic extremism. Islamic extremism began its rise in Afghanistan and the world in 1978, and 2001, in the extremists' own words, was the year of the victory of Islamic extremism in the world, which carried out its terrorist attacks on the World Trade Centre in New York City. During the jihad against the Soviets, the Afghanistan Mujahideen created an environment for foreign extremists. But after the victory and defeat of the Soviet Union, because the Mujaheddin themselves got involved in civil wars with each other, they did not have the opportunity to interact and cooperate with foreign extremists such as Arabs and others.

During the Afghanistan jihad against the Soviet Union and its puppet government in Kabul in 1972-1998, three generations of Arabs entered Afghanistan to fight and support the Afghanistan Mujaheddin. The first generation entered Afghanistan with Abdullah Azzam, the second generation with Osama bin Laden and the third generation with Ayman al-Zawahiri. Between 1982 and 1992, some 35,000 Muslim extremists from 23 Islamic countries from the Middle East, North and East Africa, Central Asia, and the Far East proved their Islam and fought along with the Afghanistan Mujahideen against the Soviet Union. Another 10,000 foreign extremist Muslims flocked to Pakistan and joined hundreds of newly established schools in Pakistan and border areas funded by General Zia's military government. Eventually, more than 100,000 Islamic radicals, under the influence of jihad, came into direct contact with Pakistan and Afghanistan. (Rashid 2002:43) But Abdullah Anas, an Algerian Arab who joined the Afghanistan jihad with Abdullah Azzam, called the figures exaggerated. He, who for some time was in charge of directing volunteers at the Office of Services (Maktab al-Khidamat), says that even if exaggerated, from 1982 to 1988, the number of volunteers was less than 4,000 Arabs. (Anas 2016)

The Arabs who took part in the Afghanistan jihad can be divided into two groups:

1) In terms of class in Arab societies
2) In terms of ideology

In terms of social classification, most of the Arab youth who took part in the Afghanistan jihad belonged to the lower classes of Arab societies, the majority of whom were poor and more than 30 per cent of whom were imprisoned for criminal and political crimes. (Perez 2007: 2) It should be remembered that in the beginning only poor Arabs, students, taxi drivers, and primitive tribes from countries such as Egypt, Saudi Arabia, Algeria, Sudan, Iraq, Yemen, Palestine, Kuwait, Turkey, Jordan, Syria, Libya, Tunisia, Morocco, Lebanon, and Pakistan had come for the war. No Saudi princes and other Arab sheikhdoms were willing to accept the rigours of the Afghanistan mountains. (Rashid 2002:194) Simultaneously, with the invasion of Afghanistan by Soviet forces, regular religious uprisings threatened the Arab sheikhdoms, especially Saudi Arabia. These rebels called the rulers of their countries tyrannical, authoritarian, corrupt, and slaves of the West, and considered any revolt against them that would overthrow them necessary.

Ideologically, the opportunity to travel and join the Afghanistan jihad was facilitated for those most-extremist Arabs, who threatened the monarchical interests of the Arab world; Saudi Arabia, more than any other Arab country, played a key role in this. It reduced the cost of plane tickets for Saudi volunteers by 75 per cent. Many works and writings by most scholars clearly show that the Arabs and other extremists who took part in the Afghanistan jihad, and still are active throughout the world, are considered a threat to all humanity.

Of course, it is worth mentioning that the Arabs who took part in the jihad in Afghanistan were later called *Afghan Arabs.*

1.8.5 The Taliban Islamic Emirate (1994-2001)

Political developments after the Soviet withdrawal, the inability of jihadist leaders to establish an inclusive government, and the spread of divisions among various jihadist groups affected the emergence of the Taliban within Afghanistan society. In this turbulent situation and with the continuation of fierce clashes between Mujahideen groups in different cities and provinces, some students in Pakistani religious schools formed a group called 'Islamic Tehreek-e-Taliban' led by Mullah Mohammad Omar Mujahid in September 1994 with the aim of 'fighting evil and corruption and the establishment of an Islamic system based on Hanafi jurisprudence". They gained a foothold along the border of Spin Boldak in Kandahar province in Afghanistan in the south of the country and quickly expanded their influence.

The regime established by the Taliban in Afghanistan from 1996 to 2001 was recognized only by Pakistan, Saudi Arabia, and the United Arab Emirates. During this period, a Saudi billionaire, Osama bin Laden, organized some of the foreign fighters fighting the Soviets in Afghanistan in the 1980s into an 'international terrorist network' called al-Qaeda.

Bin Laden supported the Taliban while planning and directing al-Qaeda's international terrorist activities. Militants loyal to bin Laden fought alongside the Taliban and took part in attacks on civilians. In December 2000, the UN Security Council decided to punish the Taliban regime for using its controlled areas in Afghanistan to train international terrorists and harbouring al-Qaeda leader bin Laden. (UN Doc. 2000: SC/684) The Taliban Islamic Emirate was completely and utterly extremist. They banned work and closed schools for women and girls and were hostile to all kinds of modern tools. They have changed the education system of Afghanistan completely; they removed the experimental sciences and replaced them with religious subjects.

1.8.6 Islamic Republic of Afghanistan (2001-2021)

In 2001, the Taliban were defeated and a transitional government of the Mujahideen and democrats came to power. In January 2004, the new constitution of Afghanistan was approved by the Loya Jirga. Article 1 of the

Constitution of Afghanistan defines the political system of Afghanistan as follows: "Afghanistan shall be an Islamic Republic, independent, unitary and indivisible state." Article 4 of the Afghanistan Constitution also recognizes national sovereignty in Afghanistan as belonging to the nation, and the nation of Afghanistan consists of Pashtun, Tajik, Hazara, Uzbek, Turkman, Baluch, Pachaie, Nuristani, Aymaq, Arab, Qirghiz, Qizilbash, Gujur, Brahwui, and other tribes. (Afghanistan Constitution 2004, 1:4) Article 4 clearly states that Afghanistan is a multi-ethnic country and so far no transparent and unbiased official census has been conducted in Afghanistan to know which ethnic group is the majority. When Afghan and foreign writers claim that a certain ethnic group in Afghanistan is the majority, they are far from the truth and have ignored the principles and rules of academic writing. So far, no official institute has conducted a census in Afghanistan so that based on its results, we can state which ethnic group is the majority in Afghanistan. However, my point is that given the ethnic context in Afghanistan, the leadership of the post-Taliban government in Afghanistan had ethnically dealt with Islamic extremism and terrorism, neither ideologically nor in accordance with the principles of the Afghanistan Security Doctrine.

According to the 2004 constitution, Afghanistan's political system is a centralized presidential system. That is, the constitution gives unconditional authority to the President of the Republic of Afghanistan. Chapter three, Article 60 clearly states that "The President shall be the head of state of the Islamic Republic of Afghanistan, executing his authority in the executive, legislative and judiciary fields in accordance with the provisions of this Constitution." Although suppressing the Taliban and other Islamic extremist groups has been a priority of the post-Taliban government in Afghanistan, since 2007 former Afghanistan President Hamid Karzai has named the Taliban as brothers hundreds of times and sought to directly and indirectly support and strengthen them. Hamid Karzai's logic was that the majority of Taliban fighters are Pashtuns and that he also is a Pashtun from Kandahar. Thus, from 2007 to 2014, ethnicity has been dealt with the phenomenon of Islamic extremism in Afghanistan, and this caused the Taliban and other terrorist groups to come to life again and continue their crimes and killings.

Ashraf Ghani Ahmadzai said in an interview with one of the Afghanistani private TV channels on 11 November 2013: "98% of Bagram prisoners speak one language, and a few per cent of the night raids on the houses of speakers of one language". (Ahmadzai 2013) Analysts believe that Ashraf Ghani's indication that 98 per cent of prisoners speak one language, was Pashto. This was because the Taliban and other terrorist groups were/are active in the Pashtun areas of Afghanistan (south and southeast). Ashraf Ghani is also a Pashtun ethnic and became president in 2014 based on a political agreement with the interposition of the USA and the UN. Ashraf Ghani also dealt ethnically with the phenomenon of Islamic extremism. Dr. Ghani, as an anthropologist, instead of sociologically and problematically searching for scientific and national solutions with the assistance of contemporary knowledge and technology, is in the shadow of tribal thinking and racial supremacy in various forms that support Taliban terrorism. Instead of rooting out why the focus of violence is mainly in southern Afghanistan, wherever Pashtun live, there are Taliban and other terrorist groups equally active. (Amirzadeh 2013)

This the end of the second chapter. Chapter three will discuss the theoretical perspective and Afghanistan's geopolitics: interplay of strategic location and extra-regional influence. This chapter will have four parts. The first explains the theoretical framework for this research and has chosen constructivism as the most applicable theory for this research. The second part will explain the geopolitical location of Afghanistan and driven impulses. Part three will explain the strategic depth of regional actors in Afghanistan and finally, part four will examine challenges to state-building in Afghanistan.

1.9 CONCLUSION

In Islam, there are two major jurisprudential schools of thought: textualist and rationalist. Textualist schools of jurisprudence rely fully on the primary and fundamental sources of Islam, namely, the Quran and Sunnah, to derive and deduce religious rulings, rejecting any other form of interpretation or analysis in this process. From the perspective of these schools, religious texts should be used directly, without interpretation or independent reasoning (*ijtihad*).

On the other hand, rationalist schools take a more flexible approach to religious sources. In addition to the Quran and Sunnah, they also utilize secondary sources such as consensus (*ijma*), analogy (*qiyas*), and independent reasoning (*ijtihad*) to derive religious rulings. These schools believe that the understanding and interpretation of religious matters should consider the context of time and place and involve the use of reason and independent interpretation.

The conclusion is that extremism in Islam is directly related to the methodology and process of deriving religious rulings. Most Islamic extremists are jurisprudentially and intellectually aligned with the textualist schools, as they offer limited space for flexibility and interpretation in religious texts. This rigid approach can contribute to the rise of extremist tendencies.

NOTES

1. The entire phrase or the initial letters are used after all the Prophets' names. The whole phrase will be used when a Prophet's name is used in speech, but the initials will be used more commonly in writing or print, especially in religiously-oriented or authored publications aimed at a Muslim readership. The term has been used once in the context of this book.
2. Jabal al-Nour is located in the Hejaz region of Saudi Arabia, just outside Mecca. Jabal al-Nour translates to "Mountain of Light." Prophet Muhammad received his first revelation through Angel Jibreel (Gabriel) in the Hira cave on this mountain. Prophet Muhammad used to climb this mountain often even before receiving his first revelation from Allah.
3. The first Caliph of Islam after the Prophet's death.
4. Companions of the Prophet, Arabic Sahabah or Ashab, in *Islam,* are followers of Prophet Muhammad who had personal contact with him, however slight. In fact, any Muslim who was alive in any part of the Prophet's lifetime and saw him may be reckoned among the Companions.
5. Sub companions are those who saw and met the companions or *Sahaba*.
6. Abu Hanifa, in full, Abu Hanifa al-Nu¿man ibn Thabit, (born 699, Kufa, Iraq—died 767, Baghdad), Muslim jurist and theologian whose systematization of Islamic legal doctrine was acknowledged as one of the four canonical schools of Islamic law (sect or madhabs). The Hanafi school of Abu Hanifa acquired such prestige that its doctrines were applied by a majority of Muslim dynasties.
7. The definition varies from different sources. However, there is a difference according to some sources: and according to Oxford in which Islamism represents a form of Political Islam that relates to "Islamic militancy or fundamentalism." Meanwhile, Oxford Bibliographies calls political Islam "any interpretation of Islam as a source of political identity and action." Thus, political Islam can be any form of political ideology based around Islam, which can include Islamic democracy, Islamic socialism, and other political ideologies that are not necessarily militaristic or fundamentalists. Again, some sources use the term interchangeably, but many in academia use one for extremist Islamic ideologies and the other to describe all Islamic political ideologies. What is meant here is that "Islamism" and "political Islam" are used with the same meaning and they are interchangeable with each other; which is the study of violent and non-violent Islamic groups seeking to gain political power and change society.
8. The Fergana Valley is located in Central Asia across eastern Uzbekistan, southern Kyrgyzstan, and northern Tajikistan.

9. Salafi Wahabi are those Islamist extremists who excommunicate other Muslims.
10. Salaf means returning to the beginning of Islam.
11. Ghazi is an Islamic religious term that refers to someone who participates in war against the infidels and has killed a number of infidels. Vice versa it is "Shaheed" martyr, meaning someone who participated in the war and was killed by infidels.

Chapter 2

Afghanistan's Geopolitics: Theoretical Perspective and the Interplay of Location and Extra-Regional Influences

2.1 Introduction

The first chapter examined Afghanistan, Islam, and Political Islam through a critical internal lens, highlighting the historical, ideological, and societal dynamics shaping the Afghanistan's political landscape. Building on this foundation, Chapter two turns to the theoretical framework of the study and evaluates these themes through the lens of Structural Realism, one of the most influential theories in international relations. By emphasizing the role of the international system, power distribution, and security competition, this chapter situates Afghanistan within its strategic geopolitical location at the crossroads of multiple regions. Structural Realism helps explain how Afghanistan's position has invited sustained intervention by regional and extra-regional powers, whose balance-of-power calculations have consistently constrained Afghanistan's political autonomy and state-building efforts.

2.2 Afghanistan's Geopolitical Location

Afghanistan, which had gained geopolitical importance to the West during the Cold War in the face of Soviet threats, lost its geopolitical importance at some point after the Cold War or in other words, after the collapse of the Soviet Union and the restructuring of the international system from bipolar to unipolar. The West, especially the USA was busy celebrating its victory, and Afghanistan which played a key role in the US victory was forgotten but the developments after 9/11 played an important role in reviving Afghanistan's crucial geopolitical and geostrategic role in the region and the world. This importance will be maintained in the course of political developments in the international system over the next few decades both at the hegemonic level of the USA and at the level of regional systems. Afghanistan's geopolitical position in the heart of several geopolitical regional systems such as the Indian subcontinent, Central Asia, the Greater Middle East, the Persian Gulf, and China will remain.

Afghanistan's position in the geopolitics of the New World System requires an understanding of what is happening in the Middle East geopolitical region as one of the most important geostrategic systems for the great powers, as well as an understanding of events in South Asia, especially where Afghanistan, Pakistan, and India are connected. These two geopolitical areas must be seriously considered. In fact, the geopolitical importance and role of Afghanistan depends first on the geopolitics and geo-economics of the Middle East at a macro and primary level in the geo-strategy of the new world system and then on understanding the developments of South Asia as a geostrategic region where India and China are connected. In fact, Afghanistan is influenced by several regional systems in terms of its geopolitical position. The Greater Middle East is the most important system at the first level, the Persian Gulf regional subsystem in particular, and the Southwest Asia system is the central and internal system that directly affects Afghanistan. Besides, China as an independent region and Central Asia also have impacts on the position and importance of Afghanistan.

Hence, Afghanistan, due to its geopolitical position, has always undergone extensive and profound changes and has been considered by regional and global powers but due to the lack of a strong government in Afghanistan, it could not take advantage of this position. Conversely, countries in the region and the world were/are able to derive their absolute and relative gains through Afghanistan's geopolitical position. How can these events be considered from a theoretical perspective? And more importantly, what theory can best explain this? The academic evidence is that the theory of realism is one of the mainstream theories in International Relations (IR) and has the ability to better explain the issues of war, peace, and power in Afghanistan, the region, and the world. Realism as a dominant theory in international relations is divided into several variants such as classical realism and structural realism (neorealism).[1] However, despite their different classifications, all realists agree on the three core principles that underlie realism. They are: states are the main actors in international politics, survival, and self-help. Therefore, the present study examines the issues of this in the form of the structural realism theory.

2.3 REALISM

Realists believe that the dominant theory in International Relations is the theory of realism because it provides a complete and effective explanation of the war that prevails in the international system. Although this idea has been criticized, it must be admitted that at least after World War II, realism has been a dominant theory in international relations.

On the other hand, the phenomenon of war and cooperation between actors in the international political arena is one of the most central issues that has become one of the main topics of international studies in Westphalia since the formation of the nation-state system and due to the crucial role which 'Power' has in and how these two phenomena occur and has always been an inseparable link between the three concepts conflict, cooperation, and power; the result of its various functions directly affected another concept called 'security' with different dimensions. Therefore, the analysis of international peace and security is possible only in a framework that can study and analyze the phenomenon of conflict and cooperation and related issues.

2.3.1 Structural Realism

Structural realism derives from the important theory of Kenneth Waltz, *Theory of International Politics*, and refers to the argument of realists who see the reason for the conflicts in the anarchic structure of the international system. In *Theory of International Politics*, Waltz gives a structural or systematic explanation of international politics. In his view, international politics is the realm of necessity and the politics of power. (Griffiths 1992: 71) He argues that the anarchy that governs the structure of the international system is often equated with a state of war. Structural realists believe that the possibility of adventure war is likely to occur in an anarchic environment. Thus, even if statesmen seek peace, the structure of the international system can lead countries to war. (Butterfield, 1951: 21)

Waltz in his book, *Man, the State and War*, attempts to explain the phenomenon of war and conflict in International Relations. He believes and refers to them in three images, which are: human nature or the first image that traces the roots of war in the belligerent nature of man or certain human beings. This means that the first image focuses on human nature and places the possibilities of peace and war at the level of individual biology and psychology. In this study, humans are either prepared for war or cooperation. States is his second image in which he tries to describe war based on the belligerence of certain states with specific political ideologies and regimes. This means that the second image explains the rise and fall of war and cooperation by focusing on the internal characteristics of each state. Whether we cooperate or not depends very much on the nature of the political systems in which we live. So, it makes a big difference whether it interacts with a government that values us or with a government that opposes it. Simply put, the second image shows that government behaviour is shaped by the nature of its domestic politics. So we should expect a democratic state to function significantly differently from a communist or authoritarian equivalent. The structure of the international system, or the third image, explains the occurrence of war based on the anarchic nature of the international system. (Moshirzadeh 2013: 108)

However, many structural realists are dissatisfied with explanations that rely solely on the first and second images. For these theorists, priority is given to the third image, which focuses on the international system rather than human nature or internal personality of states. They define the international system as 'international anarchy.' Anarchy does not necessarily mean that world politics is characterized as you think, by chaos, disorder, and endless war. Rather, the term 'international anarchy', in a more formal sense, refers to the absence of a world government or high authority. The term 'international anarchy', rather than necessarily implying disorder, refers to a structure in which international politics operates; in particular, a structure in which there is no higher authority. (Dunne et al. 2013: 78) Waltz in the 'Theory of International Politics', considers the first two ideas reductionist, because they reduce the character of the international system to the character of its constituent units, namely, individuals and governments, and introduces an acceptable explanation as a structural or systematic explanation. (Moshirzadeh 2013: 109)

He argues that the structure of International Politics is defined in terms of three components:

1. The organizing principles,
2. Determination of the functions of units or components, and
3. Distribution of capabilities or power.

The organizing principle of the international system is anarchy, that is, a system without a central and high authority, which as a result of the international environment is self-help in the sense that there is no higher authority to provide security for its members and individuals [states]. (Dunne et al. 2013: 78) All states must rely only on their own power for security, and change occurs only when anarchic space gives way to a non-anarchic structure. With regard to the determination of the functions of units or components, the main concern of all states is security; everyone should seek survival, and the ultimate goals of each state should be their own survival and security. The distribution of capabilities in the international system is different between units. For this reason, if the capability is between two great powers, it is a bipolar system, and if it is between several great powers, it is a multi-polar system, and since the anarchy and the functions of the units are constant in the international system, what matters is the distribution of capabilities. (Waltz 1979: 88-108) In other words, Waltz believes that the behaviour of actors in the international system depends on the distribution of power, and it is this structure that limits behaviour. This restriction is achieved through a two-dimensional structure, that is, either through the socialization of actors in the form of rewards or punishments they receive for their behaviour or through competition in which states have to maintain behaviour and demonstrate their rights and the ability to compete with others. (Dunne et al. 2013: 79)

Regarding cooperation, Waltz argues that in an anarchic environment, the possibility of cooperation is very limited, although states may gain benefits economically from cooperation and possibly economic revenues are typically overshadowed by political revenues, and states are always concerned about the greater profits of others. Thus, although the absolute gains of cooperation may be high, what are more important are the relative gains that, if detrimental to them, hinder cooperation. Therefore, this is anarchy that limits the amount of cooperation and its areas. Regarding stability in the international system, Waltz also argues that among the types of power distribution, the bipolar structure is more stable, and here he contrasts with Morgenthau, who considers a multi-polar system with a stable balancing factor.

2.3.1.1 State

According to realists, the main actors in international relations are States, and sovereignty are their special feature. The concept of power lies in this definition, and the internal dimension of power is stated in the famous saying of Max Weber, who believes that the "state means the right to legitimately use physical power within a given territory". As he said, the freedom of the people in return for the guarantee of their security by the government, or in other words, the security deal with the freedom that takes place in the form of an unwritten contract between the people and the government. Therefore, in terms of realism, every state has a government (Donelan 1992: 25).

Realism assumed that the issue of security and freedom has been solved within the state (domestically), but does not assume the same for the external environment, and believes that in relations among independent states, there is insecurity, danger, and threat to the existence of the states. States compete with each other for security, markets, influence, and prestige in an anarchy environment. The nature of this type of competition is also a game with zero-sum results. Thus, the competitive logic of power politics shapes agreement and cooperation. The first action of the state is to organize power internally, and the second is to gather power in the international arena which is the place of the power struggle. Therefore, the definition of power in terms of realism, as Morgenthau puts it, is *"man's control over the thoughts and actions of other human beings".* (Morgenthau 1948: 26). Realists point out two important points about the concept of power: first, that power is a relational concept, meaning that power is not used in a vacuum but in relation to another, and second, that power is a relative concept and states not only calculate their own power, but also have to measure the ratio of their power to the power of other actors.

Structural realists have sought to provide a more accurate and complete definition of power because traditional realism has faced unanswered questions about the concept of power, including why governments struggle for power. Is it essentially power that is the goal or the means to an end? Kenneth Waltz tried to define it more precisely by focusing on the concept of capabilities rather than on power. He believed that capabilities could be categorized based on population, territory (geography), number of resources, economic facilities, military force, and political stability. (Waltz 1979: 131)

Realists believe that only states are actors in the international system and others are not, and those other actors have to move in the direction of an international system whose rules are shaped by states. Realists also believe that the economy and the free trade system depend on the existence of a dominant power that is willing to bear the burden of managing this system. This view of realists is known as the Hegemonic Stability Theory and emphasizes that the international economic order depends on the existence of a dominant state, which means that if the dominant actor does not wish it, there will be no stability or cooperation, and interaction among states. In this regard, cooperation will be possible when the dominant state has willed it.

2.3.1.2 Survival

Survival is the second issue that realists from all tendencies believe is the main and ultimate goal of states is survival in an anarchic environment of international politics. The ultimate concern of states is security. In the realm of realism, security is a precondition for other goals, whether it is necessary to win over others or just to maintain its independence. Waltz argues that apart from the motivation for survival, states' goals are extremely different. (Waltz 1979: 91) In answer to the question of whether the goal of the state is to secure the state or to increase power, defensive realists and offensive realists give different answers depending on which point of view we accept. Therefore, the prospects for security and cooperation in international relations will be different. Defensive realists such as Waltz and Grieco believe that states see security as their primary goal and are therefore satisfied with the power to ensure their security, and they do not seek to maximize their power, especially when their security is at stake. (Grieco 1997) Offensive realists like Mearsheimer believe that the goal of governments is to achieve a hegemonic position in the international system. According to this view, states have always sought a hegemonic position in the international system, and if they can, they seek to disrupt the distribution of power and gain the first place for themselves, even if it jeopardizes them. (Mearsheimer 1994: 12-150)

2.3.1.3 Self-help

In *Theory of International of Politics*, Waltz argues that war and conflicts are unique features of international politics because, in such a situation, citizens do not have to defend themselves at home while in the international system there is no superior government to prevent the use of power. Therefore, security can only be achieved through self-help. In the structure of anarchy, self-help is necessarily the rule of action. In other words, the security of each state depends only on its own power and strength, and this self-help and efforts of states to ensure their security may lead to insecurity in other countries and cause them to feel more insecure; the situation is the same in what is called a security dilemma.[2]

Realists disagree over the security dilemma and how to escape it. Structural realists believe that the security dilemma is a permanent condition in international politics, but classical realists believe that this problem can be mitigated even in conditions of self-help through a balance of power.

Structural realists believe that the balance of power is created by chance, even if there is no conscious policy to strengthen the balance of power. Waltz believed that the balance of power was created without the will of the states because in an anarchic system, coalitions were created spontaneously with the aim of controlling and balancing power in the face of threatening states. In any case, all realists agree that this balance for the stability and security of the system, whether accidental or planned, is not continuous and stable. Therefore, states can, at best reduce the worst consequences of the security dilemma, but they cannot eliminate it. The reason for this unsolvable situation is the lack of trust among the actors of the international system. In other words, what causes disruption and lack of cooperation between countries is the lack of trust and suspicion among states, which not only creates the ground for cooperation but also strongly hinders the facilitation of any kind of cooperation. Kenneth Waltz refers to Rousseau in his book *Man, the State and War*:

> *Assume that five men who have acquired a rudimentary ability to speak and understand each other happen to come together at a time when all of them suffer from hunger. The hunger of each will be satisfied by the fifth part of a stag, so, they "agree" to cooperate in a project to trap one. But also, the hunger of any one of them will be satisfied by a hare, so, as a hare comes within reach, one of them grabs it. The defector obtains the means of satisfying his hunger but doing so permits the stag to escape. His immediate interest prevails over consideration of his fellows.* (Waltz 2001: 167-8)

With this allegory, Waltz considers the lack of trust of some countries as a factor to undermine collective action and considers distrust as an obstacle to cooperation. Liberals see the solution to this problem as the establishment of international institutes and structural realists agree with them on this issue, accepting that institutes can be facilitated with cooperation under certain conditions, but at the same time believing that in the system, self-help is harder to achieve and strengthen cooperation, and more depends on the power of states. In other words, from this point of view, cooperation is a function dependent on power and is a kind of dependent variable. (Baldwin 1993: 302) According to structural realists, the reason for this is the importance of relative gain.

Joseph Grieco, who focuses on the concept of relative and absolute gains in his works, believes that states are interested in increasing their power and influence (absolute gains). (Grieco 1997) Therefore, they work with other actors in the international system to increase their capabilities. At the same time, states are concerned about the achievements of others in this cooperation, in the sense that the degree of power and influence those other actors gain (relative gains) is important to any states in cooperative action. Structural realists believe that there are two obstacles to international cooperation: fraud and the relative gains of other actors. In addition, when states fail to abide by laws that encourage cooperation with others, other actors may abandon multilateral action and act unilaterally, given the relative gains in the survival of a state. According to Grieco and other structuralists, the question is not whether all actors benefit from cooperation, but who will gain the most if cooperation takes place.

2.4 Afghanistan from the Perspective of Structural Realism

In the theory of realism, the states are the main players in the international system, and all states are operating in an anarchic environment that lacks central authority and supremacy. Therefore, the ultimate goal of any state is its survival in the international system, and a state will survive that has enough power to protect itself in the anarchic system. Hence, the international system is a scene of struggle for power, the rise of power, and the display of power among states.

Afghanistan, as a state in the structure of the international system, cannot move apart from the international order and has always been influenced by international developments. Examining the situation and position of Afghanistan in the structure of the international system based on the view of structural realism requires analysis and study at three levels of analysis: state, regional, and global.

2.4.1 State Level

As mentioned above, Kenneth Waltz believes and categorizes the capabilities (power) of states based on population, territory, resources, economic opportunities, military force, and political stability. This is in contrast to most realists who believe that the domestic issue of states is resolved and concentrates only on the role of governments in gaining power in the international system. According to the Waltz division, Afghanistan possesses a large quantity of natural resources, which have managed to stay intact up till this point because there has not been a national consensus or the establishment of a national government. Some scientists even speculate that the country's natural resources may be contributing to the ongoing conflict in the country. Since 2001, it has positioned itself better among surrounding countries in terms of military might. Between 15 August 2002 and 15 August 2021, Afghanistan's armed forces (army, police, and intelligence) numbered 280,000. With the help of the USA and NATO, they were outfitted with cutting-edge equipment and armaments. It should be noted that due to political reasons, no precise, impartial, official census has been carried out in Afghanistan to date, making it impossible to obtain accurate population estimates. However, unofficial estimates place the country's population, excluding Afghanistani refugees, between 30 and 35 million as of 2010.

In terms of political stability, Afghanistan has never had sustainable governments in its history since there was the lack of national arrangement. So far, no leader or governing authority in Afghanistan has succeeded in uniting the population or fostering consensus on any of the country's key issues, including national interests, national identity, and related fundamental matters. Hundreds of incidents have taken place in Afghanistan, but none of them have united these people; on the contrary, they have widened the gaps between the Afghanistan people. The policies of the regimes that have ruled Afghanistan and the actions of politicians have always led to divisions among the Afghanistan people. Article 4 of the Afghanistan constitution lists fourteen ethnic groups who are inhabitants, but in fact, the number of ethnic groups living in Afghanistan is more than what is stated. (Afghanistan Constitution 2004, 1: 4) The people of Afghanistan have been suffering for at least four decades and all the ethnic groups of Afghanistan have suffered together which was/is shared pain, but never have the people of Afghanistan been able to stand united and fight against the pain along with each other. The internal situation in Afghanistan can be examined from what Thucydides and Morgenthau have defined, and precisely the evil nature of human beings in Afghanistan can be seen objectively. Afghanistan is politically fragile and the cause of this fragility is its deep ethnic gaps. The domination and monopoly of political power by a particular ethnic group in Afghanistan has weakened political stability and this has had a direct impact on Afghanistan's interaction at the regional and international levels. Therefore, what Waltz defines as the power (capabilities) of governments is lacking in Afghanistan and that is why it has performed poorly at the regional and international levels. Despite good opportunities in the structure of the international system, it has never been able to pursue a dynamic foreign policy at least at the regional level. This weakness has caused the countries of the region and the world to make good use of the situation in Afghanistan.

2.4.2 Regional Level

From a geopolitical point of view, Afghanistan is a buffer zone, margin, and collision zone of at least four areas of the world. The nature of this kind of geography and regions like Afghanistan is tied to conflicts, confrontations of great powers, and the arena of rivalries between neighbours and regional powers. On the other hand, the Afghanistan region is in the throes of terrorism, confrontation between Iran, Saudi Arabia, China, Russia, and the USA, and finally, the historic Indo-Pakistani conflict, which unfortunately has a direct and indirect effect on developments in Afghanistan. Regarding the political-military developments in Afghanistan, there is now no political agreement among Afghanistan's neighbours and the surrounding area. As such, Afghanistan's stability and security are at odds with the regional circumstances, particularly the political-security objectives of Afghanistan's neighbours. The absence of regional consensus has increased interference from neighbours and other external actors in Afghanistan. This growing involvement is a result of the confrontational policies of the Afghanistan government, the military presence of the USA and NATO, and the excesses of the Afghanistan government's political and security policies.

The power of states depends on what Waltz mentioned above, in the sense that political stability, wealth, and resources lead to the power of states at both the national and regional levels. Afghanistan, despite its abundant natural resources equivalent to wealth has never had political stability. Among other internal factors, one of the main elements of war and conflict in Afghanistan is its geopolitical location, and, on the other hand, the lack of active diplomacy in the Afghanistan foreign policy apparatus that can/could convince neighbouring and other sovereign active actors that the geographical location of Afghanistan poses no threat to them. Afghanistan's geopolitics is such that the actions of each sovereign actor have provoked the reactions of other actors, and according to one of the assumptions of structural realism that "states can never be certain about the intentions of other states", each action of one actor has been severely misunderstood by another actor in Afghanistan.

For example, the Afghanistan diplomatic apparatus has so far failed to make it clear to Pakistan that any kind of political, economic, or military interaction between Afghanistan and India does not mean enmity with Pakistan although India has always used cautious diplomacy in its policies towards Afghanistan and Pakistan. Conversely, Pakistan has reacted aggressively against Afghanistan in connection with India's slightest movement. In '*A History of Peloponnesian Wars*', Thucydides mentioned the misunderstandings between the Athenians and the Spartans, and believed that the main cause of the war was the suspicion of both sides. This is exactly what Afghanistan is facing today, and this is the situation in related to all other sovereign actors in Afghanistan as well. The US military presence as a world power and hegemon in Afghanistan has provoked the sensitivity and reaction of China, Russia, and Iran, and during the US presence from 2001-to 2021, unwanted and indirect alliances were formed against it in order to maintain the balance of power in the region. Although most of these coalitions were not formal, they were practically aligned with each other. Moreover, another assumption of realism states that the ultimate and supreme goal of any state is its survival. Therefore, every state is trying to increase its power and according to E.H. Carr, "The most serious wars occur because one state becomes militarily stronger or prevents others from becoming militarily stronger." (Carr 1964: 111)

2.4.3 International Level

At the international level, Afghanistan, because of its geopolitical position, has always been in the spotlight of major world powers. In the nineteenth century, for example, it was a buffer zone between Russia and Great Britain. During the Cold War, the US-Soviet proxy battlefield, and after 9/11, it became a convenient location for US policy in Asia. Although the reason for the US presence in Afghanistan was the war on terror and al-Qaeda, in fact, it meant control of China, Russia, and Iran. From 2001 to 2021, the USA controlled the politics and developments in Central and South Asia through its presence in Afghanistan. This has led regional powers such as China and Russia, according to the theory of realism, to strike a balance of power in Asia in the form of regional security organizations such as the Shanghai Cooperation Organization. The balance of power is essentially a fundamental guarantee of the survival of the system of sovereign states. Although Shanghai's ostensible philosophy is resolving members' border disputes and fighting against terrorism and separatists within its territory, China and Russia, on the other hand, have sought to limit US policy in the Middle East and in their spheres of influence.

Thus, Afghanistan has always had a strategic position in world politics for major powers, but the bitter fact is that Afghanistan has never been able to use this position to its advantage due to the lack of a strong and stable government. According to geopolitical principles, the great powers, in addition to sufficient naval and air power, need a secure land base in their strategically defined areas. Therefore, in international calculations and in terms of time and conditions, the international community deals with Afghanistan from one of these five angles in international politics.

1. Afghanistan as a buffer zone to prevent war between the great powers.
2. Afghanistan is the playground for proxy wars and groups of sovereign actors in the region.
3. Transit corridor to Central Asia and South Asia.
4. Military strategic depth.
5. The source of instability and the burden on the international community.

Each one of these characteristics will be discussed in more detail in the following pages specifically in para 3.6 (*Sovereign Actors in Afghanistan: The Strategic Calculus*).

2.5 Geopolitical Location of Afghanistan and Strategic Regional Context

2.5.1 Afghanistan Heartland Asia

Most geographers believe that as long as human beings are placed and divided into certain units and forms such as country, government, or region, in other words, as long as there is a separation between human beings, the struggle for survival will continue with intensity and weakness and this struggle for survival requires that every country and government be equipped with the elements of power. According to the paradigm of realism, one of these elements is having a suitable geographical location. (Morgenthau 1948: 80) The heartland is a good position for strong and weak states to try to dominate. The author of the Heartland theory is Sir Halford John Mackinder. According to him, there are points on every continent that dominate them as the heart and centre, and these points are so important that any superpower or any other country would try to dominate them. Before entering into the main discussion, it is necessary to know that Mackinder was a realist and his ideas are reflected in the writings of most realist scientists. (Wu 2018: 5)

Mackinder's main doctrine was that "Whoever rules the Heartland commands the World-Island; whoever rules the World-Island commands the World". According to Mackinder, the pivot area includes the river basins of the Volga, Yenisey, Amu Darya, Syr Darya, and two seas (the Caspian and the Aral). (Ismailov & Papava 2010: 85) The Amu Darya is part of Afghanistan and originates from its mountains and is the common border between Afghanistan and Tajikistan.

Afghanistan also has the position of heartland in Asia, which has been tried and dominated by various countries over the centuries. Based on the Heartland Theory, Afghanistan is located in the centre of Asia and is the heart of gravity of the Mackinder Doctrine in the Middle East in terms of geographical strategy and has a unique strategic position. According to Mackinder's theory, whoever rules this part of Asia will mean his domination of Asia and Eurasia. However, today's heartland, in addition to the features of Mackinder's natural heartland, is an ideological heartland, a human heartland with an extraordinary power of faith. Whoever dominates this heartland (Central Asia and Afghanistan...) can change world politics and will play the main role in international politics. In fact, Afghanistan is part of the Central Region or Heartland of Asia.

Sometimes, the central or heartland location, while having facilities and benefiting from geographical facilities, also appears dangerous and sensitive. It is possible to compensate the regions and countries that have such a feature and for historical and political reasons it has imported injuries and the latter is verity for Afghanistan. According to Spykman, Afghanistan is still in the heart of Asia. Its proximity to major powers such as Russia and China has proven its central position, and this central position is appropriate and a factor for greed and for its occupation. Sometimes, geopolitical situations are strategically valued due to their location between two important regions (two great powers), and this particular situation attracts the attention of the great powers. Afghanistan is one of the countries. In the meantime, the Russians have always made great efforts to reach the 'ice-free' shores for over a thousand years, but each time they have faced a show of strength of other regional and global powers.

Therefore, the geopolitical location in Afghanistan attracted the special attention of the Russians, and with the coming to power of Lenin, the Russian thesis of achieving warm waters was realized, and Afghanistan became both a target and a means for them. Because the Soviet Union is a country surrounded by icy waters, reaching the warm waters (the Indian Ocean and the Persian Gulf) has always been exciting and stimulating for that country. Reaching hot springs and owning water ports required passing through lands that, while rich in resources and mines, should be strategically suitable Afghanistan has had these conditions in every way and the US presence continued to be based on such strategic assessments.

Figure 1: The Countries of Central Eurasia[3]

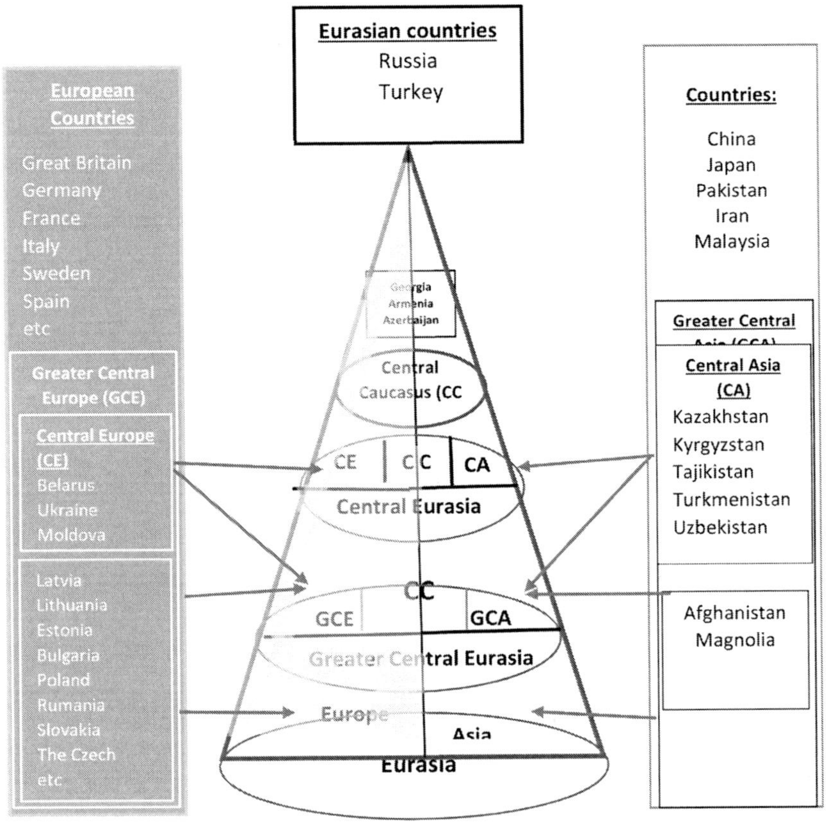

2.5.2 Afghanistan and Regional Geographical Systems

Examining the geostrategic position of Afghanistan in the New World Order[4] requires understanding the relations and position of Afghanistan in relation to the geopolitical regions of Asia. In fact, Afghanistan, which is geographically part of the regional system of South and Southwest Asia, gets the most impact from this system. In the next phase, the geopolitical system of the Greater Middle East has expanded its sphere of influence into Afghanistan. If before 9/11 Afghanistan's position was influenced by the role and link between the South Asian and Middle Eastern systems, now Afghanistan itself is defined as the centre of a regional system called the Greater Middle East although the geographical logic of Afghanistan is less visible in the Greater Middle East. Afghanistan, in reference to the Central Asian regional system, also accepts many influences, both in terms of its relational role and its role of proximity to this geographical system. In addition, China has strategic interest in Afghanistan due to its geographic proximity, as well as Afghanistan's position as a connecting point between the Persian Gulf and the Central Asian regional system.

Figure 2: Influence of Afghanistan's position on the regional geographical systems of South Asia, the Middle East, Central Asia, and the geopolitical region of China

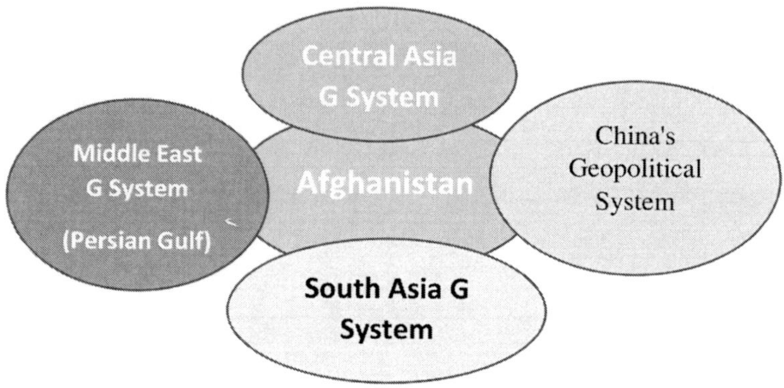

Thus, it is right to assess Afghanistan's geostrategic significance in the light of the regional shifts in geographical systems as well as its significance in the geopolitics of the emerging global order. However, as mentioned, the continuity of Afghanistan's geostrategic importance and position in the regional system of South Asia and the Middle East is more important and fundamental. These regions need to study and process the developments that can be predicted from the perspective of global and regional policies of the new system.

2.5.3 South Asian Regional System

According to Goldstein's definition, Afghanistan is part of the geopolitical space structure of South Asia. (Goldstein & Pevehouse 2013-14: 25) Afghanistan, Pakistan, and India are some of the most significant nations in this system. However, India occupies the centre of this structure, with Pakistan and Afghanistan at the periphery. The USA also serves as the primary intervening force in this region, continuing its role from 9/11. Afghanistan occupies a major position in this system and in relation to the new global order; it is regarded as one of the cornerstones of US foreign policy in Asia and the wider globe. The USA has acknowledged India's nuclear capability, economic expansion, and demographic potential and accepted its pivotal position in South Asia.

The relationship between Afghanistan and Pakistan is complex and delicate. Pakistan views Afghanistan's security and stability through the lens of its own national security concerns and insists on maintaining Afghanistan's political, economic, and military reliance on Pakistan. Pakistan has often opposed developments in Afghanistan influenced by US policies in the Middle East and South Asia, leading to ongoing stalemates in the region's security efforts.

For nearly five decades, ties between Afghanistan and Pakistan, as well as between India and Pakistan, have been tense and fragile. This regional structure is facing numerous obstacles and contradictions as a result of this issue. Afghanistan's location in South Asia may be significant due to the role of the USA as a system actor and the nuclear might of Pakistan and India in the area. However, as previously indicated, the conflict between India and Pakistan as well as Afghanistan's ambiguous and chilly relations with Pakistan pose a significant threat to US dominance over the system.

As the USA's strategic allies in South Asia, Pakistan, and Afghanistan experienced a brief rapprochement as a result of its presence and intervention in the system. Resolving the Afghanistan-Pakistan conflict in the light of the continuation and regional systems of the new system has not been out of reach, although the complexity and depth of obstacles and problems in improving relations between the two countries, in the long run, should be considered subject to fundamental changes in the policies of both sides and depends on Afghanistan's foreign policy being dynamic and multifaceted.

The problems of India and Pakistan are very complex and it is extremely difficult to resolve them. In fact, resolving the Afghanistan-Pakistan conflict is largely dependent on resolving the India-Pakistan conflict. The USA seemed to have sought to reduce the level of conflict and tension between India and Pakistan in line with India's balanced and harmonious regional policies. However, both sides have not expected that the USA would make a real effort to resolve the two nuclear disputes definitively. The USA has sought to maintain friendly relations with both Pakistan and India without interfering in the continuing confrontation and threats between them. Pakistan's threats to India caused the latter to seek control of the area of operations in organizing the political and economic activities of the subcontinent, especially in the SAARC region of which India, Pakistan, and Afghanistan, along with several other South Asian countries are members. All these factors obscure the prospect of a definitive solution to the Afghanistan-Pakistan conflict.

Therefore, it has to be expected that Afghanistan in such circumstances could take full advantage of this opportunity to resolve its disputes with Pakistan. But it has to be emphasized that US support for resolving these conflicts depends entirely on the commitments and demands of the leaders of both countries, otherwise the US presence could only provide a temporary effort to forget the Afghanistan-Pakistan conflict.

The expansion and concentration of Islamist extremist groups and international terrorism from Iraq and the Middle East to South Asia are the main causes of Afghanistan's geostrategic significance in this region. The USA lost 20 years of battle and accomplishments against terrorism in favour of its reckless exit from Afghanistan, which diminished the country's standing and prestige internationally. The US win against terrorism and fundamentalism could have improved its standing and reputation among nations across the globe. After 15 August 2021, the regional power dynamics shifted in Pakistan's favour.

2.5.4 The Persian Gulf Regional Subsystem and Afghanistan

For great powers like the USA, China, and other states in the region, the Persian Gulf is one of the most crucial areas. The USA now plays a protective role in the Persian Gulf and the surrounding region because of the enormous amount of oil produced there and the significant reliance of major world powers on energy supplies from the region.

Afghanistan serves as a bridge for communication and trade between Central Asia, South Asia and the Persian Gulf. It also plays a geopolitical role in the interactions of regional powers like China, India, and Iran with the Persian Gulf. These factors account for the interaction between Afghanistan and the Persian Gulf regional sub-system.

2.5.5 China Regional System

Despite having a modest shared border of about 73 to 93 km, China is one of Afghanistan's strongest neighbours. As one of the world's most populous and powerful economies, China greatly influences the significance of Afghanistan's geopolitical position in the region. In order to influence the regional situation through active and generally economic engagement in regional unions and organizations, China has a special interest in defining its independent geopolitical position in the world while maintaining positive relations with the USA. China's policy and strategy towards Afghanistan can be assessed in two stages: 1. from 2001 to 2021 during the Republic. 2. On 15 August 2021, when the republic in Afghanistan collapsed and the Taliban regained political and military control, a shift that led to China's approach to the country. During the first phase (2001-2021), China's focus on Afghanistan was primarily centred on security and strategic interests, aligning its policies closely with those of Pakistan. However, after the fall of the republic, China's approach expanded beyond security and strategy to include economic ambitions and a desire for greater influence and dominance in Afghanistan and the broader region.

China has a stronger focus on the Central Asian region and is keen to participate in regional organizations that involve countries from this area. Consequently, China plays a significant role in the Shanghai Cooperation Organization (SCO), where the presence of major members like Russia and India, along with observer members such as Afghanistan and Iran, underscores the regional importance of the SCO. For the USA, as a global hegemon, the expansion of this organization and its acceptance of new members is a critical development. Although China's involvement in Afghanistan's reconstruction projects, particularly in the commercial sector, has grown significantly in recent years, Afghanistan's importance for China under its new strategy remains largely focused on territorial and security concerns. Despite the expansion of economic ties, the relationship between the two countries is primarily shaped by these strategic interests.

The USA has been very cautious about China, which occupies a high position on US strategy. Therefore, during its stay in Afghanistan, the USA tried to reduce China's manoeuvring power and focus on Afghanistan, especially in Central Asia, by engaging China in the Taiwan issue. Afghanistan plays a prominent role in US strategy because it has less permeability from China than Central Asian countries. The current balance (2001-2021) and future developments in power relations between China, India, and Pakistan with US involvement play a crucial part in Afghanistan's position in the geo-strategy of the new system.

2.5.6 Central Asian Regional System

Although Central Asian countries gained independence from Russian rule after the Soviet Union's collapse, the region is still largely seen as a sphere of Russian influence, due to Russia's political resurgence. The formation of the Commonwealth of Independent States, centred around Russia, has reinforced its dominance in this area. However, as previously mentioned, China's economic rise has led to the strengthening of ties with Central Asia, especially through the Shanghai Cooperation Organization. The main threat, however, comes from US activities in Central Asia and its agreements with these countries, particularly the creation of the NATO Partnership for Peace in Afghanistan and Central Asia, which has heightened Russia's vulnerability.

If the USA persists in its strategy of fostering relations and cooperation, particularly with China in Central Asia, while also addressing Russia's security concerns, Afghanistan could potentially gain acceptance in regional organizations linked to Central Asian countries. This acceptance could play a significant role in stabilizing Afghanistan's political landscape and enhancing its economic conditions.

Therefore, it can be said that the importance and role of Afghanistan with Central Asia is more in terms of communication and geo-economic situation than can be established between this regional system with South and East Asia economically. What is important is that ensuring security and stability is both necessary and consequential. Afghanistan would greatly benefit from this scenario. Its reliance on Central Asia for economic and geo-economic needs would ultimately result in Afghanistan becoming geopolitically dependent on and closely affiliated with the regional subsystem.

2.5.7 The Middle East

In international talks, the Middle East's geo-economic significance has always been highlighted and this was also the case throughout the Cold War. Nonetheless, the significance of the Middle East appears to be growing in the wake of the 9/11 attacks. Despite the region's growing reliance on oil, the USA and other major powers in the region appear to be interested in the Middle East for security and political reasons as well as for other reasons.

Following 9/11, the USA invaded Afghanistan and then Iraq due to the threat of terrorism and fundamentalism. The significance of Afghanistan for the Middle East, apart from economic concerns, relates to also cultural (ideological) and security challenges.

2.6 Sovereign Actors in Afghanistan: The Strategic Calculus

Russia and Eurasia, Iran and the Middle East, including the Gulf States, South Asia and lastly the major trans-regional powers like the USA and China have traditionally placed Afghanistan at the intersection of at least four geopolitical and security arenas. By utilizing the resources of Afghanistan's land and people and taking advantage of its social and political divisions, this creates a favourable environment for hostile rivalry in Afghanistan's geography and territory.

As previously stated, there are five viewpoints and tactics that the major powers along with neighbouring states have about Afghanistan. The majority of their objectives are predicated on one or more of the following strategies in Afghanistan:

2.6.1 Buffer Zone

Over the years, Afghanistan has served as a buffer zone for major countries. In the 19th century, it served as a buffer zone for the Soviet Union and Great Britain, which led to the establishment of Afghanistan's contentious borders with its neighbours and rivalry between Russia and the USA during the Cold War, which led to the collapse of Afghanistan's military and economic institutions and four decades of civil conflict.

2.6.2 Playground for Proxy Wars

In situations where weak states act as a buffer zone between superpowers, powerful neighbours or regional powers can take advantage of the situation to further their own national and regional agendas. This leads to the emergence of proxy groups who can defend their own interests or engage in combat with their adversaries within the buffer zone. As a result, for four decades, the majority of the countries in the region formed proxy groups in Afghanistan to protect their interests. For example, during 1994–1995, Pakistan and Saudi Arabia fully aligned with the USA and the United Kingdom, which gave rise to an extremist Islamic group known as the Taliban. Although the USA withdrew its assistance to the Taliban following the events of 11 September

2001, Pakistan continued to provide the terrorist organization complete financial and military backing as well as sanctuary for the Taliban and their families until 15 August 2021. Pakistan's approach towards supporting the Taliban and other extremist proxy groups has been harsh, violent, and destructive for Afghanistan. In contrast, China's role has aligned with Pakistan's policies in the region. On the other hand, India has pursued a softer, more civil, and humane strategy to protect its interests in Afghanistan. India's influence in Afghanistan has largely been characterized by a soft-power approach, which has been effective and aligned with the interests of both India and Afghanistan.

Similarly, Iran has primarily utilized the Shiite communities of Afghanistan as proxy groups, and most of Iran's interactions with them have taken place on a bilateral basis. Among Afghanistan's Shiites, Iran is often regarded as a regional actor that protects and advances their political and social rights. In contrast, the United States maintains a broader strategic perspective on Afghanistan and has increasingly invested in democratic and Western-oriented Afghanistani stakeholders to advance its policies in both the country and the wider region.

2.6.3 Transit Corridor to Central Asia and South Asia

Geographically, Afghanistan is situated at the crossroads of four of the world's most populous and wealthy regions: South Asia, Central Asia, the Middle East, and the Persian Gulf. It serves as a connecting point between these regions. More broadly, the area surrounding Afghanistan can be classified into two regions. First, the internal region, which encompasses all six of Afghanistan's neighbours—China to the northeast, Pakistan to the south and east, Iran to the west, and Tajikistan, Uzbekistan, and Turkmenistan to the north. The second region is the outer area, which is made up of the majority of the countries in East, West, Central, and South Asia. Afghanistan serves as the link between these four Asian regions. Besides, Afghanistan plays a key role in the Asia-European commerce network.

Afghanistan is the hub and axis of continental commerce, which enters the country from all points in India, Southeast Asia, Europe, Russia, the Middle East, and China. Afghanistan is situated on the main East-West commercial routes of the enormous Europe-Asia area. Afghanistan served as a junction for commercial routes to the Middle East, Europe, China, and India for centuries.

2.6.4 Military Strategic Depth

Pakistan is always concerned about an Indian military attack on it because of the territorial tension with India. Given its geographical vulnerabilities, such an attack could potentially lead to the fragmentation of Pakistan. As a result, Pakistan has consistently viewed the southern and south-eastern parts of Afghanistan as its strategic military depth. Moreover, other influential actors in Afghanistan also tend to adopt a military approach in their strategies towards the region. For example, on 17 April 2017, the USA, in cooperation with NATO, deployed the 'Mother of All Bombs' (MOAB) in Nangarhar province, eastern Afghanistan. Although the official Afghanistan government statement claimed that the bomb targeted ISIS positions, it was, in reality, a test of America's new weaponry on Afghanistan soil.

2.6.5 The Cause of the Unrest and Burden on Global Society

Afghanistan is viewed by the majority of nations worldwide, particularly those in Europe, as a source of instability on the global stage and a burden on the international community. This perspective is based on two main factors. Initially, the majority of Afghanistani immigrants enters Europe via Turkey and Greece, which has typically caused issues for European nations. Second, international smugglers transport the majority of the drugs generated in Afghanistan into European markets, posing a potential hazard and contributing to a growth in organized crime that jeopardizes the national security of most European nations.

Tragically, given the events of the previous forty years and the absence of a strong stable authority, only a small number of nations consider Afghanistan to be a reliable and stable partner and ally. As a result, a thorough analysis of the strategic considerations made by independent regional and trans-regional actors in Afghanistan is essential.

2.7 The United States of America

As the world's leading economic and military power, the USA played a pivotal role in Afghanistan after 9/11. Following the attacks, President George W. Bush declared a war on terror, obtaining the support of NATO and the international community in this effort. The primary goal and strategy of the USA in Afghanistan were to combat terrorism and eliminate al-Qaeda's safe havens. Additionally, the USA aimed to include state-building and the stabilization of democracy in Afghanistan among its objectives.

Four presidents—Bush, Obama, Trump, and Biden—took office between 2001 and 2021, and they all had somewhat distinct approaches to diplomacy and strategy in Afghanistan. For instance, George W. Bush's strategy in Afghanistan aligned with the USA's long-term strategy in Asia, aiming to limit and control the spheres of influence of China and Russia in South and Central Asia. This strategy was largely continued during Obama's presidency, with some adjustments. However, since taking office, Trump has questioned America's long-term involvement in Afghanistan, pointing to pressure from the American people. Thus, Trump's goal was to bring an end to the longest-running US conflict in Afghanistan. As an independent and sovereign nation, the USA has the right to re-evaluate its foreign policy and interests. However, it was a strategic error for the country to elevate terrorist organizations like the Taliban on a global stage and foster support for them in the region by pulling out of Afghanistan without due consideration.

To fully understand the reasons behind the swift and irresponsible withdrawal on 15 August 2021, we will need time to assess the situation. However, some analysts speculate that the USA was aware of Russia's impending military action and invasion of Ukraine on 22 February 2022. It seems that the USA may have withdrawn from Afghanistan based on strategic calculations and recognized that it could not effectively engage in two active conflicts—Afghanistan and Ukraine—simultaneously.

It should be noted that the USA pursued its goals and strategy in Afghanistan (2001-2021) on two levels. One, on the domestic level or Afghanistan itself; the second, on the regional level. At the domestic level, the USA's goals and strategy were:

1. Dismantling al-Qaeda and the safe havens of other terrorist organizations on Afghanistan territory (failed)
2. Establishing a governing system and state-building (failed)
3. Strengthening and promotion of democracy (failed)
4. Prolonged stay as a regional hegemon in Afghanistan

At the regional level, US policy and strategy in Afghanistan focused on three geopolitical areas:

2.7.1 South Asia

1. Addressing the potentially serious disputes between Pakistan and Afghanistan in order to support the regional campaign against extremism and terrorism.
2. The intentional continuation of the battle between India and Pakistan in order to maintain control over India.
3. Prolonged stay in Afghanistan as a result of its close proximity to China as well as its desire to maintain dominance over Central Asia, East Asia, and the South Asian Canal.

2.7.2 Central Asia

1. Created a secure trust in terms of security for Central Asian states so they may utilize the Afghanistan-Pakistan corridor to securely connect to open waterways and transit to South and East Asia.
2. Closely examined China-Russian relations in the light of US strategic initiatives and objectives in Afghanistan and Central Asia.
3. Addressing the ethnic disputes in Afghanistan, as there is an opportunity for Central Asians to become negatively involved there.

2.7.3 The Persian Gulf

1. The USA aimed to control the Persian Gulf energy resources by leveraging Afghanistan's strategic location, extensive logistics, and operational facilities.
2. The USA viewed Iran, situated between Iraq and Afghanistan, as a potential threat to the secure transit of energy from the Persian Gulf, influencing its regional strategy.
3. The potential for Afghanistan to serve as a backup route for the flow of energy from Central Asia to the high seas.
4. Making use of the religious potential of the Persian Gulf and Arab nations in Afghanistan in the light of Iran's ambitions to increase its influence in the region.
5. The mutual security dependency between Afghanistan and the Persian Gulf, as well as the influence of security on the development of a commerce route connecting Central Asia to the Persian Gulf via Afghanistan and positive ties with the Gulf's Arab states.

2.8 CHINA

Before 15 August 2021, China employed a largely complex strategy, often in coordination with Pakistan, to address political and security issues in Afghanistan. Like Russia, China was dissatisfied with the US presence in Afghanistan and its influence in the region. Consequently, China established covert connections with the Taliban, working in collusion with Pakistan. This involved indirectly providing financial support to the Taliban through channels associated with Pakistan's Inter-Services Intelligence (ISI). During the Soviet invasion of Afghanistan in 1979, the USA actively opposed Soviet actions, contributing to the Afghanistan resistance and exerting pressure on the Soviet Union. China, meanwhile, successfully assessed and responded to these geopolitical shifts. However, during the US presence in Afghanistan, China capitalized on the economic opportunities in the region, benefiting from the free security provided by the USA.

In South Asia and Central Asia, China has pursued three general strategies through Afghanistan:

1. China's clear-cut, direct interests first prioritise and ensure they remain protected.
2. Initiatives to help settle disputes in the area so that its economic plans may be more effectively carried out.
3. Effort to meet its long-term strategic objectives.

However, the following are the main strategic objectives China has for Afghanistan:

1. Utilizing the natural resources of Afghanistan (lithium and copper)
2. China and Pakistan's joint manoeuvre zone in South Asia
3. Limiting India's influence in Afghanistan because of border problems and the strategic competition China and Pakistan have with India
4. Establish dominance in Central Asian markets through its influence in Afghanistan.
5. China trying to manage and control the activities of Uighur separatists and Muslim groups within its borders, using Afghanistan's geopolitical situation to its advantage.
6. Protecting China's commercial assets in Pakistan including the Gwadar Port.

7. Filling the security void left by the USA and NATO's departure from Afghanistan and the surrounding area.

2.9 IRAN

Iran shares a long border and many cultural ties with Afghanistan, making any developments in Afghanistan directly impactful on Iran's national security. The political, social, and economic relations between the two countries have deep historical roots. However, Iran's strategy towards Afghanistan has always been inconsistent, leading to a lack of a unified approach. Various factors have contributed to the fluctuations in Iran's multi-layered foreign policy regarding Afghanistan. For instance, despite significant ideological differences, Iran, which had recently undergone the Islamic Revolution and had an entirely Islamist-run government, coordinated with Saudi Arabia and the USA to help the Afghanistan Mujahideen during the Soviet invasion of Afghanistan. Iran allowed talks with the Taliban in 1995 after the latter had taken over a large portion of the country and Iran perceived a Sunni Islamic state operating in its neighbourhood as a threat to its national security. In response, Iran initiated negotiations with the Taliban while simultaneously offering political and military support to the Afghanistan National Front, led by Ahmad Shah Massoud, who was actively fighting against the Taliban. Additionally, after the events of 9/11, Iran played an active role in the state-building and reconstruction of Afghanistan, supporting the Afghanistan government in the international community. Simultaneously, Iran welcomed the Taliban, a designated terrorist group, by hosting them in Tehran. This clearly demonstrates the multi-layered nature of Iran's policy towards Afghanistan and highlights the contradictions within its foreign policy regarding the country.

Iran's foreign policy towards Afghanistan is contradictory, yet it nonetheless supports relative political stability in the country since it has long-term interests there, unlike Pakistan. Iran's success or failure in Afghanistan has a direct impact on its interactions with Russia and China, as well as its efforts to mitigate US pressure and sanctions, as a regional actor in the Persian Gulf and Central Asia. On the other hand, Iran's national security is gravely threatened by an increasing number of Afghanistani refugees into the country as well as the smuggling of narcotics and weapons from Afghanistan. Iran's approach to Afghanistan may therefore be summed up as follows:

1. Addressing the Helmand River water supply issue, which is the primary source of water supply limitation in Iran's Sistan region, has turned into a political standoff between the two nations.
2. Guarding shared borders and preventing the flow of weapons and drugs into Iran and from Iran to European nations.
3. Under severe Western pressure, Iran prioritizes securing its economic interests in Afghanistan, making its markets a key focus of its strategy.
4. As Iran and Saudi Arabia vie for leadership in the Islamic world, each promoting different interpretations of Islam—Shiite and Sunni extremism, respectively—Iran aims to prevent Saudi Arabia from gaining influence in Afghanistan.

2.10 INDIA

India is a rising and influential power in the South Asian region, with South Asia being a top priority in its strategic plans. India views Afghanistan as an integral part of South Asia, which gives Afghanistan special significance in Indian foreign policy. According to India's grand foreign policy doctrine, countries are divided into three concentric circles, with the first circle encompassing its immediate neighbours, including Afghanistan. Within this circle, India tries to establish regional hegemony, enabling it to counter the presence of other powers in the region. Afghanistan serves as a strategic mediator for India in its confrontation with other powers, particularly Pakistan. Additionally, Afghanistan acts as a platform for India's influence in Central Asia. After 9/11, recognizing Afghanistan's strategic position, India sought to expand its cooperation with the country, leading to a strategic alliance that allowed India to establish a foothold in Afghanistan. This alliance enabled India to leverage Afghanistan's position as a gateway to Central Asian countries.

India's strategic depth in Afghanistan is demonstrated by its access to Central Asia, its multibillion-dollar aid in rebuilding Afghanistan, its training of Afghanistani security forces, the opening of four consulates across the country, and finally, Pakistan's political siege of the country. Given its awareness of Afghanistan's geopolitical location, India is attempting to increase its dominance and take use of its strategic location to obtain access to strategic Central Asia. Relations between India and Central Asia used to be primarily based on shared cultural interests, but following the fall of the Soviet Union and the establishment of the Central Asian republics, India's foreign policy began to place more and more emphasis on Central Asia due to practical concerns like stopping the flow of weapons and drugs, preventing Islamic extremism and terrorism, gaining economic advantages, securing energy resources, and so forth. India lacks direct access to Central Asia; hence, collaboration with Afghanistan is required to accomplish India's long- and medium-term objectives in Central Asia.

Afghanistan's standing in India's foreign policy has also been strengthened by the country's continuous conflict with Pakistan over Kashmir. As they share Pakistan as an adversary, India, and Afghanistan have positive political and cultural ties. Pakistan firmly backed terrorist organizations in both Afghanistan and India after it conflicted with that country; in fact, Pakistani authorities actively advocated for the Afghanistan Taliban. The Pakistani military has attempted to use the Taliban to establish its strategic depth in Afghanistan fearing an Indian siege.

India acknowledged the US-led and international community engagement in Afghanistan following 9/11, which resulted in positive improvements to India's foreign policy. India carried out its plans to strengthen its strategic depth in Afghanistan and lessen Pakistan's influence there following the events of 11 September 2001. The Indian government undoubtedly has a variety of interests in Afghanistan, the most strategic of which are as follows:

1. Reducing Pakistan's power as a competitor in Afghanistan and South Asia.
2. Addressing and countering the threats of Islamic extremism and terrorism.
3. Leveraging Afghanistan as a bridge and access point to Central Asia.
4. Increasing the influence inside the region.
5. Reducing China's sway over Afghanistan and the surrounding area.
6. Enhancing the security framework of South Asia by integrating Afghanistan into this system.

To accomplish its objectives, India must cooperate with Afghanistan in a regular setting.[5] Delhi would provide the foundation for its direct presence in Central Asia by integrating Kabul into the South Asian security complex. This would also reinforce the India-based security paradigm in South Asia and increase Delhi's strategic depth within Afghanistan's borders.

2.11 PAKISTAN

The foreign policies of states are dictated by their national objectives and interests which serve as the guiding principles for their actions on the international stage. Based on their definition of friend and enemy, national objectives, or national interests, states follow their foreign policy doctrines. Put in another way, nations continually undermine their adversaries in order to maintain stability. The government of Pakistan used the same principle to guide its foreign policy against Afghanistan. The Pakistani government has actively contributed to Afghanistan's destabilization for at least the past forty years, while also providing support to terrorist organizations operating there. As it seeks to maintain its strategic depth in Afghanistan, the Pakistani government has a variety of interests in the country. There are three components to Pakistan's strategic depth in Afghanistan: political, military, and economic.

2.11.1 Strategic Military Depth

Pakistan is geographically well-positioned in South Asia, yet its shape is narrow. Because of this geographically flaw it lacks a substantial military and geographical backup. Following their ongoing hostilities and their three previous wars over Kashmiri, India and Pakistan have tense and antagonistic relations. The Indian Army developed the *Cold Start Doctrine* after the Kargil War in 1999, and the Pakistani military believes that in the event of a new conflict, it will use it to launch a swift attack that would split Pakistan into its northern and southern regions. This will result in the communication channels between the Pakistani army and all its armed units being severed. The Pakistani military is seeking strategic depth in Afghanistan as a result of political and military dissatisfaction. From the perspective of the military, *"strategic depth is an area where it is a good place for a retreating army to regroup and at the same time not be threatened by the enemy advancing, and this retreat can provide enough time for military cohesion and plan for the army"*. Thus, Pakistani strategists think that Pakistan has to have a strategic depth in Afghanistan if the Indian army's goal is to split the nation. As a result, Pakistan has traditionally regarded the regions of Khost, Kandahar, Ghazni, Nangarhar, and the south and southeast of Afghanistan as its strategic depth inside the country.

Map 1: Pakistan Conflict Map 2019

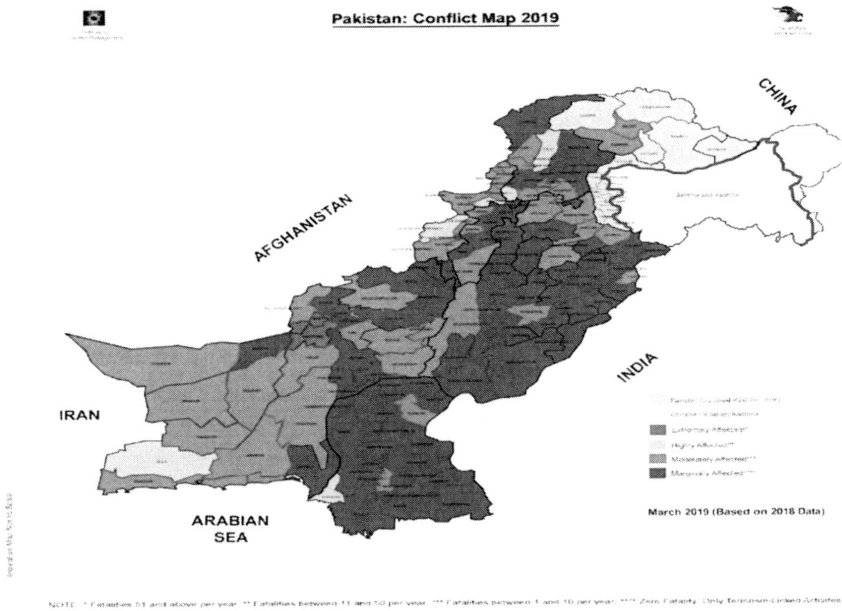

Source: Institute of Conflict Management

2.11.2 Pakistan's Political Strategy

The Durand Line is the source of Pakistan and Afghanistan's territorial disputes. Pakistan considers the Durand Line a settled issue and treats it as the official international border between the two countries. Nonetheless, the Durand Line is not acknowledged as a boundary by Afghanistan. Afghanistan argues that in 1893 the boundary was drawn by British India, and the agreement was made before Pakistan had its own government. The Durand Line issue remains unresolved from Afghanistan's perspective. Additionally, since the border itself is a contentious matter between the two countries, it has resulted in the division of Pashtun communities on both sides. This division has fuelled separatist sentiments among Pakistani Pashtuns, creating a significant political conundrum for the government of Pakistan.

Pakistan has placed its strategy of assisting Afghanistan's Pashtuns, some of whom are Islamic extremists (Taliban and Salafist), beyond its foreign policy towards Afghanistan for the past forty years in order to be able to handle both the Durand Line and Pashtunistan separatists. Pakistan gave the Taliban enormous political, military, and financial backing in 1995 when they took over control of Afghanistan. Pakistan never stopped helping the Taliban and foreign terrorist groups like al-Qaeda, ISIS, etc., after 2001, even with the USA and other international nations stationed in Afghanistan. In contrast to Afghanistan and India, Pakistan has used ideology as a tool in its foreign policy towards the region and even the entire world. Evidence suggests that between 2001 and 2018, the USA paid Pakistan $ 1 billion per year to keep terrorists under control. Pakistan has thus twice (1995–2021) provided extraordinary support to the Taliban, its proxy group in Afghanistan, in an effort to gain political power there because it believes that an independent, stable, and self-sufficient Afghanistan government is not in the interests of the region. Pakistan views Afghanistan's weak government as advantageous for it.

2.11.3 Pakistan Economic Strategy

It is debatable what Pakistan's economic interests are in Afghanistan. Pakistan hopes to sell its exports to Afghanistan and other Central Asian nations. Major actors have been competing for gas and oil pipelines in and out Central Asia in recent years due to the region's huge and mostly untapped energy resources. Geographically speaking, Afghanistan is close to the region of the Middle East and Central Asia that is abundant in energy. Pakistan needs energy to boost its economy, and despite its many issues, the TAPI gas pipeline will give the country access to adequate energy for the next 50 years. The pipeline was intended to be finished by 2019, but because of Afghanistan's and the region's fast changes, not much has happened.

The China-Pakistan Economic Corridor (CPEC) is a key component of China's Belt and Road Initiative (BRI), aiming to connect Central Asia with South Asia through Pakistan and Afghanistan. As a result, the security situation in Afghanistan has a significant influence on Pakistan's economic interests. Waltz, a prominent theorist of the school of structural realism, posits that states not only strive to enhance their military power but also seek to bolster their economic strength.

Map 2: TAPI Route Map

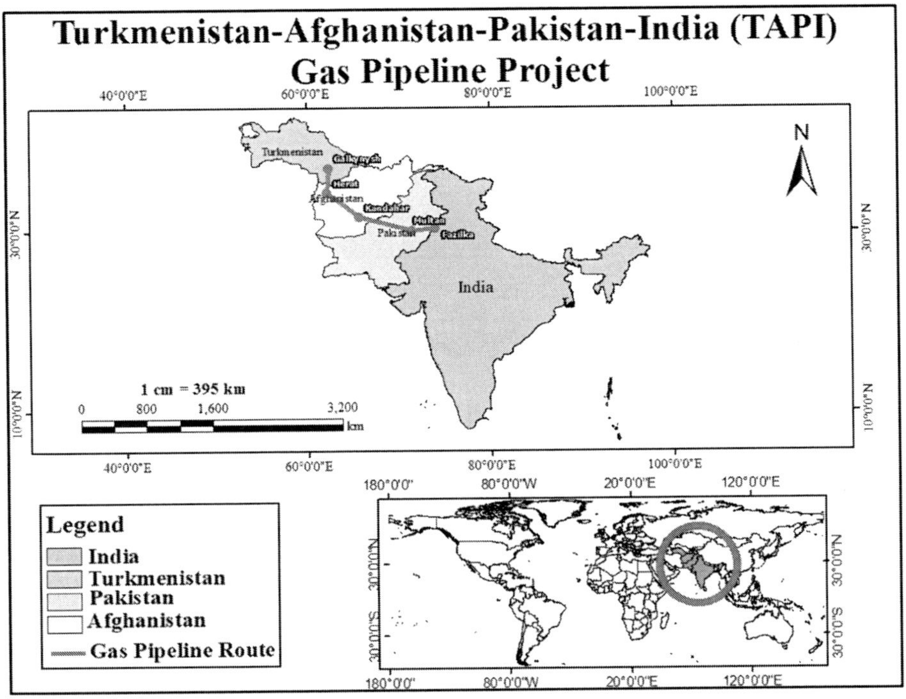

Source: Author based on TAPI Roadmap

2.12 THE IMPLICATIONS OF THE COLLABORATION OF SOVEREIGN ACTORS IN AFGHANISTAN

All the key players in Afghanistan share similar strategies in certain areas. If these actors cooperate, it could lead to regional convergence, creating a win-win situation for all involved. Afghanistan, in particular, stands to gain the most from this collaboration. Security and regional economic development are two powerful drivers that could foster this convergence among the sovereign states in Afghanistan. Given its strategic location, Afghanistan has the potential to significantly contribute to regional convergence and economic growth. The successful model of regional economic integration in Europe over the past few decades has inspired similar efforts among developing nations. For Afghanistan and its neighbouring regions, such convergence holds particular importance, offering opportunities for enhanced cooperation and economic development.

2.12.1 BRI and the Role of Afghanistan

The Belt and Road Initiative (BRI) is a global development strategy launched by the People's Republic of China. It aims to connect Asia with Africa and Europe through a network of land and maritime routes. The primary objectives of the BRI are to enhance regional integration, boost trade, and stimulate economic growth across the participating countries. By investing in infrastructure projects, China seeks to create a modern Silk Road, fostering stronger economic ties and cooperation between regions. (European Bank 2021)

In addition to its economic benefits, this initiative establishes the foundation for fostering greater social and cultural interaction and ties together sixty-four sovereign states and 4.5 billion people worldwide. This project will have a significant impact on the economic growth of every country along its path and greatly contribute to the integration of Asia. By ensuring prosperity, stability, and security across multiple regions, the BRI represents a win-win cooperation among Asian, European, and African nations. It marks a turning point in international convergence, linking significant economic interests with broader global objectives.

Two millennia ago, the Silk Road traversed across Afghanistan. Between China and the regions that are now known as Afghanistan, there has long been a route for traders, pilgrims, and commercial caravans. Afghanistan has traditionally served as a vital route connecting India and China, the Far East, Central Asia, and the Middle East, as well as serving as a hub for social and commercial exchanges. This path is crucial for Afghanistan, of course. Afghanistan can export to nations in Europe and the Far East by using the Silk Road. Through projects linked to the Silk Road, both Chinese and Afghanistani investors can explore investment opportunities in each other's countries, fostering mutual economic growth. The Wakhan-Badakhshan Corridor in Afghanistan is a crucial gateway on the Silk Road, and its revival is essential for boosting economic and commercial development in Afghanistan and the broader region. This corridor not only facilitates trade but also strengthens the region's strategic importance in the context of the Belt and Road Initiative. (Dunning 2021)

Economic and trade relations between Afghanistan and China are growing, with significant investments being made. In 2008, the Hamid Karzai administration signed a 30-year agreement with a Chinese joint venture, MCC, to mine high-grade copper at Mes Aynak. This site is estimated to contain up to 12 million tons of copper, highlighting its substantial mineral wealth and the potential for major economic benefits for both countries. (Kullab 2022) In early 2012, the Afghanistan government signed an agreement with the China National Oil Company to explore and extract oil and gas reserves in the Amu Basin, located in northern Afghanistan. This agreement marks another significant step in enhancing economic ties between Afghanistan and China, focusing on developing Afghanistan's energy sector.

It is important to keep in mind that the projected value of Afghanistan's diverse mining deposits exceeds $ 3 trillion. Gas, minerals including iron and copper, and a variety of valuable and ornamental stones are abundant in Afghanistan. In addition, an evaluation conducted recently at the World Institute of Taste and Quality in Brussels revealed that out of three hundred varieties of saffron from various nations, Afghanistan saffron was deemed the best in the world. (Jahanmal 2019) China's involvement in the import of Chinese commodities into Afghanistan and the export of Afghanistani items to China is particularly significant for both sides.

2.12.2 The Economic Relations of Central and South Asia and the Strategic Role of Afghanistan

The potential for regional integration between Central and South Asia holds substantial economic benefits. Currently, trade between these two regions is minimal, largely due to the high transportation costs associated with their geographic distance. India, the third-largest energy consumer globally, (Sbesta 2020) and Pakistan, with its projected increasing energy demand, could greatly benefit from the resources available in Central Asia. Central Asian countries like Turkmenistan and Uzbekistan have significant gas reserves, Kazakhstan is a major oil producer, and Kyrgyzstan and Tajikistan have substantial hydropower production capabilities. Enhancing connectivity and trade between these regions could unlock their economic potential and address mutual energy needs.

Afghanistan is positioned to offer the most direct, cheapest, and efficient energy corridors connecting Central Asia with South Asia. All proposed corridors between these regions will traverse Afghanistan. Notably, the

Turkmenistan-Afghanistan-Pakistan-India (TAPI) pipeline project is underway, aiming to transport up to 33 billion cubic metres of natural gas annually from Turkmenistan through Afghanistan to Pakistan and India. Recently, the government of Bangladesh has also shown interest in joining this initiative, further extending its potential impact.

For exporting Turkmenistan gas to Pakistan and India, the TAPI route is the most efficient option. The alternative, the Turkmenistan-Iran-Pakistan-India route, is significantly longer, making it less practical compared to the direct TAPI pipeline.

For future exports of Uzbekistan's natural gas to Pakistan and India, the most viable and efficient route would be through Afghanistan, which is significantly shorter than the alternative routes. Additionally, Afghanistan provides the most direct path for power transmission lines between Central Asia and South Asia. The CASA-1000 project, currently in progress, aims to transfer 1,000 MW of electricity from Kyrgyzstan and Tajikistan to Pakistan via Afghanistan using a 1,227-kilometre transmission line. This route is the best option for the project, with no more advantageous alternatives.

Thus, Afghanistan has the potential to serve as the hub for a unified Central Asia-South Asia energy market. This integration could be transformative for both regions, driving substantial economic growth and development across the entire area.

Map 3: Wakhan Corridor

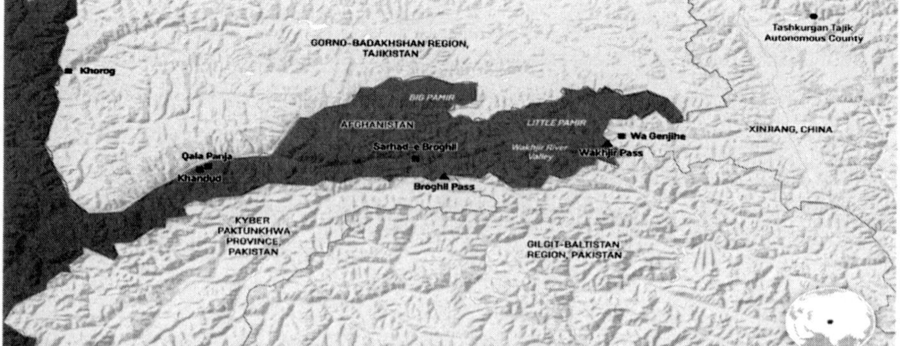

Source: The Karakoram

The next chapter will be the continuation of this chapter with a different topic. It will discuss two important issues. First, it will explain the clash of the strategic depth of sovereign actors and its outcomes for Afghanistan and will answer the tough questions relating to it. Second, it will examine the challenges to state-building in Afghanistan and will have an in-depth analysis. The second part will answer the question: why has Afghanistan not had a stable and independent government (economically and politically) over the past decades?

2.13 CONCLUSION

Due to its strategic location at the crossroads of four regional security complexes—South Asia, Central Asia, the Persian Gulf, and China—Afghanistan has long attracted the attention of various regional and global powers. This geopolitical position has not only fuelled the interests and competition of major powers but has also been a key factor in the continuation of prolonged wars in the country. However, most members of these security complexes have concluded that Afghanistan, due to its internal weaknesses, does not pose a significant threat on its own. The primary concern for regional and global actors is the potential use of Afghanistan territory by their rivals to increase influence or harm their interests.

These concerns are rooted in the theory of realism in international relations. According to this theory, international politics is a realm of power struggles, and the primary priority of states is to ensure their survival in an unstable and anarchic environment. As a result, countries are constantly suspicious of each other's intentions and goals within the international system, and this uncertainty leads to defensive and pre-emptive reactions. Consequently, any involvement or interaction by a foreign actor with Afghanistan triggers responses from other players.

A clear example of this situation was the presence of the USA in Afghanistan from 2001 to 2021, which raised concerns and reactions from China, Russia, and Iran. These countries, feeling threatened by the potential risks posed by the US presence, responded by establishing proxy groups within Afghanistan. The result of these competitions not only weakened the Afghan government but also escalated unrest and complicated the security situation in the country.

On the other hand, the weakness of Afghanistan's diplomatic apparatus was another factor contributing to this situation. The Afghan government was never able to effectively communicate to regional and global actors that its interactions with one country did not mean hostility towards others. For example, Kabul failed to assure Pakistan that its closer ties with India did not pose a threat to Islamabad. This diplomatic failure led Pakistan to continue supporting armed groups such as the Taliban and other terrorist organizations in Afghanistan, further weakening the country in the process.

NOTES

1. John Mearsheimer divides realism into two parts: classical realism and structural realism. According to him, classical realism, in which Machiavelli and Thucydides are prominent scientists, believes that the desire for power and the will to overcome others is the most fundamental aspect of human nature and the selfish and self-centred behaviour of governments is only a reflection of the personality of those who are governing the state. In fact, Thucydides reduced realism to the human nature. Thucydides focused on anarchy and self-help in the international system of ancient Greece, emphasizing how the Spartans and Athenians competed with each other and gained political power and influence over allies. Thucydides claims in his landmark work "*A History of the Peloponnesian War*" that the main spark for the war between Athens and the Spartans was ignited by the fear in the two sides of each other. The Spartans feared the growing power of the Athenians and their expansionist policies, and the Athenians thought that a ruthless and vast military power was trying to compete with them for the whole of Greece. These misconceptions between the two sides resulted in nothing but fighting. The result of this struggle was the weakness of both the City-States and the destruction. He believed that it was the psychology of fear and misunderstanding that led the two nations to a bloody catastrophe and that the neglect of the psychological factors involved in Athens and Sparta was the real cause of the war. In any case, the reduction of realism to the natural condition of man is also reflected in the works of thinkers such as Morgenthau. According to Mearsheimer, structural realism, which considers itself dependent on this type of realism, sees the cause of war and peace in the structure of the international system and not in human nature, that is, structuralists look from the top to down in the international system.
2. Security Dilemma, which in security literature refers to the security puzzle has a simple meaning. In the international environment in the face of what is rightly or wrongly considered a threatening environment. To defend their country against foreign threats, national leaders take actions that they consider defensive, such as strengthening the army, increasing the military budget, and so on. These leaders consider their actions to be purely defensive, and think that their intentions and motives are just as clear to their neighbours and other countries, when they are not. In fact, what distinguishes an offensive weapon from a defensive weapon is the intention of the owner and depends on which side of the barrel you look inside. The problem of policymakers in dealing with this security dilemma has two aspects: a perceptual aspect and a documentary aspect. In the real world of security, the true intentions of the enemy cannot be easily understood. And reciprocity against a government depends on the perception that is gained after examining their actions. In other words, governments tend to attribute

the actions of others to the inherent characteristics of themselves or their leaders, and underestimate the role of environmental factors in the behaviour, such as the strengthening of the former Soviet military in Eastern Europe, because it was fear of NATO power not because of the expansionist goals of the Soviet Union. In any case, the security dilemma is a problem that exists in the system of international anarchy and affects the behaviour of governments.

3. This figure, reshaped from: Ismailov, Eldar & Papava Vladimer,. 2010, "Rethinking Central Eurasia". Central Asia- Caucasus & Silk Road Studies Program, A Joint Transatlantic Research, and Policy Centre, p. 102.
4. The post-Cold War situation was such that the United States allowed the victorious superpower to introduce the doctrine of the *New World Order* as a strategic policy of the American government in the 20th and 21st centuries. In a radio address to the world during the summer of April 1991, then-President George W. Bush declared the theory of the New World Order as America's post-Cold War national strategy, adding that the world had come to the conclusion that neither multipolar nor bipolar systems, but only a unipolar system that can ensure world peace and security, and now the USA deserves to lead a unipolar system more than any other country because of its unrivalled economic and military power. However, some scholars of international relations believe that the period of 1991-2001 can be considered as the period of the *New World Order*, but after 2001, due to the formation of the hierarchy of power, the term *New World System* should be used.
5. The ideal scenario is for Afghanistan to have an independent elected government formed through the votes of its people. However, at present, following 15 August 2021, the Taliban—acting on behalf of Pakistan and several other countries—has taken control of Afghanistan. As of 29 May 2022, no country in the world has officially recognized the Taliban government. Consequently, Afghanistan lacks a popularly elected and legitimate representative government.

Chapter 3

Search for Strategic Depth and Challenges to State-building

3.1 INTRODUCTION

In the second chapter, the theoretical framework was discussed in three parts. In the first part, structural realism was evaluated. Based on the findings of this research, structural realism was found to be the most suitable theoretical framework. In the second part, the impact of the geopolitical location of Afghanistan on its peace and stability was discussed. It was found that throughout its history Afghanistan has never been able to use its golden location (geopolitical and geostrategic) to its advantage. In contrast, Afghanistan's geopolitical location has always had a negative impact on its stability. In the third part, the role and strategic goals of sovereign actors in Afghanistan the USA, China, India, Pakistan, and Iran are evaluated.

Based on the framework of this research, the third chapter discusses the *Clash of Respective Strategic Depths of Sovereign Actors in Afghanistan*. This chapter consists of two parts. The first is about the political and social challenges facing state-building in Afghanistan examined from both internal as well as external perspectives. From the external perspective, it focuses on the impact of the conflict of interest of sovereign actors in Afghanistan. From the internal perspective, the chapter examines the relevance of the concepts of the modern nation-state and governments in the context of Afghanistan. The overall objective is to examine the biggest socio-political challenges facing Statebuilding in Afghanistan from 2001 to 2021. It is, therefore, necessary to briefly review the peculiarities and also the way of formation of modern post-Westphalian states, so that the process of formation and the obstacles of state building in

Afghanistan can be examined in its light. The second part of the chapter is devoted to the conflicts between the strategic goals of several sovereign actors (the USA, China, India, Pakistan, and Iran) in Afghanistan and their impact on the state-building process in Afghanistan.

3.2 CONCEPTUAL BASIS

3.2.1 Examining the Terminology of Nation-States

The terms 'Nation-State, 'State-Building and 'Nation-Building'[1] were conceptualized as modern categories in the political-philosophical thought and political-social developments of contemporary European centuries, the period in which nationalism emerged as a process of these developments and the rule of kings was replaced by the idea of the formation of the nation-state. Until the 15th and 16th centuries, different authorities—sultans, the Church, feudalists, and lords—ruled Europe. But in the middle of the 17th century, the Peace of Westphalia (1648), at the end of the thirty-year religious wars of Europe, weakened the power of the Church. (Teschke 1999: 20) Subsequently, the state gradually became the main source of political authority, thereby creating a framework for modern international relations. Political thoughts around the concept of the modern state and nation-state evolved in the Age of Enlightenment and the Renaissance of Europe arose from the intellectual developments of previous periods of history and were influenced by the civilization of different lands, from ancient Greece to India and China and up to the Islamic civilization in the Middle East, and other ancient civilizations in North Africa.

The transformation in the field of thought and political knowledge of Western society, especially Europe, was one of the important consequences of the Renaissance. Many different scientists have presented various theories on this matter. The term 'Nation-State' secured an important place in the text of these theories. The foundation of modern states was laid on the basis of new political ideas and knowledge. In the new process of political and social development, the 'State' and the 'Nation' were mutually consolidated. Vassals and subjects were gradually promoted to the nation and citizens, and the autocratic and absolutist government system became a modern state with the characteristics of accountability to the Nation and Citizens. New mechanisms were formed. Civil society, elected parliaments and legislation, and law enforcement were created by these institutions and have evolved over time.

3.2.2 State

In general, the state can be defined by two definitions, classic and modern, but due to the different ideas and views of political science and law scholars and the difference in schools of thought and ideology, a single image of the modern definition of the state is not presented. There is not even the same expression and image of the state within every school of thought and ideology. For example, ancient philosophers such as Aristotle consider the state as a political association between the elements of society. (Aristotle 1944: 1.1252a) Scholars such as Hobbes, Locke, and Jean-Jacques Rousseau consider the states as the result of a social contract. (Muhammad 2020: 123) Communists following the thoughts of Karl Marx (1818-1883) consider the state to be the product of class struggles between opposing social forces. (Obo and Coker 2014: 533) There are different and even contradictory views in the definition of Islamic sects, especially the current Islamist movements, about the state and the mechanism of state formation, which talk about the similarity of Islam with politics and the necessity of forming an Islamic state. In the classical definition, the state is the highest manifestation of the power relationship and the exercise of sovereignty in society. In this definition, the state is not formed based on a social contract, but by the use of power tools and the effectiveness of these tools stabilize the role and presence of the government in society.

The modern state is also divided into numerous and diverse states in terms of its nature and characteristics. Some modern states are totalitarian and despotic. Many ideological states, such as the communist single-party[2] states, are considered modern ideological states. However, the ideal modern states that succeed in forming a Nation in the country under its rule and complete the process of Nation-State formation are modern national states. Although, some political and social scientists, such as Anthony Giddens, an English sociologist, defined states as principal actors within the global political order and believed that sovereignty is the most prominent characteristic of modern states. (Giddens 1990: 66-71) Based on this definition, ideological states that cannot be national states are not considered modern states either but some scholars believe that ideological states, especially left-wing Marxist states, are non-national modern states, although in modern ideological states, national democratic political culture is absent. Despite this, modern ideological states have two features—nationalism and sovereignty. Modern national states grow in the context of democracy and people are citizens in the territory of a modern national state, while in classical states and in traditional and ideological totalitarian governments, they are subjects of the government and rulers.

3.2.3 Nation

The term 'Nation' entered political and legal knowledge as a modern category in the Renaissance era. The concept of Nation in this category comes from the word which has Latin roots in European languages and means birth. Some define the Nation with the State and some talk about the Nation without the State. Contemporary scientists and philosophers of political science consider the nation not as a specific ethnic and religious identity, but as a political thought that gives national and trans-ethnic identity to the country's nationals and citizens. Anthony D. Smith narrated the definition of according to Ernest Renan (1823-1892), the French historian, linguist, and philosopher who considers the Nation as a kind of spiritual solidarity that is created and maintained by a distinct historical consciousness. He believes that the homogeneity of nations from a 'racial' and 'ethnic' point of view is an illusion and believes that different nations have followed different paths for their emergence.

> A nation is a great solidarity, created by the sentiments of the sacrifices which have been made and of those that one is disposed to make in the future. It presupposes a past; but it resumes itself in the present by a tangible fact: the consent, the clearly expressed desire to continue life in common. The existence of a nation is a plebiscite of every day, as the existence of the individual is a perpetual affirmation of life. (Smith 1998: 10)

The idea of the Nation draws the members of society from dependence and loyalty to small local, tribal, and ethnic identities to a new inclusive and broad identity called the Nation. It is a people organized; a people united. In this respect, a Nation gives an idea of an organization to the people within a territory. In the modern sense, as Eric Hobsbawm cited, "a nation is the totality of individuals united by living under a common law and represented by the same legislative assembly." (Hobsbawm 1996: 1066)

3.3 National Identity

In the modern and scientific definition, National Identity neither refers to ethnic and tribal identity, nor does it refer to religious and racial identity, and it is not the reflection of these identities at the internal or external level of a state. National Identity is the official and legal affiliation of an individual or a community to the nation-state. It is a cultural term. Common history, common geography, common political and economic structure, common culture, common interests, and losses are considered components of National Identity in a state. Moreover, Eugene Tartakovsky believes that 'National identity' is a subjective construct, differing from the concept of 'nationality,' which is an objective marker of an individual's belonging to a nation. (Tartakovsky 2010: 1851) According to him, 'National Identity' is a subjective conviction (self-categorization) as to which nation one belongs to, and includes positive and negative emotions towards that nation. These commonalities create a common national spirit for the residents and citizens of the country, and their relationships are formed in the light of this common spirit despite social and cultural differences.

National identity is a citizen's identity that is formed by the political thought that believes in the identity of the citizen in a country, not by homogenizing the descent identity and integrating all the descent and cultural identities into a majority and dominant descent identity. Reducing national and civil identity to descent and ethnic identity, even under the pretext of a majority of an ethnic group in a country, fuels political instability and social crisis. As Hobsbawm put it, the concept of a single, exclusive, and unchanging ethnic or cultural, or other identity is a dangerous piece of brainwashing. Human mental identities are not like shoes, of which we can only wear one pair at a time. (Hobsbawm 1996: 1067) Descent(ism) is an ideology that sees society as black and white, and two groups of right and wrong. In the mirror of this ideology, one sees peers as superior and rightful in the field of political, social, and economic power, and considers other ethnic and descent groups to obey and serve them. In this respect, this is the same ideology of fascism, racism, and apartheid, which not only has no scientific and human foundation but led to very bloody conflicts such as World War II.

3.4 NATION-BUILDING

Jochen Hippler believes that the term 'Nation-Building' is markedly vague and inconsistent. However, he gives two clarifications:

> First, *Nation-building is, on the one hand, a process of socio-political development, which ideally—usually over a longer historical time span—allows initially loosely linked communities to become a common society with a nation-state corresponding to it. Such a process can get off the ground as a result of political, economic, social, cultural, and other dynamics. However, it is not automatic that such nation-building processes will proceed successfully. They can involve extremely different dimensions and instruments, such as economic integration, cultural integration, political centralization, bureaucratic control, military conquest or subjugation, creation of common interests, democratization and establishment of common citizenship or repression, and acts of 'ethnic cleansing'.* Second, *Nation-Building can, on the other hand, be a political objective as well as a strategy for reaching specific political objectives. Internal or external players strive to create or strengthen a political and social system constituted under a nation-state where this appears to serve their interests, where it fulfils particular functional requirements to a greater degree than a previously existing arrangement, or where it strengthens their power or weakens that of their opponents.* (Hippler 2005: 6-7)

If the concept of nation is accepted as a socio-political idea, and not as an ethnic, religious, or racial entity, it would be difficult to limit and specify the elements that make up the nation. Despite that, homogeneity in the identity of citizens and residents of a state facilitates the formation of nation-building while heterogeneity leads to difficulty and complexity. However, in the nation-building process, the feeling and belonging to different cultural and social identities, which reflect heterogeneity, give way to the common national feeling and identity in a specific geographical unit called the state.

Among the components that make up the elements of the nation, language, ethnicity, and religious identity are considered the most influential factors. Some contemporary Western theorists and philosophers point to the role of language in the formation of the nation. There is no doubt that language plays a significant role in the formation of a nation and the success of the nation-state formation process, but even though the common language facilitates and accelerates the process of nation-building and nation-state, it will never lead to the creation of a united nation. The USA, England, Australia, and Canada all speak the English language, but they are not a single nation. The countries of Latin America and Spain in Europe also have a single language, but they are not considered a single nation. Twenty-three Arab countries, with a common Arabic language in Asia and Africa are similar examples. Each one of them is considered a separate nation. Though Switzerland has four (German, French, Italian, and Romansh) official languages, it is considered a single Swiss nation. (The New Swiss Constitution, Inter-Parliamentary Union, No. 179-1st Half-year 2000/ASGP Review)

In Hippler's belief, nation-building will only be successful in the long term if it stems from an integrative ideology. Fundamental restructuring of politics and society requires special legitimation regarding the justification of policy as well as social mobilization for its ends. He mentioned the formation of Pakistan and Israel as good examples of his claim. Moreover, he explained that the second prerequisite for a successful nation-building process involves the integration of a society from the loosely associated groups that existed previously and considered the development of functional state apparatus as a crucial component of nation-building. (Hippler 2005: 7, 8, 9)

Sometimes, the Nation is defined and exists with the State, but without the State, it is not possible to talk about the Nation. With this approach, every country that has a State also has a Nation. However, this view is not accepted by some political science scholars, and they sometimes talk about a nation without a state and a state without a nation. Of course, a nation cannot be built without a state. The Nation-Building process must be completed by the modern national State characteristics and there is no law of natural evolution to complete this process.

3.4.1 Methods of Nation-Building and Nation-State Formation

Contemporary scientists and philosophers, especially after the Renaissance and the Age of Enlightenment in Europe, when the terms of nation and nation-state building became common, presented different methods for its formation. However, despite clear and diverse views on this matter, each society and country takes different paths in the nation-state process. Different social, cultural, and economic conditions and even geographical locations add to the diversity and multiplicity of these methods. Some scientists and theorists of political science consider nation-building and state-building as two distinct and separate processes and some talk about the intertwining of both. Considering the different and diverse forms of the nation-state in different states, many examples and models can be studied and observed. Among these, two examples are significant and important:

3.4.1.1 European Model

Precedence or delay of the nation-state is two separate ways of forming the nation in the first step or forming the state before the formation of the nation. In Western Europe, the supremacy of the nation (bottom-up) over the state was implemented to some extent. Although in the model of the nation's superiority over the state, the intertwining and mutual influence of the state and the nation was evident, and it is not possible to study and observe the formation of both phenomena in a space of time separately.

3.4.1.2 American Model

However, the model of the state's priority over the nation (top to down) is more common in the world than the nation's priority over the state. The formation of the state in the United States of America is an example of this model. There, first a strong development-oriented state is formed legitimately with the formation and strengthening of civil institutions and enters into the process of nation-building. By adopting national policies, these kinds of states aim to form civil society and citizen-nation in a pluralistic society. Some Third World countries followed the same model. In this model, favourable factors, and contexts such as cultural similarities, descent, economic progress, and abundant natural resources facilitate and accelerate the formation of the nation-state.

Moreover, the model of the precedence of the state or state-building over nation-building in the world, there are various examples. Different societies and states around the world have used different methods in accordance with their cultural and social diversities, and economical and political potential in the direction of the priority model of state-building. This part is not devoted to evaluating the models of nation-building, but focuses on which methods were suited for Afghanistan from 2001 to 2021.

This model is usually used in the context of foreign power assistance or intervention. The model of nation-state building with foreign aid is a top-down model or a model of the state's priority over the nation. In this model, the government is formed with the help and intervention of the country or foreign actors and international organizations and then pursues the process of nation-building. Examples of nation-state building after World War II took place in Japan and Germany. Later, at the beginning of the 21st century, this experience began in Afghanistan, Iraq, and some other countries such as Kosovo, East Timor, and Sierra Leone.

3.5 Challenges to Afghanistan State-Building: An In-Depth Analysis from an Internal Perspective

3.5.1 Bonn Accord 2021

On 13 December 2001, following nine days of discussion and debate, the participants at the Bonn meeting in Germany signed a three-stage agreement that laid the foundation for the establishment of a new system after twenty years of civil war in Afghanistan. According to this historic agreement, the key figures and groups involved in Afghanistan's affairs agreed to the establishment of a six-month interim government, followed by a transitional government and then the holding of elections. Furthermore, they agreed to help ensure security in Afghanistan after years of instability and war, and desired that the International Security Assistance Forces (ISAF), which later gave way to NATO, be deployed in Afghanistan. The agreement stipulates that *"the right of the Afghan people to freely choose the political future of their country based on Islamic principles, democracy, pluralism, and social justice"* is guaranteed. Furthermore, after the Bonn agreement, at the international level, they restored Afghanistan's permanent seat in the United Nations, and at the domestic level, approved the general disarmament of irresponsible armed groups and handed over all control of the country to the 'interim government'. (UM Doc. 2001: S/2001/1154)

After the Bonn Agreement, the expectation of the political elites and the public was that this agreement could end one of the most controversial political problems in Afghanistan in the past three decades, which was the equal division of political power, and lay the foundations of state-building based on inclusive participation and social justice that would reflect the collective will of the people of Afghanistan. But after 20 years, it became clear that the political structure that was created in Bonn for state-building in Afghanistan in 2001, contained defective contents and that the executive method and its agents had a serious problem—that everything that had been built in the past twenty years had been, destroyed and Afghanistan was in the same situation as before. On 15 August 2021, the Taliban as a terrorist group regained political power, the army and government institutions fell apart, and the freedoms of the Afghanistan people, especially women, were again denied.

From the point of view of realism, the Bonn Agreement has many disadvantages. Here are some of its shortcomings. The first was that the influence of the Western states, led by the USA, on the process of the Bonn negotiations and the formulation of the provisions of the agreement was too much, and such an action by the Western states was justified by the aid and support of the Afghanistan government and people. In fact, such an approach hindered the freedom of action by Afghanistani elites in plans and proposals, and initiatives. It means that the Bonn negotiation process and its outcome were not completely pure and Afghanistani. The second defect was that the negotiations related to the Bonn Agreement were not comprehensive negotiations with the presence of representatives of different ethnic, religious, and racial groups, and that only the main parties involved in the internal conflict had been allowed to participate in the conference. The third flaw of the Bonn Agreement was that it rendered Afghanistan completely dependent on foreign actors, relying on them to provide funding, formulate policies, and build institutions for nearly two decades. This situation indicates that Afghanistani statesmen either failed to assume responsibility or were unable to take meaningful initiative in the post-2001 period. All these shortcomings plus ethnic divisions caused the process of state-building in post-Bonn Afghanistan to falter.

Considering the Bonn Agreement and its shortcomings, the findings of this research show that there are other serious and historical challenges beyond the Bonn Agreement, which are the major obstacles to the state-building process in Afghanistan. Also, the findings of this research point out that the shortcomings of the Bonn Agreement are the continuation of the political and historical mistakes of the Afghanistani statesmen who have committed such mistakes intentionally or unintentionally for years and never wanted to eliminate the main obstacles to state-building in Afghanistan. Therefore, it is necessary to examine the obstacles here.

3.5.2 Internal Barriers

Historical and empirical evidences indicate that the process of state-building in Third World and developing countries has not been successfully completed and that they have been faced with important crises such as identity crisis, legitimacy, nation-building, and ultimately ethnic and religious violence. Challenges facing state building in Afghanistan have two internal and external dimensions. In the internal dimension, elements such as ethnic divisions, identity crisis, active and deep-rooted violence caused by the identity crisis, cultural poverty, and extreme traditionality of the society are among the important obstacles to state-building in Afghanistan. Furthermore, there are two opposing indigenous views. One is the Pashtun-oriented view that considers the presence and intervention of foreign forces (American and NATO forces) in Afghanistan as an intervening element in the state-building process in Afghanistan. (Taraki 2010) Second, the non-Pashtun-oriented view believes that the method implemented by the international community, especially the USA, in the direction of state building in Afghanistan from 2001 to 2021 was not suitable and applicable in accordance with the social and political conditions of Afghanistan. Also, this view believes that despite the fact that no foreign forces have been present in Afghanistan for many years, the politicians of Afghanistan who were of Pashtun descent, have failed in the formation of a comprehensive and inclusive national government since 1747, and instead of forming a national government, have tried to form an ethnic government and went forward to the hegemony of ethnicity.

3.5.3 Failure in Forming of a National Government

Afghanistan has some of the main and necessary components for the formation of a nation and a modern national state: common history, common geography, common political and economic destiny, and common religion. These commonalities are a favourable platform on which a modern national state can be formed. In this respect, nation-state building is one of the main duties of the governments, but those governments will be able to accomplish this task only if they have national thoughts and national policies. How can a modern national government be created in the multinational society of

Afghanistan and how can the process of forming a nation-state be completed? The answer to this question lies in the formation of a nation of citizens based, not a nation based on the identity of ethnic groups. In the process of political, economic, social, and cultural development, it is possible to achieve the formation of a nation-state and a civil society, a society where the identity of people is established as citizens, not based on their descent and language ties. The main question is whether Afghanistan has ever had a national government or not. To answer this question, it is necessary to know the process of state-building and its obstacles since the emergence of Afghanistan as a political identity. Accordingly, there are two main existing discourses about the formation of the government in Afghanistan. I will evaluate that both discourses are dominant, and at the same time, are in opposition to each other.

3.5.3.1 Single Discourse (The Official Discourse of the Afghanistan Government)

In his book, *Deconstructing the Official Discourse of State Formation in Afghanistan*, Mujib Rahman Rahimi believes that the first discourse is the exclusive ethnic discourse of the Pashtuns in Afghanistan, which has shaped the narrative and the official vision of the Afghanistan government in relation to state formation for years. This discourse includes colonial and post-colonial discourse, and it has benefited from colonial knowledge to strengthen itself. Over time, Afghan (Pashtuns) statesmen have gradually reproduced colonial knowledge based on their ethnic interests, which has led to official discourse with the help of colonial knowledge as the main source for foreigners who want to know about Afghanistan. The official discourse about the formation of the government in Afghanistan claims that Afghanistan existed as a political identity until the 10th century BC and divides it into historical Afghanistan and contemporary Afghanistan. According to this discourse, historical Afghanistan was called Ariana in ancient times and Khorasan in the post-Islamic period. However, modern or contemporary Afghanistan was democratically[3] re-established in 1747 by Ahmad Shah Abdali. Therefore, Afghanistan, with a distinct historical and cultural background, has existed as an independent national state since its inception. (Rahimi 2014: 182)

3.5.3.2 Principles of Single/Official discourse

Rahimi mentions fourteen principles for the government's official discourse, a few of which are briefly mentioned here in order to make it clear that the main topic of this section, which focuses on the challenges of state-building in Afghanistan, can be carefully examined. (Rahimi 2014: 444, 445, 446)

1. Afghanistan is portrayed in the official discourse as a democratic political identity in which the government is formed based on public participation, voting, persuasion, and consensus by Jirgas that manage society. In this narrative, the country is regularly and permanently invaded by foreign powers and the enemies of Afghanistan and sometimes it causes the fall and collapse of the government, but the brave and free people of Afghanistan or Afghans always fight, defeat the enemy and restore their national government.
2. Strongly argues that Afghanistan was founded by Afghans (Pashtuns) and they constitute the absolute majority in this country and the Pashto language should be its official and national language.
3. The official discourse believes that the Pashtuns are the natural rulers of this country and that no other than the Pashtuns has the right to rule over this land.

   Based on the third principle, from 1947 to 2021, except for three periods (Amir Habibullah Khan Kalkani from January 1929 to November 1929, Babrak Karmal from 1979 to 1986, and Professor Burhanuddin Rabbani from 1992 to 2001) (Balkhi 2020: 62) that the Tajiks ruled, all the other rulers of Afghanistan have been of Pashtun ethnicity. Therefore, one of the objective political facts in Afghanistan is that when the Pashtuns were at the head of political power, they always tried to keep the top of power from the hands of other ethnic groups, and this is a fundamental and accepted principle among the Pashtun elites. Even when the question of transferring political power from the Pashtuns to the Tajiks or other ethnic groups comes up, the secular Pashtuns form an alliance with the extremist Islamist Pashtuns such as the Taliban, and the democrat Pashtuns with communist Pashtuns in order to protect their political position. For example, on the one hand, Hamid Karzai was the president of Afghanistan from 2002 to 2014 and the chief of the armed forces, and on the other hand, he called the Taliban his brothers at the same time. In such a situation, it is clear that a soldier who was fighting to protect the system, of which Karzai was the president, lost his morale on the battlefields in the face of the enemy (Taliban). It is here that in a society where ethnicity is the main factor for political, social and economic interactions, not only does the process of nation-building and state-building not take place, but no political theory is the answer. There are war documents and claims that show that the Taliban were transported by unknown helicopters during the night and fought against the Afghanistani army during the day. What these documents reveal is that on the one hand, the head of the country's political and military power, who was the centre of the command of war and peace, was in the hands of Pashtuns, and on the other hand, the majority of those who fought against the Afghanistan government (Taliban) were Pashtuns. Therefore, it was not possible in a country that had an active army, police, and intelligence and its airspace protected by the USA for unknown helicopters or from a third country to come and equip the Taliban on the battlefields. Apart from ethnicity, there was nothing connecting the battlefields of the Taliban with the citadel of the Afghanistan presidency.

4. It allows Pashtuns to communicate with foreign countries while establishing a relationship but if done by other ethnic groups or their leaders would be considered national treason;
   In 2010, President Karzai's office secretly received millions of dollars from the Iranian government and gave it to members of parliament, Pashtun leaders, and Taliban commanders. (Filkins & Rubin 2010; Shalizi 2010) Until this issue became public President Karzai called it a donation from the Iranian government to the Afghanistan government. Meanwhile, all aid from the international community, including Iran, had to go through transparent and legal channels. This is an example of hundreds of cases in the history of Afghanistan (1747-2021) and the Pashtun rulers have always justified their external dependence and given it a national aspect because they held political power. A large amount of Iranian money was given to Taliban commanders, which strengthened them and enabled them to destroy and kill more people of Afghanistan and disrupted the US objectives in Afghanistan. Karzai and those involved who received money illegally and without transparency from Iran were never prosecuted but were

supported by extreme Pashtunists at various levels. Therefore, the Pashtuns have always used their political power to do whatever they wanted that would lead to the strengthening of their ethnic political position within Afghanistan, even if it was in contradiction with the national interests and of the people of Afghanistan.

5. The extremists of this stream believe that only Pashtuns are the native and original inhabitants of this country and other ethnic minorities in Afghanistan are immigrants who migrated to this country at different stages. Based on this, they are not pure and native like the Pashtuns, and can be returned to their original lands if needed.
6. The ethnic nationalist and Pashtunist elites who support and promote this monopolistic discourse in the post-2001 government system under the leadership of Hamid Karzai and Ashraf Ghani Ahmadzai have tried to return to the 1960s by using the logic of difference and pass the era of displacement. (Rahimi 2014)[4]
7. The official discourse believes that Afghanistan is the only Pashtun state in the world and other ethnic groups living in this country have their own independent states in the region: Persians, Tajiks, Turks, and Uzbeks, respectively, have their own authority and governments in Iran, Tajikistan, Turkey, and Uzbekistan. Afghanistan cannot be exempted from this and the Pashtuns have a right to have Afghanistan as their territory and government. Accordingly, it asks all ethnic minorities to accept the Afghan/Pashtun identity of the state;

In fact, this principle is the foundation of the official discourse and is an attempt by the Pashtun elites to use the tools of political power to impose their ethnic identity on other ethnic groups in Afghanistan. For this purpose, they started the policy of ethnic assimilation (homogenization) combined with a violent approach in Afghanistan. According to this point of view, for all Afghanistan citizens and regardless of which ethnic group they belong to, the term 'Afghan' should be applied but this was not acceptable to the majority of other ethnic groups because, terminologically and historically, the word 'Afghan' means 'Pashtun' and its generalization and extension to other ethnic groups mean denying the identity of others. Identity(ism) exists in the world, and most states, instead of the policy of eliminating identity (ism), have a scientific and tolerant view in order to preserve the stability of their society. However, in Afghanistan, there is still a policy of exclusion and a security perspective on identity issues.

In this respect, after two years (2012-2014) a new law, 'The Population Registration Act' was approved by the parliament in order to distribute Electronic National Identity Cards (known as the e-Tazkira) to Afghanistan citizens. The new law solved the identity problem of Afghanistan citizens to a large extent, but it faced a strong reaction from the Pashtuns for two reasons. The first was that the Pashtuns claimed/are that they form an ethnic majority in Afghanistan and therefore always considered themselves entitled to the presidency or the top of political power. With the implementation of the new law and the electronic registration of all Afghanistan citizens, statistics would be obtained for the entire population of the country and ethnic groups, and the Pashtuns knew that their claim that they are not an ethnic majority would be proved invalid; as a result, they would lose the top of political power position. Second, the ethnic assimilation (homogenization) process initiated by Pashtuns would be failed for ever in Afghanistan. Karzai and Ashraf Ghani, who became presidents on the basis of ethnicity, prevented the implementation of this law and considered it a disgrace for themselves, and strongly opposed it. Ashraf Ghani later modified the aforementioned law with a presidential decree for the purpose of Pashtun hegemony and added that all Afghanistan citizens shall be called 'Afghan'. When in a multi-ethnic society, one ethnic group wants to have everything from beginning to end, it is clear that in such a society there will be friction and conflict, and the process of nation-building and state-building will face severe social obstacles.

According to Rahimi, the official discourse has gone through five historical stages in order to become the official and dominant discourse of the government centred on the Pashtuns of Afghanistan. These five historical stages are: 1) the nucleation and establishment of the discourse between 1880 and 1919; 2) the enrichment of the discourse between the years 1919 and 1928; 3) the complexity and progress of the discourse between 1930 and 1978; 4) the stage of placeless and diversity of the discourse; and 5) trying to go back to the past and re-impose the official discourse between 2001 and 2010. (Rahimi 2014: 123)

Historical facts have shown that any socio-political narrative and knowledge that has political, financial, and military support will prosper, dominate and survive, even if that narration and discourse is incomplete, biased, and forged. Therefore, one of the prominent and important features of the official discourse is that it has always used foreign economic, military, and cultural resources and facilities for its survival and domination. For example, the official discourse of the British colonial knowledge about the formation of the government in Afghanistan has been significantly used and enriched, and localized. History, symbols, and myths were redefined with the support of political power.

As Rahimi demonstrated, the colonial knowledge of Afghanistan was founded by Mountstuart Elphinstone.[5] Elphinstone was the first British ambassador in 1808 and 1809 to the court of Shah Shuja, King of Kabul. He was obliged to negotiate a treaty with the ruler of Kabul and succeeded in his mission. However, the biggest achievement of his trip was collecting a lot of information about Afghanistan. This information is available in nine volumes under the title '*Kabul Sultanate Report*' in the India Office of the British Library. Elphinstone and his companions in the East India Company, as the first colonial group to study Afghanistan, laid the foundation of the knowledge of the colonial discourse about Afghanistan. (Rahimi 2014: 197) Quoting Elphinstone, Rahimi writes the purpose of his trip to Kabul as follows: In 1808, reports from the British delegation were received from Fars and other sources, which indicated that France decided to drag the war to Asia. Based on this, it was decided to send a delegation to the Sultanate of Kabul. (Rahimi 2014: 199)

The fact is that what Elphinstone wrote about Afghanistan and its people in the '*Kabul Sultanate Report*' is a part of Afghanistan's reality, not the whole reality. Nonetheless, the reason is that when Elphinstone was assigned by the British government to go to Afghanistan and collect information about it and its people, the only possible way for Elphinstone was to enter from the south and eastern part of Afghanistan, where mostly the residents of these areas are Pashtuns. When he reached the throne of Kabul, the king of Kabul was Shah Shuja and he belonged to one of the Pashtun tribes. Therefore, Elphinstone did not go to other regions of Afghanistan where the majority of residents were Tajiks, Hazaras, and Uzbeks, or he did not want to go, or he could not go due to mission, political or economic reasons; all three possibilities exist. Therefore, Elphinstone's report reflects a small part of the facts of Afghanistan, and generalizing the findings of this report to the whole of Afghanistan is unscientific, incomplete, and far from reality. However, in general, the information that Elphinstone wrote about Afghanistan forms most of the principles of the official discourse, and that is why the official discourse has reproduced and localized colonial information and knowledge in order to protect and survive.

3.5.3.3 Pluralist Discourse

The pluralistic democratic protest discourse includes Tajiks, Hazaras, and Uzbeks, which are on the opposite side of the official discourse (single discourse) and has challenged the official discourse. Rahimi believes that the pluralistic discourse has challenged the imposition of a monopolistic ethnic identity, the discrimination of some elites of one ethnic group against other ethnic groups. The pluralistic discourse provides the basis for the formation of a democratic narrative and conception, based on citizenship rights, social justice, and equality which forms the content of the second narrative or pluralistic discourse. (Rahimi 2014: 21) Rahimi still believes that this discourse is more rooted in the era of placeless; on the one hand, it considers the structural disorder and on the other, it challenges the official and Pashtun-centric discourse.

The pluralistic democratic protest discourse has emerged in reaction to the official monopolistic and repressive narrative. Therefore, this discourse not only challenges the dominance of the Pashtuns but is also involved in a bitter ethnocentric confrontation with the Pashtunists and accuses them of injustice and adopting discriminatory policies. In addition, these tensions are revealed when the Pashtun-run government enters into a political transaction with one of the ethnic groups using the logic of difference to obtain the necessary majority. The pluralistic protest discourse, in contrast to the monopolistic ethnocentric official discourse, is still scattered, irregular, and in the stages of formation and suffers from the lack of necessary complexity and political coherence. (Rahimi 2014: 453-454)

3.5.3.4 The Principles of Pluralistic Discourse

Rahimi continues and states some principles for pluralistic discourse. In summary, they are:

1. The democratic pluralist protest discourse tries to challenge the fundamental claims and hypotheses of the official narrative; these two

ties Afghanistan and Afghans together and question the emergence and governance of Jirgas and its democratic process. The pluralistic discourse believes that the official discourse is based on forgery, lies, and history-making by ethnic rulers and Pashtunists;

2. Strongly argues that the official narrative is Pashtun-centric and exclusivist and does not represent the ethnic and cultural diversity of the country, especially the identity of other ethnic groups;
3. It is believed that the official narrative and ethnocentric nationalism supported by the government were forcibly imposed on other ethnicities by Pashtun governments without the consent and will of the people;
4. Recognizes the Pashtuns are one of the main ethnic groups of the region, but rejects the claim of the establishment of contemporary or modern Afghanistan by Ahmad Shah Durrani in 1747. Contrary to this, the pluralistic discourse argues that Afghanistan as a political unit with its current international borders was created by the British and Russian empires in the 1880s, and even the name 'Afghanistan' was invented by the British and imposed on them without the consent of the country's inhabitants.
5. Pluralistic discourse believes that the Pashtuns are one of the newly arrived tribes in this region. They gradually expanded their sphere of influence from around the Sulaiman Mountains (Koh-e-Sulaiman), which is located in Pakistan today, to other areas. In this regard, sometimes they occupied new areas in Khorasan or Eastern Iran as a result of migration, sometimes in the company of world explorers as war forces;
6. It supports the recognition of pluralism and the representation of this plurality in state symbols and policies such as national history, national symbols, state emblems, historical figures, national celebrations, schools, universities, armed forces, national institutions, and the administrative system of the country;
7. Pluralistic discourse claims that Western nations and governments, especially Britain, do not know about the pluralism and diversity of the country, under the influence of the power of colonial discourse or Pashtun governments or Pashtunist elites, or they are deliberately prevented from understanding this issue. (Rahimi 2014: 449- 491)

Confirming Rahimi's point of view that the pluralist discourse is in the stage of formation and does not yet have the necessary political complexities, a few other things should be mentioned. First, the pluralist discourse consists of Tajiks, Hazaras, Uzbeks and other ethnic groups in Afghanistan, and each has a different approach in challenging the official discourse of Pashtuns. For example, the Hazaras and the Uzbeks of Afghanistan have the same and similar approach, which is that they want to share in political power. They tell the Pashtuns that all the power is not theirs, and they should also share in a corner of the country's political power; they never claim to challenge the hegemony of the Pashtuns and say that they want to be the first persons in the country.

By contrast, Tajiks are the only ethnic group in Afghanistan that has challenged the hegemony of Pashtuns. Historical evidence shows that the Tajiks at least two or times overthrew the Pashtun supremacy and gained the top of political power in Afghanistan. Once, in January 1929, Amir Habibullah Khan Kalakani overthrew Amanullah Khan, the revisionist king of Afghanistan Ahmad Shah Massoud, former defence minister of Afghanistan, supported Burhanuddin Rabbani as the president of Afghanistan in 1992. It shows that they not only did they want an equal share in the political power of the country; they also wanted to be at the top of the political power.[6] They have shown this at least twice in the modern history of Afghanistan. In other words, Pashtuns believe that Hazaras and Uzbeks are more of a political nuisance than political rivals. However, they consider Tajiks their main political rivals and believe that they have a higher political potential than Hazaras and Uzbeks. However, after 2001, the Tajiks have lost the leadership capacity to take the top of political power, and the claimants to the leadership of this ethnic group mostly traded away the aspirations of the Tajik people. However, among the Tajiks, the motivation to take the top of political power is very high, and considering the conditions, new leaders will emerge from among them.

3.5.4 Social Configuration

The social structures of every society have an influencing role in the social and political developments of that society and even the behaviour of its politicians and people, and it is considered an important part of the culture of formation of society. Considering the ethnic and tribal structure of Afghanistan society, the political culture of this society is strongly influenced by its social structure, and this culture has a direct influence on the political behaviour of politicians and even the way in which people look at politics. In this sense, in the history of Afghanistan, politics and social behaviours have been strongly influenced by ethnic and tribal structures, and at some historical points, with the intensification of ethnic and social divisions, we have witnessed some political conflicts in society and especially among the elites. Unfortunately, due to the deep impact of tribal structures on the behaviour and political culture of society, Afghanistani politicians have sometimes made instrumental use of this element and strengthened the tribal and ethnic structures in society.

Loya Jirga[7] is one of the structures greatly affecting the process of political development in Afghanistan. It is a local and tribal tradition that is specific to Pashtuns. Pashtun tribes, especially in the eastern regions of Afghanistan, have permanent jirgas, which are the place for collective resolution of various social issues, local and tribal disputes, and even criminal cases. Women usually do not have the right to participate in jirgas, even though most jirgas are used to determine the fate of women in Pashtun tribes. Loya Jirga slowly entered the political structure of Afghanistan, and the evidence shows that relying on the hegemony of Pashtuns, the Afghanistan governments have gone to the Loya Jirga in seven instances to approve the constitution and six instances to decide on Afghanistan's foreign policy. In effect, jirgas have become a tool to legitimize the wishes and ideals of Pashtunists so that they can impose their wishes and will over other ethnic groups of Afghanistan.

However, the Loya Jirga has an ethnic and tribal basis, which is never the answer to the contemporary problems of Afghanistan. Modern states in the 21st century hold referendums to solve their fundamental problems and refer to the votes of the general public, including women, men, and all ethnic groups while the Jirga is composed of a small group representing all the people of Afghanistan and decides the fate of the general public. Most of the participants of Loya Jirga forget the actual purpose of their assembly and end up approving the demands of the government. Jirga is a good instrument to implement the goals of the official discourse, and, for this reason, it has faced strong opposition from other ethnic groups in Afghanistan. Other ethnic groups consider the decisions of the Loya Jirga to be illegitimate.

Historically, there are more historical gaps in the social structure of Afghanistan society. It is strongly an ethnic society and different ethnic groups live in it, but due to the fact that the nation-building process in the modern sense has never been successfully completed in this society, the tribal and ethnic structure still plays a very effective role in its political culture and behaviour. After 2001, it was expected that with the international and domestic developments that took place in Afghanistan, with the cooperation of the international community, a kind of transition from tribal and ethnic structures to the nation-building process would take place in Afghanistan; but unfortunately, in the short term, Afghanistan has witnessed a kind of return and re-emergence of ethnic approaches and the influence of tribal and ethnic structure on politics and governance in Afghanistan. Therefore, it can be said that the infrastructure of political and social life in Afghanistan still has deep ethnic and tribal roots, which may become stronger and weaker under the influence of some external and sometimes internal factors, but it is still hidden as fire under the ashes. Unfortunately, factors such as the geographical situation of Afghanistan, where the majority of the people of this country live far from urban life, and on the other hand, the low level of literacy and awareness of the people, as well as external factors, have had an effect on accentuating ethnic and tribal attitudes in the politics and government of Afghanistan. Therefore, after 2001, despite the presence of the international community in Afghanistan, due to the different views that foreigners had on it, each of these countries tried to have the companionship and convergence of some ethnic groups in Afghanistan with them, and from this point of view, the country witnessed the strengthening and continuation of the ethnic and tribal structure in the politics and government and political system.

Ethnic divisions in Afghanistan are such that one tribe does not tolerate the historical, cultural, and glorious heritage of another tribe. Every ethnic group tries to have all their material and spiritual things accepted by other ethnicities. The history, culture, mythology, and personality of one ethnic group are not accepted by other ethnicities. For example, Ahmad Shah Abdali is a hero in the eyes of the Pashtuns of Afghanistan, but not in the eyes of the other ethnic groups, or Ahmad Shah Masoud is the national hero of Afghanistan in the eyes of the Tajiks, but not for other ethnicities. Likewise, Abdul Rashid Dostum is a hero for the Uzbeks of Afghanistan and Abdul Ali Mazari the Hazaras. The ethnic policies of the past governments of Afghanistan have caused the destruction of the connecting elements of Afghanistan's ethnic groups in general and have pushed ethnic jealousy to the point of enmity.

There is no connecting element that can unite all the ethnic groups of Afghanistan and form a united nation. Religion, culture, geography, and shared history are important elements that unite nations, but in Afghanistan, none of these have been able to surpass the element of ethnicity. This element is the basis of any kind of political interaction and this is the reason why the ethnic divides in Afghanistan are increasing day by day.

3.6 National Identity Crisis

The generally stated definition is: "National identity is a set of features, affiliations and geographic, historical, cultural, epic, and ethnic ties that includes human life, which members of society are proud of.". According to the mentioned definition, national identity is not something that happens or exists in a vacuum, that is, it is not a subjective and abstract issue but, a social process that crystallizes in the objectivity of society and the objectivities of the national sovereignty structures. Therefore, if we do not have a precise definition of national culture, governance structure, and national interests, we will not achieve national identity. Therefore, national identity means the awareness and feeling of great national solidarity, loyalty to it, and sacrifice for it. In other words, national identity, like other individual and collective identities, is formed in our imaginary struggle with others—Arab against Afghanistani, Afghanistani against Pakistani, and Pakistani against Iranian. Therefore, national identity shows itself as a prominent concept when the feeling hidden in national societies is based on a well-directed destination and awareness, the basis for a political, cultural, and economic plan.

National identity, which can be called fundamental identity, is realized if the members of a society, regardless of family, ethnicity, gender, language, religion, and region, consider themselves belonging to it and are obligated and committed. National identity is created in society when the general spirit is formed. It is in this case that the sub-national identities are affected by the national identity and lose colour in front of it.

Crisis means imbalance and instability in any state and situation that endangers the desired situation. If the people of society separate themselves from any identity ties or do not hang onto them when there is no need, life will be ambiguous for them. If people are cut off from their affiliations, or if the political government defines some of the identity-building factors as its vital and essential component and the citizens reach for other component ties, the society will experience an identity crisis. As a result, the individual and social life of a person is severely damaged and can lead to its destruction. In the process of political development, an identity crisis occurs when a society finds that what it has accepted so far as the physical and psychological definitions of its 'collective self' cannot be accepted under new historical conditions. Afghanistan is facing a severe identity crisis and has not yet been able to define a national identity that is acceptable to all Afghanistan people, and this is one of the biggest obstacles to state-building in Afghanistan. The factors that caused a national identity crisis in Afghanistan are as follows:

3.6.1 The Name of Afghanistan

The name of each country is effective in creating an identity and a suitable framework for national integration and unity. The selection of the name of a country has a special sensitivity due to its political and emotional burden, which helps to find the reason for the creation of the states and the government. Choosing a meaningful name so that it creates a complete umbrella and comprehensive coverage for all the people of a nation is important to instil a sense of belonging among them and motivate both sides to consider themselves part of each other. Choosing names that represent a part of the citizens reflects that part only, even if it was the majority and this will lead to national unity, and cohesion facing the first basic challenge. The sub-minority does not feel attached to it and considers itself separate from the body of the nation. Gradually, this belief is institutionalized in them, and in favourable conditions, it manifests itself in the form of a special political ideal, and becomes a problem for the government.

As far as Afghanistan, as it is known today, is a country composed of different ethnic groups, only one of which is the Afghans (Pashtuns). Using the name of Afghanistan as the name of the entire country in the first step refers to a kind of monopoly of power, imposing the identity of Afghanistan on non-Pashtuns, and denying the existence of other inhabitants of the land. For this reason, this name is never accepted by some other ethnic groups, and this is a fact that is less reflected outside Afghanistan; however, it is an absolute reality inside Afghanistan. Of course, the role of colonialism and colonial knowledge and its reproduction by Pashtun politicians is prominent in this topic. Therefore, one of the main factors of the identity crisis in *Afghanistan* is the name of the country itself, which has created the grounds for division, divergence, and non-dependence among the ethnic groups living in this country.

Afghanistan is a relatively new name although Pashtuns claim that the name first originated in 1747, during the reign of Ahmad Shah Abdali. However, historical documents show that he referred to himself as the king of Khorasan. Afghanistan was referred to as 'Ariana' and 'Khorasan' in more reliable historical documents before 1749. Before the advent of Islam, Afghanistan was called Ariana and after that, it was called Khorasan, which was wider than the current geographical borders and covered all the different ethnic groups. The current name 'Afghanistan', for other ethnic groups in Afghanistan, is the biggest obstacle to nation-building and state-building.

3.6.2 Constitution and National Anthem

In the words of Thomas Paine:

> *A constitution is a thing antecedent to government, and a government is only the creature of a constitution. The constitution of a country is not the act of its government, but of the people constituting a government. It is the body of elements to which you can refer and quote article by article; and which contains the principles upon which the government shall be established, the manner in which it shall be organized, the powers it shall have, the mode of elections, the duration of parliaments, or by what other name such bodies may be called. the powers which the executive.* (Thomas 1791)

From this definition, it can be inferred that the constitution provides legitimacy to the government, and at the same time, limits its power. Therefore, the constitution imposes restrictions on the government's power and guidance on how to exercise it. Furthermore, the constitution is a national bond and a social contract that is concluded between the government and the people. It determines the rights and duties of citizens, the structure of political power, duties, and competencies of the pillars of the government.

Afghanistan's constitution (2004), however, has many drawbacks. It is important to mention the two most important drawbacks. First, there is a claim that Afghanistan is seen as a fraudulent political system (from the formation as a political identity to elections), a fake constitution, ethnic structures based on tribal thinking, and an imposed mono-ethnic identity, and that the constitution is considered a charter of injustice, promoting ethnic disunity and consolidating the foundations of legal tyranny. Afghanistan is the first country in the world that has two constitutions; one is the original version approved by the Loya Jirga on 4 January 2004 and the other is a fake version of official gazette 818 approved on 26 January 2004. Now the people know what betrayal has taken place and which articles of the constitution have been falsified deleted, altered, and modified. According to Hafiz Mansoor, a member of the constitutional Loya Jirga in 2004, the published Constitution No. 818 in the official gazette and in force has incorporated 52 changes in the finalized Constitution of the Loya Jirga. Even according to Mansoor, the Loya Jirga ended without approving the constitution. (Mansoor 2018)

Article 20 of the Constitution of Afghanistan states that *"the national anthem of Afghanistan is in Pashto language and with Allahu Akbar and the names of ethnic groups of the Afghan"* which shows the supremacy of one ethnic group over the others. The majority of non-Pashtun ethnic groups are against this article and consider it in line with the ethnic hegemony of the Pashtuns. Participants of other ethnic groups in the constitutional Loya Jirga believe that article 20 of this constitution is a total of several other articles that have been falsified contrary to the decision of the Jirga and that the then president of Afghanistan, Hamid Karzai, who is a Pashtun, is a participant in this falsification.

Second, Article 64 defines the authority and duties of Afghanistan's president. According to this constitution, Afghanistan's political system is purely centralized and the president is at the top of the political, military, and financial apparatus. This could lead to corruption and misuse of national property towards ethnic hegemonizing whereas, according to the unwritten political contract, the president shall be of Pushtun ethnicity. This was what happened during the presidency of Karzai and Ashraf Ghani Ahmadzai from 2001 to 2021. Ashraf Ghani took over the absolute political, military, and economic power of the country by relying on the centralized political system of

Afghanistan. He used to give economic contracts to his relatives and army and police commanders were appointed in payment of bribes which caused a decrease in the quality of work and war on the battlefields against the Taliban, which ultimately led to the failure of the government and army.

3.6.3 Political Tyranny

The political system in Afghanistan has always been authoritarian and totalitarian in nature. Autocratic governments in Afghanistan have had different faces and different forms, but the common feature and general characteristics of all of them are: taking over political power by one ethnic group with or without external powers, erasing social and religious differences, attempting to popularize language and culture of one ethnic group through force, military campaigns, and finally, massacres and human disasters, are the most important factors that have always caused the security crisis in Afghanistan and provided the ground for several factions. All this has taken place through Afghanistan's tyrannical rulers.

It is obvious that autocracy appears under any name and form; it causes instability in society and a deep division of social layers. In a society where ethnic tyranny and social divisions exist, not only can stable security, unity, and national identity not be formed, but talking about them is also ineffective. In its political life, Afghanistan has never experienced positive and peaceful political competition combined with national programs.

3.6.4 Ethnocentrism

The meaning of this word is a tendency based on which the behavioural and intellectual standards of ethnicity are presented in a privileged and superior position over other ethnic groups. An ethnocentric attitude, which carries suspicion and a negative view of other ethnic groups, is considered one of the serious causes of ethnic conflict among Afghan ethnic groups. Because ethnocentrism sees the behaviour and beliefs of other ethnic groups from the perspective of the culture and vision of the ruling ethnic group, it leads to a kind of positive attitude towards its own culture and a negative attitude towards the culture of other ethnic groups, and ultimately leads to cultural ethnicity imposition. Finally, ethnocentrism is a tendency to change other cultural values based on one's own culture. In simpler terms, ethnocentrism means giving superiority to one's own tribe and culture and making it superior to other nations and cultures.

When a racial and ethnic group believed that it deserves political power over other ethnic groups and its members are more intelligent than other ethnic and racial groups, it causes social and political conflicts among the residents of that society. Unfortunately, in Afghanistan society, ethnocentrism and tribalism have been important elements and fundamental factors that hinder unity and national identity. This issue is considered a big obstacle in the way of fraternity and equality and rights of other ethnic groups. Furthermore, it is also the source of discrimination and exclusivity in Afghan society. In this respect, society members are divided into first-class, second-class, and third-class citizens. There is a spirit of ethnocentrism and exclusivism in Afghanistan society, and it is not specific to a particular tribe, but this spirit of ethnocentrism weighs heavily on the side of the Pashtuns of Afghanistan as compared to other ethnicities, because they have used political and military power for years in order to support their ethnocentrism.

In addition, ethnicism has caused the other ethnic groups to be underprivileged in political and economic points except for the Pashtuns in Afghanistan. Throughout history, especially after 2001, power has been divided from top to bottom based on ethnic composition, and most of the cabinet ministers of the Afghanistan government had to be Pashtuns. Recruitment and selection in the structure of the army, police, and civil institutions, even entering governmental universities—all had to be based on ethnic composition. Therefore, when a Tajik, Uzbek, Hazara, Nuristani, Imaq professional, etc., comes to the conclusion that s/he can no longer become the president, minister, or head of the military and civil institutions of Afghanistan, it is clear that not only national identity will not form, but will also cause huge social and political grudges. Therefore, after 15August 2021, and the Taliban's dominance again, the political and social atmosphere has been prepared for redefining everything (constitution, name of Afghanistan, political structures, national anthem, etc.) in Afghanistan. If all Afghanistani want to form a single modern nation, they must all redefine themselves and their assets.

3.7 Challenges to State-Building: External Perspective

As mentioned earlier, the second part of this chapter is devoted to the clash of the strategic depths of sovereign actors in Afghanistan and the consequences of their rivalries, and how these clashes have affected the state-building process in Afghanistan. This part examined the challenges of the state-building process in Afghanistan from an external perspective and the USA, China, India, Pakistan, and Iran are case studies in this part.

The external obstacles in the way of state building in Afghanistan have historical roots due to the competition of regional and global powers at least in the last two centuries. In the nineteenth century, Afghanistan was a buffer zone between the Russian and British empires, and its borders were determined by these two empires. Each government tried to show a more appropriate regional role by influencing the Afghanistan government. With the Soviet invasion in 1979, the position of Afghanistan in the policies of the West, especially in the foreign policy of the USA was elevated, and the country became an area of conflict and competition between the two superpowers. After 9/11, with the ever-increasing development of China's comprehensive power, the nuclearization of India and Pakistan, Iran's efforts to obtain nuclear weapons, the revival of Russia, and the abundant energy resources in Central Asia, affected Afghanistan's geopolitics and geo-economic location. The USA and the international community found Afghanistan as a fragile state and gave themselves the right to intervene in it in 2001. It means that Afghanistani were never able to create a native national government based on their needs and will.

However, if the issue is examined from the structural realism point of view, it will be concluded that: the state is a legal entity and a territory is formed by a fixed population and government, and it has the exclusive right to the legitimate use of power and its sovereignty is recognized by other governments in the international system. From this point of view, the 'state' is the main actor, and 'sovereignty' is its distinguishing feature, and the meaning of 'sovereign state' is inseparably connected to the use of 'power' to show the relationship between 'violence' and 'state' in its domestic dimension. The best definition we can use is Max Weber's definition of the state, "the exclusive right to legitimately exercise physical power within a defined territory." From the realist's perspective, the international system is anarchic, and the only way for states to survive is within their capabilities. Furthermore, a government that has enough power survives in the international system. Therefore, it is necessary for governments to organize first at their domestic level and then at the international level. Nonetheless, Afghanistan has never had a systematic arrangement at the domestic level and has not been able to organize itself. .It has always appeared weak at the international and regional levels, and this has caused it to be attacked and invaded by regional and global powers for the following reasons:

1. The specificity and aggressive structure of some ruling political regimes at the international level.
2. Gaining political, economic, and cultural influence in weak and crisis-stricken countries.
3. Supporting fellow races and ethnic groups abroad.
4. Separation and annexation of regions of the country in question.
5. Regional competitions, taking advantage of rival weaknesses and reducing the country's political, economic, and military capabilities, through internal conflicts, and affecting the country's political life.
6. Proxy role of neighbouring countries and regional powers as an ally or tool to stimulate and encourage great powers.
7. Transferring the crisis outside the borders and regionalizing the dimensions of the crisis.
8. Taking advantage of an ethnic conflict as one of the foreign policy tools in political dealings with a rival country (something Pakistan has been doing in Afghanistan for many years).

Therefore, obviously, the process of state-building in Afghanistan has been affected by regional and global power competitions, and here the role of several sovereign actors is studied case by case.

3.7.1 The United States

According to David Lake, the USA employed three models[8] of state building in the last century, and each of these versions was based on a political theory and responded to specific local needs and conditions. The first version that Lake named State Building 1.0 started in the 1890s. When the USA first began trying to change the shape of foreign regimes, the model that dominated until the end of the Cold War emphasized the creation of loyal and politically stable subject states. In this version, whenever loyalty to the USA conflicted with local interests, Washington tolerated and supported authoritarian governments, and democracy was a means to an end. In the same way, the second version is named State-building 2.0. In this version, it was the efforts of the USA to create a new world order after 1990. According to this version, it attempted to build broad popular support for fledgling governments by building democratic institutions and advancing economic reforms. State-building 3.0 was an attempt to fill the gaps between the first and second versions that were implemented in Afghanistan and Iraq. Lake doubted in 2010 that this version would become one of the permanent features of the politics of the USA. This model is based on the social contract theory and its main principle that legitimacy comes from the effective provision of the basic needs of citizens. (Lake 2010)

Based on the third version, Francis Fukuyama agrees with Lake and believes that in order for legitimacy to be based on providing for the needs of the citizens the USA had to do two things in its state-building process, *Reconstruction,* and *Development*. According to Fukuyama, *Reconstruction* is something that foreign powers are historically able to do. Post-war Japan, Germany, Italy, and Western Europe in general were examples of successful American reconstruction efforts. Although the post-war *Reconstruction* efforts of the USA in Bosnia and Kosovo were weak and confusing, it was later able to return these countries to their pre-war state. However, *Development* is highly problematic, both conceptually and as a pragmatic policy. The self-confidence of Americans in their ability to help and develop poor countries was high immediately after World War II and then plummeted during and after the Vietnam War. According to Fukuyama, the early American self-confidence in its ability to promote development came under the pressure of a variety of 1970s and 1980s. State-building was carried out without regard to the democratic legitimacy of the states involved, involved foreign donors in violating the human rights of recipients, and failed to prevent coups, revolutions, and wars that led to political collapse. (Fukuyaman 2006: 4-5)

According to the historical background of the US's state-building in the last century, the functions of the USA in the direction of state-building in Afghanistan can be divided into two phases. The first phase started in 2001 and ended in May 2011 with the killing of bin Laden, and the second phase covers from 2011 to 2021. Based on the findings of this research, the first stage of the US state-building in Afghanistan was associated with revengeful feelings and excitement that had roots in 9/11, not based on state-building recognized standards. The US actions at this stage are so vague and confusing that it is difficult to understand its intention in the direction of state-building in Afghanistan. As Fukuyama also points out that when the USA decided to attack Afghanistan in December 2001, there was no clear and organized framework for state-building in Afghanistan and no unity of command in US government institutions such as the United States Department of State and Defence. The US's main goal in the first phase was to defeat terrorism and al-Qaeda, and war was the only option on the table. In this respect, there was consensus and unity of command among the Americans only on the issue of the war on terror, not on the issues of state-building in particular. This problem is well understood when evaluating the costs of the USA in the war on terror in Afghanistan. America has spent more than 2.3 trillion dollars in the war against terror in Afghanistan, (Watson Institute 2022) including 850 billion dollars in the direct war on terror and 85 billion dollars in training and equipping the Afghanistan National Army. These numbers clearly show America's sense of revenge against terrorism, not state-building based on democratic principles.

The second phase includes the new strategy of the USA, which had defined its presence in Afghanistan for the future, which was after the death of bin Laden in 2011. This stage includes the efforts of the USA to withdraw its forces from Afghanistan in a dignified manner, and the death of Bin Laden legitimized these efforts, strategy, and subsequent actions of the USA at the domestic and international levels. One of these efforts is the beginning of direct political interaction of the USA with the Taliban and providing diplomatic concessions at the regional level to the terrorist group that had mobilized the international community to overthrow them a decade ago. In June 2013, under the guidance and support of the USA, Qatar established a political office for the Taliban under the name 'Political Office of the Islamic Emirate of Afghanistan', while inside Afghanistan there was a government that was based on the elections This was the first step in the direction of destroying the governmental institutions, a government that the USA had invested in cooperation with its international partners for a decade. The establishment of the political office of the Taliban in Qatar actually meant the recognition of the government of a terrorist group in exile, although the USA openly and even in the Doha Peace Agreement stated several times that this did not mean the recognition of the Taliban. Based on this bilateral approach which had been taken by the USA, China, Russia, and Iran, as major regional powers, followed the USA by granting diplomatic concessions to the Taliban and rolling out the red carpet for them.

The US state-building in Afghanistan also had positive points, but several factors failed it in Afghanistan, the most important of which are:

3.7.1.1 Competition with Regional and Global Powers

As Lake also points out in his article, various reasons have been influential in the strategy and policies of the USA from the last century until now. For example, the US state-building process on the Caribbean coast, which began in 1992, was not intended to support weak and fragile governments for the sake of domestic and regional political stability, but factors such as the ideological competition between the two great powers; the East which was led by the Soviet Union and the West, led by the USA, have been the main factors in state building in the mentioned regions. At that time, both world powers were trying to have subordinate, follower, and local governments in the world. Although the world situation changed after the Cold War, Afghanistan is not an exception to this rule. The US state-building process in Afghanistan has been influenced by two factors in this matter. The first factor was the revenge of the USA against al-Qaeda and its supporting groups, and the second was the desire to be present in South Asia in order to control China, Russia, Iran, and the Central Asian states. That is, the US state-building in Afghanistan was not based on the fact that this country had spent years of war and all its institutions and infrastructure had been destroyed so that the Americans can rebuild. Revenge and competition thwarted US state-building efforts in Afghanistan. From 1898 to 2021, the USA made 17 case attempts in state-building, of which only in four has democracy been stable after ten years, or in other words, only four out of 17 have been successful, and all others have failed. As such, Afghanistan is one of the failed state-building processes of the USA in history.

Table 1: The U.S. State-building

Target Country	*Period*	*Years of the first national election*	*Number of years from intervention to election*	*Democracy after ten years?*
Cuba	1898-1902	1901	3	No
Panama	1903-1936	1952	49	No
Cuba	1906-1909	1908	2	No
Nicaragua	1909-1933	1912	3	No
Haiti	1915-1934	1930	15	No
Cuba	1917-1922	1918	1	No
Dominican Republic	1916-1924	1924	8	No
West Germany	1945-1949	1949	4	Yes
Japan	1945-1952	1946	1	Yes
Dominican Republic	1965-1966	1966	1	No
South Vietnam	1964-1973	1970	6	No
Cambodia	1970-1973	1972	1	No
Grenada	1983	1984	1	Yes
Panama	1989	Restoration	-	Yes
Haiti	1994-1996	1995	1	No
Afghanistan	2001-2021[9]	2004	3	No
Iraq	2003-present	2005	2	-

Source: David Lake, 2010, 260.

3.7.1.2 Method

The method and model of state building that the USA and its allies chose for state-building in Afghanistan were wrong. The meaning of this conversation is that the model was not inherently problematic although the top-down state-building model has worked in some countries, such as Japan, East Timor, and America itself. However, that is to say, the mentioned model was not suitable for the social and political conditions of Afghanistan. The state-building model that the USA had started in Afghanistan with the cooperation of the international community was a top-down model, which means that a strong central government had to be built first, without nation-building. Later, nation-building would be done slowly. The appropriate state-building model for Afghanistan was/is the European model, especially the French model. The French model is a bottom-up model, which means that a divided society first moves towards unity, forms a national identity, and defines all the connecting elements of a nation (name of the country, flag, national anthem, etc.) and then move towards state-building.

Depriving the People of Afghanistan of Freedom and Initiative: From the outset of the state-building process in Afghanistan—beginning with the Bonn Conference and culminating in the Doha Agreement, which precipitated the collapse of the Islamic Republic of Afghanistan—the USA systematically deprived Afghanistani elites of autonomy and initiative. Owing to its hegemonic approach, the USA consistently sought to keep Afghanistan's indigenous institutions intellectually dependent in policy formulation and materially reliant on external support from itself and the wider international community. Furthermore, through the Doha Peace Agreement, the United States largely bypassed the Afghanistan government and engaged directly with the Taliban, concluding a bilateral agreement that significantly strengthened the Taliban's morale and legitimacy, both at the negotiating table and on the battlefield.

3.7.1.3 Native agents

During the state-building process in Afghanistan, the USA tried to manage the state-building process through several Afghanistan Americans such as Karzai and Ghani. Although Karzai's political and social position was higher than that of Ashraf Ghani among the people of Afghanistan people, even so, Karzai wasted Afghanistan's golden opportunities and could not make good use of the war excitement of the USA in the direction of state-building. Instead of rebuilding and developing Afghanistan's basic infrastructure, Karzai tried to limit the political power of local forces with the support of the USA, which considered them rivals and called them 'warlords'. Karzai and Ashraf Ghani are two examples of hundreds of people who had dual nationalities who did not show any kind of dependence on the people and Afghanistan.

3.7.2 China

Examining the relations between China and Afghanistan in the past decades shows that China's distance and proximity to Afghanistan depended on China's internal conditions, regional and international developments, China's competition with other actors, and dealing with extremist threats. Therefore, the relationship interpretation based on the need assessment of two actors

(China and Afghanistan) has no place here, and this is the reason why China did not play an important and influential role in the process of state-building in Afghanistan after 2001. China's financial and technical assistance in the process of state building in Afghanistan after 2001 is very little and insignificant compared to the USA and its allies and is not comparable at all. However, China has always used a policy of caution and patience regarding political developments in Afghanistan.

Table 2: China and the USA's presence in Afghanistan

Country	*Year*	*Troops*	*Killed*	*Injured*	*Expenses in US Dollar*
The USA	2001-2021	110,000	2,443	20,666	$ 2.3 trillion
China	2001-2021	0	0	0	$ 300 million-estimate

The official relations between China and Afghanistan started in the 1950s with the recognition of China by Afghanistan. China's approach to Afghanistan has always been economic with an emphasis on security considerations. In the past decades, security considerations have always been the priority in the eyes of the Chinese authorities towards Afghanistan. An example of this is the occupation of Afghanistan by the Soviet Union, the civil war in Afghanistan, the first domination of the Taliban, and finally the presence of American forces. China, as a great power that is establishing hegemony in its surrounding environment, evaluates every move and presence of rival actors in the region from the perspective of its competition with that actor.

That is why, after 2001 and the formation of the new government in Afghanistan, China, despite its greater capabilities, only took an active and cautious policy and never wanted to get involved in security and political issues like the USA and its Western allies or keep up with the USA and participate in the war against terrorism and state-building in Afghanistan. However, Afghanistan is important for China for several reasons: 1. Afghanistan is one of the focal points in the BRI. The absence of Afghanistan in BRI China's regional economic plan remains flawed; 2. There are religious extremists on both sides of the border between Afghanistan and China, and China has been worried about the connection between the Uyghurs with ISIS, the Taliban, and other extreme Islamist groups in Afghanistan; 3. In order to expand its political influence in the region, China should expand its influence to the remaining areas such as Afghanistan, and advance its security and political goals through the economic window; 4. China was deeply concerned about the presence of China's regional and global competitors in Afghanistan and considered it a shame and a hindrance to its development policies in the region.

China's role after the Bonn Accord and the formation of the new government in Afghanistan can be examined in two stages, just like the USA. The first stage is from 2002-2011 and the second stage is from 2011-2021. The first phase of China's policies in Afghanistan was very smart and based on economic policy considering the presence of its main rival (USA). In 2002, China reactivated its embassy in Afghanistan, and in December 2003, it signed the 'Five Neighbouring Countries' agreement, which became known as the Kabul Declaration, with the aim of the neighbouring countries' respect for the sovereignty and territorial integrity of Afghanistan, and their constant support for the peace process there. Although there is no reliable information about China's aid in the direction of state building in Afghanistan, but based on available sources, it can be said that China's aid was not more than 500 million US dollars. At this stage, China was more focused on commercial issues and benefited from the free security and abundant money that the USA and its international partners had provided to Afghanistan; most of the so-called Western analysts of China enjoyed a free ride in this period in Afghanistan. In 2008, a Chinese company invested 3.5 billion dollars in copper mining in the Aynak copper mine in Afghanistan. Most of the official relations and agreements between China and Afghanistan were focused on commercial and economic issues, except for a few cases of scholarships for diplomats, police, and Afghan students.

In the second phase, which includes the last decade, circumstances and events happened in such a way that China, in addition to the economic approach, had to deal with the security and political issues of Afghanistan. One of these events was setting a timetable for the withdrawal of US and NATO forces from Afghanistan, which deeply worried China. China in keeping with its soft policy and regional economy, wanted a stable, and popular government in Afghanistan and that was why it has never displeased the internal parties involved in Afghanistan's politics. For example, China had high-level official, economic and diplomatic cooperation with the Afghanistan government, which was under the influence of the regional policy of the USA, and at the same time, had established relations with the Taliban through the mediation of Pakistan. Although China's relationship with the Taliban was aimed at grounding the USA in Afghanistan, but as an independent actor, in some cases its policies in Afghanistan clashed. As mentioned above, a strong and stable government in Afghanistan was/is in China's favour, but the main question is why China did not participate more in the direction of state building in Afghanistan after 2001 and did not cooperate with the West in a regular and clean manner.

To answer these questions it is necessary to look at the issue from a wider angle and to know the chain of coalitions and the number of independent actors such as the USA, India, Iran, and Pakistan in Afghanistan and what economic, political, and military goals each of them pursues in Afghanistan and its surrounding areas. Coalition A is between China-Pakistan-Iran and each has had economic and military cooperation and, by the way, they follow the same regional and global policies. Coalition B is constituted by the USA, India, a few Central Asian countries and NATO members. The first alliance, of which Iran and Pakistan are a part, has been pursuing dual policies towards Afghanistan for at least the last four decades, and they have not wanted a strong and stable government to be established in Afghanistan according to their internal considerations. This approach of Iran and Pakistan as China's regional allies has directly influenced China's policies in Afghanistan. On the contrary, there are very clear signs that coalition B, at least after 2001, tried to build a state in Afghanistan while pursuing its regional goals. In coalition B, of which the USA is the leader, there are problems and competition at the regional and global levels with two powers of alliance A (China and Iran). India also has conflicts of interests with China and Pakistan in the region and border problems. Therefore, considering the form and nature of these two alliances, China's competition with the USA and India has had a direct impact on China's role in the process of state-building in Afghanistan.

3.7.2.1 The field of competition between A and B coalitions

The truth is that with the collapse of the Soviet Union in the early 1990s, fundamental changes were made in various fields of international relations. Although in the first decade the USA was considered the undisputed power of the world, gradually and since the early 2000s, China entered the world stage in a more serious way and became a power in competition with the USA. Consequently, during the last decade, the competition between the two countries rapidly turned into global disputes. This exponential growth is not only expanding quantitatively, but an ideological dimension has also been added. The ultimate goal of the current competition between these two great powers is to seize global power, and for this reason, the international system is facing a growing and exponential process of competition. The competition between the USA and China has become the pattern of international relations in recent years. In fact, the importance of this competition is to the extent that it now organizes strategic spaces and real political, military, and economic dynamics. This tough competition should be seen as a conflict that imposes a new order on the international structure; a system that analyzed many developments, conflicts, and peace-building at the international level through the lens of its power.

One of the areas of competition between alliances A and B is Central Asia. Central Asia is a region rich in natural resources and has a geo-economic and strategic position, the importance of which is also expressed in Mackinder's Heartland theory, and it is located in the neighbourhood of Afghanistan with longitudinal borders. Therefore, the importance of Central Asia in international equations is an important and new issue for American policymakers; however, this process mainly started with the collapse of the Soviet Union. This is despite the fact that China had historical ties with Central Asia long before the USA entered the picture. Here, China's high dependence on oil and gas in the region, along with the link between the internal security of the Central Asian region and China's security, has made this country's involvement in the region inevitable. China's more serious entry into the region is in line with the country's geo-economic strategy, based on which strengthening trade, energy security, and creating cross-border infrastructure are prioritized, while the USA has sought security, energy, and promotion of democracy in this region. China and the USA compete in Central Asia in four areas: economic, security, political, and cultural. Also, India as a rising power is also seeking influence, a base, and a mutual market in Central Asia.

Afghanistan and the countries of Central Asia have many similarities and closeness due to geography and a long history. In short, the relations between Afghanistan and Central Asia have been in four areas of common history—

security, political relations, military relations, and economic cooperation. For example, the war between the Soviet Union and Afghanistan had a great impact on the societies of Central Asia. In the meantime, Tajikistan received the most influence. During the civil wars in Afghanistan, Uzbekistan suffered a small wave of refugees who were mostly Uzbeks. Turkmenistan also has close ties with Afghanistan due to the presence of the Turkmen minority in Afghanistan. After the formation of the interim government in 2001, all five Central Asian governments held several international meetings for a safe and stable Afghanistan. This means that any kind of political and military developments in Afghanistan affect the region and vice versa. Therefore, the consequences of the conflicts between the interests of coalition A and B members in Central Asia have also affected the situation in Afghanistan.

3.7.3 India

The prevailing belief is that India-Afghanistan relations are sustainable and unlimited. India has been one of Afghanistan's major regional allies for nearly two decades (2001-2021) and has made a great contribution to reconstruction and state-building in Afghanistan. In other words, in the years after the defeat of the Taliban and the establishment of the new political order in Afghanistan, India has been the fifth largest donor towards the reconstruction of Afghanistan. The reconstruction of the Salma Dam in Herat and the construction of the new building of Afghanistan's Parliament are two of India's biggest projects. India-Afghanistan relations have traditionally been good, and India has always tried to have the people of Afghanistan people with it. For this reason, many Afghanistani people believe that India is a friend for all seasons. India's cultural exports have helped to strengthen the long-standing ties between the two countries. According to the data published by the Ministry of External Affairs of the Government of India, from 2001 to 2021 India has helped Afghanistan in the fields of health, education, urban development, infrastructure, agriculture, transportation, higher education, and the training of military officers. India's aid in the last two decades in Afghanistan reaches more than 1 billion dollars. (Govt. India 2009)

Table 3: India Small Development Projects in Afghanistan

India	*Agriculture and Veterinary*	*Health*	*Water and Sanitation*	*Educational Project*	*Women and Family Welfare*
4 Projects	22 Projects	22 Projects	23 Projects	22 Projects	

Source: Ministry of External Affairs, Government of India, pp. 29-31.

Therefore, due to security and geopolitical reasons in South Asia, India has always been trying to form a stable government in Afghanistan and has provided full political, financial, and technical support to the government after the Bonn Conference. On the other hand, India is part of coalition B in Afghanistan and its surrounding areas and pursues the same policy as the USA in Asia, and is clearly in opposition to the two regional nuclear powers, China and Pakistan. Both China and Pakistan have tried to limit India's sphere of influence in Afghanistan and Central Asia, respectively, and most of India's projects in Afghanistan have come under direct attack by Pakistan-backed extremist Islamists.

After 9/11, India supported the national security doctrine of the USA and aligned with it in the war against terror. This was for two reasons; one, the USA started a war on a front that India had to fight alone because it had suffered several times from international terrorism that was a potential threat to India's national security; second, in addition to the war against terrorism, the USA had specific goals to control and limit the influence of China, Russia, and Iran in Asia. That is, India's interaction with the USA was a win-win game for either country. For this reason, in July 2007, the USA and India agreed on the text of the nuclear cooperation agreement known as the bilateral 123 Agreement. (Govt. the USA 2007)

In this respect, Manmohan Singh, the then Prime Minister of India, visited the USA in July 2005, and in the joint declaration issued by the latter and India during this trip India was considered an independent state with advanced nuclear technology. What was evident from the strategic defence and nuclear cooperation between India and the USA was the impact of these actions on the balance of power in Asia in the strategic relations of the USA. Although it had changed the rules of the game with India in order to create balance against China and Russia, at the same time, it helped India to become a major power and a strategic ally in Asia. This strategy was/is based on the ability of the USA to form reliable regional partners. The USA knew that a nuclear China could upset the balance of power in Asia and even the world. The nuclear agreement between India and the USA was the result of the perception of the latter that defence, economic and nuclear support, and cooperation with India can establish a balance in Asia. The main goal of the USA in concluding the peaceful nuclear deal was to turn India into a regional military power to realize the interests of both countries, which has also affected other regional powers; it also had to reconsider its security interests in the region. Accordingly, India still took the side of the USA in its nuclear disputes with Iran.

In addition, another reason for the competition between China and India is the historical and traditional border problems between the two countries. Both have strong differences in three sectors (three border areas) western, middle, and eastern. India claims the entire Aksai Chin area, which is approximately 38,000 sq km and is under the control of China. In contrast, China in the eastern sector claims the entire state of Arunachal Pradesh, which is approximately 90,000 sq km and is under the rule of the Government of India. In the central sector, both countries have small differences compared to the eastern and western sectors, and the range of differences in this area is approximately 2,000 sq km in the states of Himachal Pradesh and Uttarakhand. (Chinoy 2022: 4)

Moreover, India and Pakistan have been hostile towards each other since the latter's separation from India, and both countries have a sharp border dispute over the Kashmir issue. This border dispute between India and Pakistan caused China to take full advantage of the opportunity and become a strategic economic, military, and nuclear partner of Pakistan in the region. This China-Pakistan alliance against India caused severe military conflicts between India and Pakistan—the Kargil war in 1999, the Pulwama attack in February 2019. The last border conflict between China and India was in the Galwan Valley in 2020.

Bearing in mind these bitter disputes between India, China, and Pakistan, which have repeatedly had direct military conflicts within their territories, they are still engaged in competition outside their borders and in the region, and each is trying to control and limit the other's sphere of influence. One of the fields of competition for these regional powers is Afghanistan, and these actors pursue contradictory policies in Afghanistan according to national interests and internal and regional conditions. As India wants a stable, dignified, and popular government in Afghanistan and considers it to be in its interests in the region, it has played a constructive role in the process of state-building in Afghanistan at every opportunity. But on the other hand, Pakistan and China want a weak and subordinate government through which they can pursue their interests. China and Pakistan have always tried to limit India's sphere of influence in Afghanistan. Accordingly, most of India's reconstruction projects in Afghanistan have been attacked by extremist Islamists who were financed and equipped by Pakistan. On the contrary, India adopted a soft policy towards Pakistan, and most of the 80 per cent of India's construction projects until 2009 were in the south and southeast of Afghanistan, where most of the inhabitants are Pashtuns; They are considered one of Pakistan's influence areas.

3.7.4 Pakistan

The history of Afghanistan-Pakistan relations has many ups and downs and one can see the heritage of the colonial era in them with full confidence. Despite deep racial and cultural ties, these two countries have always had a tense history, the main reason for which is the territorial disputes between the two countries; the lasting sign of this difference is the Durand Line. On the other hand, these disputes are also rooted in the issue of ethnicity, and its symbol is the issue of Pashtunistan, which caused Afghanistan to have a negative attitude towards Pakistan's policies from the very beginning. The Durand Line demarcating the two countries was signed by Amir Abdul Rahman Khan, the king of Afghanistan in 1893, and Britain when Britain had its colony in India. Because of internal reasons and sensitivities the Line has not been accepted by most Afghanistani statesmen at any point of history.

These border and ethnic differences between Afghanistan and Pakistan have caused Pakistan to always adopt a hostile policy towards Afghanistan and has never wanted a strong and stable government to be formed there. There are many historical evidences that reveal Pakistan's hostile policy towards the formation of a sovereign and stable government in Afghanistan. For example, the communist regime of Afghanistan from 1978-1992, had a well-equipped, organized army, and a strong and efficient intelligence which had a good position in the region; for 14 years, Pakistan housed the opponents of this regime, which included extreme and moderate Islamic parties (mujahideen), trained, equipped, and financed them to overthrow the communist regime, until in 1992, the communist regime was completely destroyed. The army, intelligence, and government civil institutions were completely disintegrated and destroyed. Undoubtedly, great powers such as the USA, which played an important role in the war, also contributed to this destruction, but Pakistan was only the first regional player in the case. From 1992 to 2001, when the Islamic government under the leadership of Burhanuddin Rabbani had international recognition, Pakistan continued its hostile policy and Afghanistan witnessed civil wars followed by the emergence of the Taliban.

From 2001 to 2021, when according to the Bonn Accord, Afghanistan was experiencing state building again, with the USA, the European Union and most of the countries in the region and Afghanistan's neighbours playing a positive active role. But Pakistan continued its hostile policy and went against the regional and global plan towards Afghanistan. The Afghanistan government, the USA, the European Union, and most of the countries in the region wanted the Taliban, al-Qaeda, and other terrorist groups to be destroyed and, on the contrary, Pakistan sheltered, financed, and equipped them to fight against the Afghanistan government and the international community.

The main question is why Pakistan does not want a strong and stable government to be formed in Afghanistan. The answer to this can be evaluated in two internal and external aspects of Pakistan's policy towards Afghanistan. In the domestic dimension, among Pakistani statesmen, there were three views towards Afghanistan: 1. The view of the Pakistani military, which aims to fully merge Afghanistan with Pakistan and create a confederation, which means reaching the Amu River; 2. The view of the ISI, which has many supporters among Pakistani Pashtun officers such as General Hamidgul, Nasrullah Babar, Karneel Imam, General Asad Durrani and also clerics such as Maulana Fazlur Rehman, and wishes to establish a Pashtun religious extremist government in Afghanistan like the Taliban regime or the annexation of part of Pashtun-populated areas of Afghanistan; 3. The point of view of the democratic and moderate politicians of Pakistan is that they aim to prevent the establishment of an anti-Pakistani government in Afghanistan that would have a territorial claim on Pakistan. Unless there is a government in Afghanistan that has no territorial claims on Pakistan and wants to be friends with it, it should not be opposed. (Arianfar 2016: 225)

Aziz Arianfar believes that the Punjabi and Sindhi generals of the Pakistani army mostly have big and strategic goals in mind, such as finding a way to Central Asia, encircling Iran, and confronting India while the generals and clerics of Pakistani Pashtun descent pursue more limited goals. They are more interested in increasing the political weight of Pashtuns within Pakistan. Arianfar also believes that the views of moderate and democratic Pakistani politicians are reasonable and realistic, and to realize this view, a national government should be established in Afghanistan that does not have territorial claims with Pakistan, and in this way, understanding and reconciliation for both countries will be provided. (Arianfar 2016: 225)

In the foreign policy dimension, Pakistan has a protective strategy against India, which it wants to achieve through an alliance with Afghanistan. According to this strategy, Pakistan has two goals; firstly, it wants to create a geographical strategic depth inside Afghanistan, although the Pakistanis claim that Baluchistan has provided them with this strategic depth. And secondly, it wants to prevent India's influence in Afghanistan. In this respect, the consolidation of a stable and popular government in Afghanistan is considered by Pakistan to mean its encirclement by India, since Pakistanis know that a strong and popular government in Afghanistan will naturally have a friendly relationship with India according to its internal needs and national interests. This deep concern of Pakistan was revealed when the President of Pakistan, Pervez Musharraf, in a meeting with the President of Afghanistan, Hamid Karzai, in 2006, complained about the presence of Indian intelligence near the borders of Pakistan and accused India and Afghanistan supporting the Baloch and Pashtun separatists in the territory of Pakistan. (Kasuri 2015: 312)

In addition, Pakistan has been concerned about the activities of the Indian consulate in the southern and south-eastern regions of Afghanistan bordering Pakistan. Pakistan claimed that the Indian consulates in the mentioned areas do not have any kind of economic benefit for India, but the continuation of their activities has a high cost for India unless India is using them for other purposes against Pakistan. From 2006 to 2011, Pakistan felt besieged by India and Afghanistan. In 2011, following the death of bin Laden in Pakistan, when it was under pressure from the USA and the international community for harbouring al-Qaeda, the USA somehow evaluated itself as the winner of the war on terror and decided to withdraw its forces from Afghanistan. Pakistan was more determined than before to support and equip the Taliban and prepared itself to play a bigger role and fill the security vacuum that was created after the withdrawal of the USA and NATO forces in Afghanistan. Although this action of Pakistan was not new, there was a big difference with Pakistan's previous policies towards Afghanistan.

The difference was that Pakistan had practically understood that the physical existence of a popular but relatively weak government in Afghanistan could not be indifferent to Pakistan's covert and open interventions in Afghanistan's internal affairs. It even understood that in such a situation, Afghanistan can have regional support. Therefore, in such a situation, Pakistan was forced to invest more in the Taliban and use them once again at the right time. Among its other goals, Pakistan did this more strongly for two reasons. One, Pakistan was struggling with its internal problems at that time and political stability in Pakistan was shaky and it could not fight on two fronts both inside and outside its borders. Second, Pakistan wanted to save itself from India's blockade through Afghanistan and was still trying to bring an alternative to the Afghanistan government.

The rivalry between Pakistan and India has had a great impact on the process of Afghanistan's state-building compared to other regional players. The competition between these two countries is like water and fire, which should be destroyed if one of them is physically present. That is, if India and Afghanistan have close and friendly relations, Pakistan should be left out of the equation. And if the ruling government in Afghanistan has close and friendly relations with Pakistan, like the presence of the Taliban before 2001, there will be no place for India in Afghanistan. Both India and Pakistan follow two different policies in the direction of state-building in Afghanistan; as mentioned before, India wants a strong government arising from the processes of democracy in Afghanistan, and on the contrary, Pakistan wants a weak, autocratic, and subservient government that can be a friend of Pakistan.

3.7.5 Iran

Since the establishment of the Islamic Republic of Iran in 1357, Afghanistan has been one of the important issues and matters of its foreign policy. However, the position and importance of this country in Iran's foreign policy have not been the same. Rather, it has undergone changes due to internal situations in Afghanistan, regional, and international developments. In a way, due to the occurrence of severe and deep crises at these three levels, Afghanistan has become the most important issue and the dilemma of Iran's foreign policy. The invasion of the US-led international coalition forces into Afghanistan and then the fall of the Taliban in December 2001 is one of those historical events. Although this incident is not considered a 'foreign policy crisis' for the Islamic Republic of Iran, it has created a regional and international crisis in its surrounding security environment and has severely affected the security and national interests of Iran.

Iran and Afghanistan, which have cultural, linguistic, racial, and religious commonalities, try to manage their relations using these commonalities because the countries located in a geographical area influence each other and are influenced by each other based on factors such as geography, history, economy, and culture. A look at the relations between the Islamic Republic of Iran and Afghanistan shows that these two countries are affected by each other due to their neighbourhood. Iran and Afghanistan have a common border of 945 kilometres, and Afghanistan has a special place in securing Iran's national security and interests from three cultural, economic, and political security dimensions. After the 2002 Tokyo conference, Iran pledged more than 500 million dollars for the reconstruction of Afghanistan.

As noted, Iran's policy towards Afghanistan has had extreme fluctuations and has never had a one-handed policy towards Afghanistan. According to a number of analysts, these fluctuations in Iran's policy towards Afghanistan have been influenced by four elements: 1. the ideology of the Islamic Revolution; 2. The approach of major and regional powers to Afghanistan; 3. The approach of domestic political groups towards Afghanistan; and 4. The approach of the leaders of the Islamic Republic of Iran to Afghanistan. Due to the different interactions of these four elements, Iran's policy towards Afghanistan has been different over time. Since foreign policy is one of the tools to protect national interests, it can be said that Iran's national interests in

Afghanistan have not been fixed and defined. Of course, this also indicates that there was no unanimity of opinion regarding Afghanistan in the policy-making institutions in the Iranian government.

From the performance of the Islamic Republic of Iran towards Afghanistan in the last two decades, it is clear that the second element (the approach of major and regional powers) has had a greater impact on Iran's policies towards Afghanistan. For example, during the Soviet invasion of Afghanistan in 1978, Iran provided political and military support to the Shia parties against Pakistan, Saudi Arabia, and the USA, whose Sunni Mujahideen received financial and military support. In fact, Iran tried to prevent the influence of its regional rivals such as Saudi Arabia and Pakistan in Afghanistan. During the civil wars, Iran, along with the Afghanistani Shiites, supported the Persian–speaking people of Afghanistan against extremist Pashtuns such as Hekmatyar and later the Taliban, who were supported by Pakistan.

The fall of the Taliban in 2001 as a result of the US attack was both an opportunity and a challenge for Iran. The opportunity was due to the fact that Iran considered the existence of an extremist Sunni Islamic regime on its borders as a threat to its national security, which was destroyed free of charge by America, and, on the other hand, the role and influence of its regional rivals such as Saudi Arabia and Pakistan had been limited in Afghanistan. The forcible removal of the Taliban by the USA was an unintentional gift to Iran that created a strategic configuration with both enticing opportunities as well as dangers for Iran. (Milani 2016: 235)

The challenge was due to the fact that the place of Iran's regional competitors was taken by its global competitor, the USA. The basis of Iran's concern was that from the point of view of realism, weak states in terms of power in the international system cannot have stable national interests. In other words, their national interests are largely influenced by the national interests of great powers and their orientation. Since Afghanistan was a weak and fragile state in Iran's calculations and at the same time the USA was present in Afghanistan with political and military power, most of Iran's national interests were at risk and created a security dilemma for Iran.

From a geostrategic point of view, Iran has become very close to China and Russia in recent years due to its enmity with the USA. In recent years,

Iran has been able to obtain large amounts of advanced weapons, including MiG-29 aircraft and powerful air defence missiles from Russia. This country has also achieved the technology of producing medium-range tactical surface-to-surface, surface-to-sea, surface-to-air, and air-to-surface missiles and advanced drones. Some Western sources claim that Iran may still secretly have large quantities of chemical and biological weapons. (Milani 2016: 241)

Iran and the USA have had hostile relations for a long time over the issues of the former's nuclear program. Iran's concern about the presence of the USA in Afghanistan was more serious in three cases: 1. the direct presence of American forces on Iran's borders, along with the possibility of creating new military bases and the fear of a military attack by the USA on Iran through Afghanistan; 2. Since 11 September, the regional policies of the US government have focused more on the isolation of Iran in its geopolitical sphere and the creation and strengthening of regional coalitions against Iran and the pursuit of regime change policy. The reason for this claim is the negotiations between the USA and Afghanistan to sign a strategic agreement in July 2011. Pursuing such policies has caused Iran to counter the opposing goals of the USA in the region in a defensive response; 3; Threats caused by new geopolitical changes in the region that have emerged following the process of transitioning the region to a new political and security order. Iran's new security dilemma goes back to the process of political transition in the region and the challenges caused by the formation of a new political and security order. From this point of view, the policies and efforts of the US government in creating this order based on the national interests of the USA in the region by using affiliated or like-minded elites to contain Iran were in conflict with the national interests of Iran, because in practice it caused the presence and influence of the USA in the region. Such policies not only endangered Iran's national security but also led to the reduction of Iran's role and influence in its security environment, especially in the Persian Gulf region. Therefore, the new security dilemma was that the policies that are interpreted as an increase in regional security from the point of view of the USA were perceived as a decrease in regional security for Iran at the same time.

Bearing in mind these concerns of Iran at the regional and international level, and also the lack of consensus and unity of command and opinion among Iranian politicians, Iran has had a dual policy towards Afghanistan and has not played an effective role in the process of state-building in Afghanistan. However, a strong and stable government in Afghanistan is in the interests of Iran, and most of Iran's political elites have also understood this. A strong and stable government in Afghanistan can at least solve and manage the problems of hydro politics, drugs, and the issue of Afghanistani immigrants in Iran. Therefore, Iran's efforts for state-building in Afghanistan have become a victim of Iran's regional and global rivalries with other sovereign active actors in Afghanistan. This has caused Iran to always have a dual policy towards Afghanistan, like Pakistan. In this respect, Iran had to be friends with the Afghanistan government and its internal and external enemies at the same time. It is better for Iran to pursue a one-sided policy in Afghanistan because the differences between them are not enough to require a two-sided policy.

3.8 CONCLUSION

Throughout its history, Afghanistan has consistently faced serious challenges in forming a national government, with all state-building efforts ultimately ending in failure. These failures stem from a combination of internal and external factors, each contributing to the inability to establish a stable and effective government system.

Among the internal factors is Afghanistan's complex political and social structure. Various political regimes, the crisis of national identity, ethnic nationalism, and political despotism have been major obstacles. In addition, issues related to the constitution and the official name 'Afghanistan,' which has been a source of contention among the country's various ethnic groups, as well as the multi-layered structure and social and ethnic divisions that have weakened national cohesion, are factors that have further challenged the state-building process.

External factors have also played a significant role in Afghanistan's state-building failures. Foreign powers, through repeated interventions, have imposed political and ideological models and processes that have not aligned with the country's social and political realities. A prominent example of these interventions is the state-building process initiated by the USA and the international community after 2001. This top-down model of state-building began with institution-building, whereas in a country like Afghanistan, where the nation-building process has not yet been completed, such an approach has proven ineffective. In fact, in countries like Afghanistan, a strong national identity must first be established so that state institutions can form based on a united nation.

Afghanistan remains fragmented in terms of identity, and a well-defined national identity has not yet taken shape. While in many societies, nations form governments and protect them, this process has not taken place properly in Afghanistan. Without completing the nation-building process, any efforts to build institutions are bound to fail. In this context, the European model of state-building might be more suitable for Afghanistan, as it prioritizes nation-building. It emphasizes that without the formation of a strong national identity state institutions cannot function effectively or garner public support.

NOTES

1. Sometimes there is a misunderstanding in the concept of State-Building and Nation-Building. Some consider both concepts to be the same, and some consider them to be separate. As Francis Fukuyama demonstrated: *Europeans often criticize Americans for the use of the term nation-building, reflecting as it does the specifically American experience of constructing a new political order in a land of new settlement without deeply rooted peoples, cultures, and traditions. Nations—that is to say, communities of shared values, traditions, and historical memory—by this argument are never built, particularly by outsiders; rather, they evolve out of an unplanned historical-evolutionary process. What Americans refer to as nation-building is rather state-building—that is, constructing political institutions, or else promoting economic development. This argument is largely true: what Americans mean by nation-building is usually state-building coupled with economic development.* For more details see, Fukuyaman, Francis. 2006, "*Nation-Building: Beyond Afghanistan and Iraq*", Baltimore, USA. The John Hopkins University Press, p. 3.
2. There have been three historical forms of the single-party system: communist, fascist, and that found in less-developed countries. In the traditional communist model, the party hierarchy, then, and not the official state hierarchy, has the real power. The first secretary of the party is the most important figure of the regime, and, whether the party leadership is in the hands of one individual or several, the party remains the centre of political power. China is an example of this model. For more details, see https://www.britannica.com/topic/political-party/Single-party-systems and Lawrence, Susan V. & Martin, Michael F. 2012, "Understanding China's Political System". Congressional Research Service, CRS Report for Congress R41007. Available at: https://crsreports.congress.gov/search/#/?termsToSearch=Understanding%20China%E2%80%99s%20Political%20System&orderBy=Relevance, accessed 23 December 2022.
3. Rahimi writes that the official narrative claims that Ahmad Shah Abdali was appointed as the king of Afghanistan in a nine-day jirga. Their reason is that several Pashtun tribal leaders sat for nine days in consultation until they finally decided to appoint Ahmad Shah Abdali as the king of Afghanistan, and the official discourse, referring to this nine-day meeting, considered the method of electing Ahmad Shah Abdali as a democratic process. While jirga is a tribal mechanism to solve local problems and disputes among Pashtuns living in tribal

areas of Afghanistan rather than a political mechanism. It should also be noted that there is a clear contradiction between the official discourse and the historical book written in the court of Ahmad Shah Abdali and under his command titled *"History of Ahmad Shahi",* and that the official discourse considers Ahmad Shah Abdali as a founder *of Afghanistan,* while in the *"History Ahmad Shahi",* Ahmad Shah Abdali is mentioned as the king of Khorasan .See for more details: Rahimi, Mujib. 2021-22. "*Deconstructing the Official Discourse of State Formation in Afghanistan*". Kabul. Amiri Publication. 167-170.

4. Rahimi mentioned nine historical events that have transformed and disturbed the process, hegemony, and dominance of the official discourse, which he considers as placeless and replacement events. The nine events are: 1) the communist coup d'état on the 7thof April 1978, 2) the invasion of Afghanistan by the Soviet Union in 1979, 3) the national jihad and resistance against the Soviet occupation and the global support for this resistance, 4) the massive migration of people to neighbouring countries and other parts of the world, 5) the withdrawal of the Soviet Union from Afghanistan, 6) the fall of the communist regime in Afghanistan, 7) the victory of the Mujahideen in 1992, 8) the rise of the Taliban, 9) the events of September 11, 2001, and the intervention of the USA and its allies to Afghanistan and the region. According to Rahimi, these events had three basic consequences: A) the traditional structure of power or the symbolic order of the ruler was disrupted, B) the official discourse as the only absolute truth was challenged and shaken, C) the context and conditions for the emergence of new discourses provided.
5. Mountstuart Elphinstone FRSE was a Scottish statesman and historian, associated with the government of British India. He later became the Governor of Bombay (now Mumbai) where he is credited with the opening of several educational institutions accessible to the Indian population. Besides being a noted administrator, he wrote books on India and Afghanistan.
6. Why is the top of political power so important in Afghanistan? According to the 2004 constitution, Afghanistan's political system is a centralized presidential system. Also, in this constitution, the president is at the top of power and has unlimited powers. Therefore, each ethnic group, especially the Tajiks and the Pashtuns tries to be at the top of the power.
7. A Grand Council of religious and tribal leaders in Afghanistan.
8. Lake refers to them as models, but I prefer to name them here as the American state-building versions, keeping in mind the European model.
9. This data was provided by David Lake in 2010, at that time the USA was present in Afghanistan with a number of its military and political forces, and it was premature for Lake to judge the stability of democracy in Afghanistan and Iraq after ten years. But now, after the middle of 2021, it can be well judged for Afghanistan that the answer to the question is '*No*'.

Chapter 4

Islamist Extremism and Afghanistan: Dynamics and External Linkages

4.1 INTRODUCTION

The third chapter discussed 'The Clash of Respective Strategic Depths of Sovereign Actors in Afghanistan' It was divided into two main parts. The first part delved into the political and social challenges facing state-building in Afghanistan, from internal perspectives. It also examined the relevance of modern nation-state concepts and governance within the Afghanistan context. Nine internal elements that influenced the state-building process in Afghanistan were analysed. The second part focused on conflicts between the strategic goals of various sovereign actors (such as the USA, China, India, Pakistan, and Iran) in Afghanistan, and their impact on the state-building process in Afghanistan.

The fourth chapter attempts to elucidate the internal dynamics and external linkages of Islamist extremism in Afghanistan. It comprises five main parts. The first discusses the characteristics of Islamist extremism since 2001, elucidating how extremist groups have challenged socio-political trends in Afghanistan. The second part focuses on the strength and support base of Islamist groups among the civilian population and political elites. This section also examines socio-religious movements alongside governmental policies. The third part addresses external influences on and linkages with Islamic extremism. The fourth critically observes the manifestations of Islamic extremism and its influence on policymaking over the past two decades (2001-2021). Finally, the last part explores resistance against extremism within Afghanistan and its outcomes.

4.2 CHARACTER OF ISLAMIST EXTREMISM SINCE 2001

Extremism, regardless of its ideological or religious orientation, is characterized by distinct principles, foundations, and predefined objectives. Islamic extremism, in particular, exhibits unique traits that distinguish it from other forms of extremism. To facilitate a deeper understanding, the features of Islamic extremism are categorized into two parts. Firstly, the intrinsic characteristics of Islamic extremism that provides profound interconnectedness among Islamic extremist factions. Secondly, the functional characteristics of Islamic extremism which are analysed separately within this section. It is important to clarify that the focus of this article is to examine Sunni Islamic extremism, commonly referred to as Salafism in existing scholarly discourse. Notably, every Sunni Islamic extremist group traces its origins back to Salafism. Hence, whenever reference is made to extremist groups herein, it aims specifically to Salafi extremist factions.

4.2.1 Intrinsic Characteristics of Islamic Extremism

The inherent features of Islamic extremism are analogous among numerous Islamic extremist groups (Taliban 2.0, al-Qaeda, ISIS, etc.). These characteristics serve as foundational elements for the establishment of all Islamist extremist movements. Moreover, they foster intellectual, operational, and strategic alignments among a majority of extremist groups worldwide. Consequently, Islamic extremist groups tend to collaborate rather than engage in conflict with one another, thus reinforcing their shared objectives. These features comprise:

4.2.1.1 Literal Interpretation of Religious Texts

Within the realm of semantics, Islamic extremists adhere staunchly to appearance[ism], that is, overt display of fealty to religious doctrines. They rely exclusively on superficial and biased interpretations of primary religious texts, refusing to entertain any form of interpretation thereof, particularly in the case of the Quran, unless corroborated or elucidated by Hadith. Extremists adamantly maintain that Quranic interpretation is strictly forbidden, even for individuals possessing scholarly expertise in Islamic sciences. (Alizadeh Mousavi 2019: 99) This literalist approach has resulted in the propagation of rigid and dogmatic narratives among extremists, consequently constricting their understanding of Islam. Despite the *Quran*'s status as the foremost source in

Islam, it inherently permits diverse interpretations through the concept of 'ijtihad'. (Quadri 2012)

> *The reason for ijtihad is that the Quran is an encompassing guide for all humanity. Thus, its doctrines have to be applied to diverse social, political, and economic settings, in various time periods. Even though many of the Quran's discourses are universal, some of them require specific geopolitical implementation. Thus, through its provision of ijtihad, the Quran allows Muslims to interpret its tenets so that they can appropriately cater to changing times and diverse private and public needs in Islamic communities across the globe.* (Venkatraman 2007: 236)

Furthermore, this adherence to appearance[ism] has led extremist groups to remain static and resistant to adaptation in response to contemporary conditions and advancements. Consequently, they confine themselves to ideologies rooted in past centuries. This phenomenon is significant as these groups espouse the integration of religion and politics, perceiving them as inseparable entities. Accordingly, they find themselves intellectually stagnant, hindering their ability to realize their ultimate objective of establishing an Islamic system. In essence, appearance[ism] by extremist groups has constrained their efficacy and utilization of modern tools and technologies in pursuit of their goals.

4.2.1.2 Human Rights Violations

From the Islamic perspective, humanity is esteemed as a valuable creation deserving of respect, being endowed with consciousness, will, and authority. Islam upholds principles of human freedom and emphasizes the inherent rights and dignity of individuals, irrespective of extraneous factors such as race, language, colour, or nationality.

Islam regards both men and women as integral components of humanity, without discrimination concerning their intrinsic honour and dignity. According to Quranic interpretations, both genders originate from the same human source, and discourses concerning the inherent worth of humans encompass both men and women. Certain verses underscore the equality of men and women in facilitating human progress and spiritual fulfilment through righteous deeds, faith, and correct beliefs.

However, human rights are disregarded by Islamic extremist groups, who exclusively prioritize Islamic rights according to their ideological frameworks for subjects and inhabitants under their jurisdiction. These groups do not recognize the concept of universal human rights. Moreover, they assert their interpretation of Islamic law, which may vary across different geographic regions where they operate. For instance, during their rule from 1996 to 2001, the Taliban 1.0 regime in Afghanistan curtailed numerous basic individual and group freedoms in the areas under their control.

During the rule of Taliban 1.0, individuals were deprived of the fundamental rights to participate in political and social discourse. Even activities as commonplace as listening to music or staying informed through news broadcasts were deemed criminal offences. Religious minorities faced severe constraints in practising their faith openly. Women, who constituted a significant segment of the Afghanistan population, were systematically denied the rights to education, employment, and autonomy. Additionally, men were subject to strict dress codes dictated by the Taliban, with wearing a tie or a suit deemed tantamount to religious apostasy. The regime imposed draconian restrictions on the observance of special occasions as well. Consequently, human rights and basic freedoms held no sway in the eyes of Islamic extremist groups like the Taliban; rather, they actively opposed and sought to dismantle such rights.

According to the Office of the United Nations High Commissioner for Human Rights (OHCHR), terrorism aims at the very destruction of human rights, democracy and the rule of law. It attacks the values that lie at the heart of the Charter of the United Nations and other international instruments: respect for human rights; the rule of law; rules governing armed conflict and the protection of civilians; tolerance among peoples and nations; and the peaceful resolution of conflict. (UN Doc 2007. DPO/2439B/Rev.2: 7)

4.2.1.3 Use of Violence

The utilization of violence stands as a defining characteristic of extremist groups. While various entities, including individuals, political, social, and religious factions, as well as governments, may employ violence either for self-preservation or to accomplish preconceived objectives, within the discourse surrounding Islamic extremism, the deployment of violence emerges as a pivotal and indissoluble component during both the formative and operational phases of these groups. A multitude of Islamic extremist organizations incorporate violence into their agendas and activities. Diverse perspectives exist regarding the motivations prompting these groups to resort to violence, reflecting the complex interplay of ideological, strategic, and contextual factors driving their actions.

Colin J. Beck, who has studied terrorism in the framework of the Social Movements Theory (SMT), believes that "Terrorism, given that it makes political claims and seeks to influence political processes and outcomes, should be seen as one such mode of collective action." He continues to add that "terrorism is a tactic and a type of contention that may or may not appear in a political struggle". He believes that, political violence is often conducted by organized groups. According to Beck a social movement is, "collective challenges, based on common purposes and social solidarities, in sustained interaction with elites, opponents, and authorities." (Beck 2008:1566)

The SMT states that every social movement emerges against the grievances of societies. These grievances can have political, economic and military dimensions. So Beck also believes that:

> *In the study of terrorism, grievance and strain accounts continue to play a central role: terrorism is argued to be motivated by threatened values or idealized religious doctrine in contradiction with society's practice reactions to the strain of modernization in society, foreign military occupations and external influence, or other broad grievances.* (Beck 2008:1567)

A parallel hypothesis frequently utilized by extremist Islamist groups posits that militants' movements, in general, emerged in response to Western policies towards other nations. As Anja D. Neilsen states:

> *A related argument—an argument frequently used by the militants themselves—points to a presumed Western political, economic, and cultural imperialism vis-a-vis the rest of the world. Foreign economic, political, and military pressure combined with repressive indigenous regimes, the argument goes, create strains in society and lead to the emergence of social protest movements. Religious movements frequently become the vehicle for such protest when opposition political parties are banned as in a number of Middle Eastern countries.* (Dallgaard- Neilsen 2008: 4)

The aforementioned viewpoints predominantly emphasize indigenous social movements, downplaying the significance of external influences in their inception. This aspect complicates the discourse, as Islamist extremist groups not only fall within the purview of social movement theory but also present challenges. Alongside indigenous factors contributing to the emergence of Islamist extremist groups, foreign elements also exert influence, guiding and supporting their activities. This dynamic is particularly conspicuous in the case of Afghanistan, exemplified by the Taliban. Despite possessing inherent indigenous capabilities, the Taliban also benefit from substantial foreign support.

The rationale behind the employment of violence by Islamist extremist groups can be attributed to two primary factors. Firstly, these groups perceive violence as a retaliatory measure against Western policies directed towards Islamic nations, or as a response to indigenous leaders who align themselves with the West. Secondly, through the strategic use of violence within specific geographic regions, they aim to advance political agendas. Consequently, these groups necessitate the creation of a narrative and propaganda framework to solidify their political and religious identity. Thus, violence emerges as the most accessible and cost-effective means for them to assert their presence as active and formidable entities vis-à-vis governments

4.2.1.4 Haqqani Network

Here, the Haqqani Network is examined as a case study for two primary purposes. Firstly, it serves to elucidate the underlying rationale guiding the utilization of violence by Islamist extremist factions, thereby shedding light on the political and social standing these groups typically seek in pursuit of their ideological objectives within a defined geographical context. Secondly, the analysis aims to comprehend the violent responses exhibited by such groups towards perceived political, economic, and military grievances within societies.

Jalaluddin Haqqani was one of the prominent Mujahideen commanders in the 1980s during the jihad against the Soviet Union, who conducted military operations in the southeastern regions (Khost, Paktika, and Paktia) bordering Pakistan. He served as the Minister of Justice in the Mujahedin government cabinet. Following the emergence of the Taliban 1.0 in 1996, Jalaluddin Haqqani joined it and was appointed as Minister of Borders and Tribal Affairs by Mullah Omar. (Alemarah 2020; Stanford University 2017) After the collapse of the Taliban 1.0 government, he fled to Miran Shah, Pakistan, where he established new structures under the name of the Haqqani Network (HQN). He wielded significant influence in the southeastern regions of Afghanistan and among the Pashtun tribes residing on both sides of the Afghanistan-Pakistan border. Following Jalaluddin Haqqani's death in 2018 (Counter Terrorism 2022), Sirajuddin Haqqani, his son, assumed leadership responsibilities within this network.

The HQN is recognized as one of the most influential and violent Islamist extremist groups with extensive operations in Afghanistan. Despite its significant role within the Taliban, it maintains a distinct identity owing to its independent organizational structure and strategies. According to available documentation and evidence, the HQN boasts a considerable number of suicide fighters, ready for deployment. Its internal capabilities in the battlefield, particularly in executing suicide attacks against US forces, NATO, Afghanistan security forces, and civilians, serve to distinguish this group in the spectrum of Islamist extremist organizations. Furthermore, the proliferation of violence has contributed to the prominence of the HQN. Some Haqqani suicide attacks are:

Table 4: A Few Suicide Attacks of Haqqani Network in Afghanistan

No.	*No. Injured*	*No. Killed*	*Kind of Attack*	*Place*	*Date No*
1	14 May 2020	Pakita	Suicide/Car bomb	5	14
2	27 Jan 2018	Kabul	Militants detonate an explode an ambulance	103	235
3	20 Jan 2018	Kabul/ Intercontinental	Gunmen attack	22 – including 4 Americans	20
4	31 May 2017	Kabul	Militants/Tanker Truck 3,000 lb explosive	150	400

Source: National Counterterrorism Centre.

Figure 3: Sirajuddin Haqqani and Khalil al-Raham Haqqani wanted notice

Source: US Department of States's National Security Reward

Sirajuddin Haqqani, the current leader of the Haqqani network, holds a pivotal role in its organization and leadership, garnering significant attention from global security organizations along with his uncle, Khalil al-Raham Haqqani, who is wanted by the US Federal Police and is subject to UN sanctions. The FBI has offered a reward ranging from 5 to 10 million dollars for information leading to their apprehension. (The U.S. Department of State's National Security 2024).

4.2.1.5 Global Jihad

Jihad exists as a doctrinal concept within Islam, subject to specific conditions for its legitimate enactment. Defined within primary Islamic texts, jihad encompasses various stages and forms. However, the emergence of the term 'Global Jihad'[1] gained prominence following the Soviet invasion of Afghanistan in 1979, which attracted numerous militant extremists, primarily from Arab Islamic nations, to participate in jihad against the Soviet forces. This ideological construct of global jihad was principally articulated by Abdullah Azzam. Subsequently, in 1998, Osama bin Laden, along with a coalition of clerics, issued a fatwa known as 'Jihad Against Jews and Crusaders,' targeting Western nations, notably the USA. Since its proclamation, this fatwa has served as a foundational manifesto for extremist Islamist factions, including the Taliban.

According to the United States Institute of Peace, jihadism initially focused on overthrowing local regimes; agendas gradually expanded to include transnational or transcontinental goals. For some, the short-term focus has again moved towards local goals and strategies. Local jihadist groups have also multiplied. Jihadism now has multiple models but ISIS and al-Qaeda remain the two major global brands. (USIP 2017: 6)

4.2.1.6 Anti-Western Sentiment

Anti-Western sentiment is prevalent among extremist Islamist groups, particularly with a focus on opposition to the USA. The genesis of these sentiments can be traced back to a series of political and military interventions undertaken by the USA and its Western allies in Islamic countries. The physical deployment of American forces in Afghanistan and Iraq, as well as the establishment of military bases in Saudi Arabia and several Arab nations in the Persian Gulf, has been a significant catalyst for such sentiments. The situation is further exacerbated by the support extended by the USA and other Western nations to Israel in its conflict with Palestine. However, in the case of Afghanistan, Taliban 2.0 regarded the twenty-year presence of NATO and the USA as foreign occupation, prompting them to resist it.

4.2.1.7 Opposition to Pluralism and Social Diversity

Afghanistan is characterized by its multi-ethnic, multicultural, and multilingual composition. While the majority of population adhere to Islam, the country historically accommodated religious minorities such as Sikhs and Jews prior to the emergence of armed extremism. However, Islamic extremism has overshadowed other aspects of identity, such as nationality, language, and regional affiliations. For instance, Taliban 2.0, predominantly composed of Pashtuns, also includes a minority representation of Tajiks, Uzbeks, and Hazaras. This exemplifies how Islamic extremism has superseded ethnic diversity within the group's identity framework.

The focal point of this discussion lies in the aspiration of Taliban 2.0, an extremist Islamist group, to impose a homogenous societal structure. This vision entails uniformity across all Afghanistan ethnicities, languages, and cultures, aligning them with the Taliban's own ethos and appearance. Under this regime, men are expected to adhere to traditional attire and refrain from trimming their beards, while women are confined to their homes unless wearing a hijab and burqa. Such stringent mandates underscore the Taliban's rejection of social diversity and pluralism. Their agenda prioritizes a singular, monolithic societal framework, devoid of any deviation from their narrow interpretation of Islamic norms. This underscores the group's aversion to embracing the richness of Afghanistan's social fabric and highlights their inclination towards enforcing rigid ideological conformity.

4.2.2 Functional Characteristics of Islamic Extremism

The functional characteristics of extremist groups are different from each other, although there are common goals among them. Usually, their functional characteristics are appropriate to the conditions and geography in which these they operate. What is clear is that none of the groups (al-Qaeda, ISIS, etc.) have the ability to regularly and systematically wage war with governments for two reasons. First, they do not have enough forces for conventional wars because wherever this group conducts operations, the majority of the people of that community are against this group, which will reduce their recruitment. Second, conventional and regular wars have a high financial cost, which no group can afford. For example, ISIS focused more on frontal wars in Iraq and Syria at the beginning. After 9/11, al-Qaeda has focused on bombings and suicide attacks, which have more of a media aspect and control of public opinion. Considering the geography of Afghanistan, the Taliban after 2001 focused more on guerrilla warfare on the highways, bombings and suicide attacks in big cities, gangs in universities, schools and public facilities. Since 2014, only the Taliban have been able to fight directly with the Afghan military forces, and the political and military capabilities of the Afghanistan government have weakened with the withdrawal of American and NATO forces.

4.3 Strength and Support Bases of Islamic Extremism among Civilian Populations and Political Elites

Continuous wars and political instability in Afghanistan have facilitated the emergence and consolidation of Islamic extremism, providing fertile ground for its growth and support. The geographical landscape, coupled with the enduring ramifications of decades-long conflicts, has directly contributed to the bolstering of Islamic extremism in Afghanistan. Consequently, this section aims to explore the multifaceted aspects underlying the strength and support networks of Islamic extremism in Afghanistan.

4.3.1 Geography and Ethnicity

Afghanistan is geographically characterized by its mountainous terrain and landlocked position. The majority of its rural populace resides far from urban centres, resulting in limited access to modern scientific and technological resources. Regrettably, successive Afghan governments have failed to formulate policies to address this challenge, perpetuating the reliance on traditional educational institutions, primarily madrasas (religious schools). The dearth of access to modern scientific and technological advancements has created fertile ground for the proliferation of extremist Islamic groups.

Map 4: Taliban Control in Afghanistan in 2021

Source: Author, based on Radio Free Europe data

Map 4, as published by Radio Free Europe in 2020, illustrates the expansion of Taliban 2.0 into regions distant from urban centres, where they are actively besieging major cities in Afghanistan such as Kabul, Kandahar, Herat, and Mazar-e-Sharif. This underscores the country's capacity to harbour and propagate Islamic extremism, manifested in its geographical spread and the ongoing efforts to establish control over key urban hubs.

It is crucial to acknowledge that not all regions distant from urban centres possess the predisposition for the proliferation of Islamic extremism. The crux of the matter lies in the interplay of various influential factors, wherein ethnicity emerges as a significant determinant alongside other elements such as geography, ideology, and political dynamics. Specifically, the ethnic composition of a region plays a pivotal role in shaping attitudes towards extremism. For instance, areas inhabited by the Hazara ethnic group have historically exhibited very little inclination towards embracing Islamic extremism. Conversely, regions predominantly inhabited by Pashtuns have been more conducive to the acceptance and proliferation of extremist ideologies compared to other ethnic groups. Tajik and Uzbek regions in Afghanistan have demonstrated varying degrees of susceptibility to extremism, with tendencies falling between those of Hazaras and Pashtuns. Thus, ethnicity, in conjunction with geographic factors, assumes a crucial supporting role in the diffusion of extremist ideologies.

4.3.2 Absolute Divergence and Disharmony between Religious and Modern Education

A profound gap exists between the curricula of religious schools and modern educational institutions in Afghanistan. The content taught in these two systems starkly contrasts with one another. While modern schools integrate Islamic studies with modern and experimental sciences, madrasas solely focus on religious education, neglecting scientific and technological subjects. Adding to this difference is the fact that there are more religious madrasas than modern schools in Afghanistan. Consequently, the social outcomes of these educational systems diverge significantly. Over the course of several decades, madrasas have been instrumental in producing religious scholars, contributing to the proliferation of extremist ideologies within Afghanistan society. Conversely, the societal roles and statuses of school teachers and clerics who teach in madrasas are markedly different, reflecting distinct social perceptions and hierarchies.

This discord and potential conflict between religious schools and modern educational institutions have significantly contributed to the growth of extremism in Afghanistan society. Individuals affiliated with madrasas, who hold significant influence in society through their dominance over mosques and pulpits, play a pivotal role in either exacerbating or mitigating extremism. However, the noted disparity and disconnect between religious schools and mainstream educational establishments often result in the propagation of extremist interpretations of religion, perpetuating the survival and expansion of radical ideologies, particularly among the youth.

Addressing and bridging this gap across all sectors necessitates the implementation of effective and practical initiatives by the Afghanistan government, particularly through the ministries of Education, Higher Education, and Hajj and Islamic Affairs. Harmonizing educational programs and curricula across schools, colleges, and universities stands out as a key strategy to diminish this disparity and mitigate the radicalization of society.

4.3.3 Escalating Social Injustice

The rising prevalence of social injustice within Afghanistan society, particularly concerning political representation, employment opportunities, and access to civil and social rights, stemming from various forms of discrimination, stands out as another factor exacerbating extremism among both the populace and youth. As hundreds of thousands of educated young individuals observe a select few of their counterparts enjoying political and social advantages solely on the basis of familial, ethnic, tribal, or other affiliations, the resulting confusion and frustration regarding this inequality often serve as catalysts for the emergence of extremist ideologies and militant tendencies.

In Afghanistan, when individuals from specific backgrounds, including members of certain ethnic groups, political parties, parliamentarians, ministers, and the offspring and relatives of leaders, are perceived as the sole inheritors of political and financial privileges, it results in a stark dichotomy in society. The majority of the population, however, is left grappling with poverty, unemployment, helplessness, despair, and disillusionment, while witnessing the concentration of wealth and power in the hands of a select few. This systemic injustice drives many towards extremism and militancy as a means of expressing their grievances and seeking redress. As long as this unjust, un-Islamic, and morally reprehensible state of affairs persists in Afghanistan society, the scourge of extremism and violence will continue to thrive and spread unabated.

4.3.4 The Inability of the Government to Curb Islamic Extremists

The government of Afghanistan, particularly the Ministry of Hajj and Islamic affairs, has been criticized for its lack of a comprehensive strategy to effectively address and mitigate the activities of Islamic extremist groups over the past decade. During this period of escalating extremism, some individuals assert that certain factions within the Afghanistan government turned a blind eye towards the violent actions of extremist organizations, purportedly due to their close ties with governments known to support terrorism and Islamic extremism, such as Saudi Arabia, the United Arab Emirates, Qatar, and Pakistan.

The government's failure to stem the tide of religious extremism in Afghanistan can be attributed to several underlying factors. Chief among them is the apparent lack of resolve and commitment from statesmen over the past two decades.

From 2001 to 2021, the Afghanistan government failed to implement comprehensive policies and solutions aimed at curtailing the proliferation of religious extremism, encompassing both its soft manifestations, such as religious parties and movements, and the fight against armed extremist groups like the Taliban, al-Qaeda, and ISIS. The conflict with the Taliban, an Islamic extremist group, was often influenced by ethnic dynamics and power-sharing arrangements in Afghanistan. Consequently, this prolonged conflict led to daily casualties among Afghanistani civilians, posing a significant security threat to both the government and the people. Despite the persistent challenges, the Afghanistan government failed to devise effective strategies to counter religious extremism and mitigate the associated security risks during this period.

4.3.5 The Role of Jamiat Eslah in the Spread of Islamic Extremism

The role of the Jamiat Eslah[2] in the propagation of religious extremism is notable. Established as a social institution and officially registered with the Ministry of Justice of Afghanistan in 2003, its origins trace back to the 1980s during the Soviet Union's military occupation of Afghanistan. Over time, it has gained significant influence across numerous public universities in Afghanistan, as well as within Sharia faculties in private institutions. Professors associated with Jamiat Eslah within public universities have been observed actively disseminating extremist ideologies and endeavouring to recruit students into their fold.

A significant portion of the populace holds the belief that Jamiat Eslah maintains its own private university and maintains ideological alignment with several other private educational institutions. Among these, Salam University is often referred to as an unofficial extension of Jamiat Eslah. Professors affiliated to Jamiat Eslah are actively engaged in teaching roles across various private universities, exerting substantial influence in these academic settings.

The activities of the Jamiat Islah primarily encompass four key components:

4.3.6 Training and Skill Development

This aspect focuses on the provision of Islamic education programs, including teachings on Hadith, jurisprudence, organizing religious seminars, and Quranic education.

4.3.6.1 Islamic Cultural Programs and Publications

The Jamiat Islah disseminates its message through various channels, including Islah Radio, Islah National Weekly, as well as publications such as *Qafala*, *Marafet*, *Beineh*, and *Rahnevardan*. Additionally, the distribution of thousands of CDs, DVDs, and brochures contributes to the propagation of its Islamic cultural agenda.

4.3.6.2 Educational Initiatives

The Jamiat Islah is actively involved in educational endeavours, operating educational institutions ranging from high schools to Dar al-Hefaz[3] and madrasas, aiming to instil Islamic teachings and values in the younger generation.

4.3.6.3 Political and Social Engagement

Beyond religious and educational activities, the Jamiat Islah also engages in political and social spheres, participating in public demonstrations and advocating for its ideological and social agenda.

On 5 February 2016, the *Hasht-e-Sobh* daily published an investigative report in Farsi, shedding light on Maulvi Abdul Salam Abid, a prominent figure among Sunni Imams in Kabul. As an active member of the Jamiat Islah, he stated: "We are all Salafis, because true Salafism entails adhering to the teachings of the scholars and relatives of Prophet Muhammad." Salafists advocate for a return to the practices and beliefs of Islam during the time of

Prophet Muhammad and the caliphs who succeeded him. The term 'Salaf' is derived from Salafi and refers to the predecessors or early generations of Muslims. The resurgence of Salafism has paved the way for the emergence of certain Islamic political parties seeking to reinstate the caliphate as a political authority in the Islamic world, drawing inspiration from the early Islamic era. (Nazair & Akbari 2014)

In a follow-up to the authors' report, referencing a video released by the online section of the Jamiat Islah, a scene unfolds at a mosque in Kabul, attended by a multitude of individuals, particularly students. In the speech delivered by one of the senior members of the Jamiat Islah, he asserts, "Our primary objective is to enlighten people about authentic Islam." However, it's important to note that their interpretation of 'real Islam' may differ from mainstream perspectives. Additionally, another cleric featured in the video declares, "We are prepared to sacrifice our blood, lives, and possessions to defend the oppressed people of Palestine." (Nazair & Akbari 2014) This demonstrates that the movement not only sought to incite extremism in Afghanistan society but also propagated the concept of a global jihad.

By exploiting freedom of speech and media platforms, the Jamiat Islah actively disseminated its extremist ideologies throughout Afghanistan society. Leveraging the democratic principles enshrined in the Afghanistan constitution, such as freedom of expression and publication, this institution propagated its beliefs and agendas. However, it openly expressed opposition to the Republic of Afghanistan system, which was backed by the USA and the international community. The government's failure to promptly address the activities of the Jamiat Islah, given the nature of its ideologies, resulted in numerous challenges for both the government and the Afghanistan populace. (Nazair & Akbari 2014)

4.3.7 Hizb ut-Tahrir in Afghanistan

The Hizb ut-Tahrir is a political and ideological party established in 1953 by a Palestinian judge named Taqiuddin Nabhani, who seceded from the Egypt Muslim Brotherhood. The primary tenet and aspiration of Hizb ut-Tahrir is the establishment of an Islamic caliphate. (Hizb ut-Tahrir 2024) However, due to its lack of official registration as a political party in any country and its clandestine and unofficial operations, obtaining precise and authoritative information about the organization proves challenging. 'Tahrir,' an Arabic term, translates to 'liberation,' and adherents of this party in Afghanistan maintain that the appellation signifies their dedication to supporting Islamic nations in attaining freedom. Within the formal structure of this party, each nation is designated as a province. An Amir is appointed by the central office of the Hizb ut-Tahrir to oversee the party's affairs in each country. However, it is essential to note that the party's ideological framework does not recognize current official countries and borders. According to the party's doctrine, every province is considered part of Islamic territory, and ultimately, they envision these provinces falling under their governance as part of the caliphate when established by the party.

This party maintains a presence across a wide spectrum of Islamic nations and among Muslim communities worldwide. It staunchly rejects recognition of any existing governmental structures. While officially advocating for a transformation in the prevailing intellectual orientation of the Muslim populace to align with its objectives, and subsequently the restoration of the caliphate, the party views this approach as following the model set forth by Prophet Muhammad in establishing Islamic governance. It is worth noting, however, that the party's founder, Taqiuddin Nabhani, made several attempts during his lifetime to seize power through coups in Jordan, all of which were unsuccessful. (Ahmed & Stuart 2009)

During the Afghanistan jihad era, a number of Afghanistani and Arabs pledged allegiance to the Hizb ut-Tahrir. However, as the party did not prioritize armed conflict, it gradually lost relevance among the populace. There are accounts suggesting that following the emergence of the Taliban 1.0 regime in 1996, a delegation of Hizb ut-Tahrir members approached Mullah Muhammad Omar, urging him to proclaim a caliphate. They asserted that members of Hizb ut-Tahrir from around the world would migrate to Afghanistan and participate in the conflict. However, Mullah Omar rejected their entreaty, contending that the caliphate was an innovation supported by the practices of the Prophet's companions. Instead, he advocated for an 'Emirate' system as a superior method for governing Muslim affairs.[4] Following the collapse of the Taliban government post-2003, the Hizb ut-Tahrir capitalized on the resulting power vacuum, leveraging religious sentiments to intensify its activities in Afghanistan. This trend persists to the present day.

4.3.7.1 Hizb Tahrir Recruitment Method in Afghanistan

The recruitment strategy of the Hizb ut-Tahrir involves initially engaging with adolescents and members of the general public who exhibit Islamic sentiments. Party members target individuals in schools, mosques, universities, and other public settings, forging amicable relationships with them. Through gradual and indirect means, they seek to influence the ideological inclinations of these individuals, slowly instilling the party's principles and fostering belief in a concerted effort to establish an Islamic State. Once individuals have absorbed the ideas propagated by Hizb ut-Tahrir members, they may either independently contemplate the next steps or be prompted to do so by the party's advocates. Members of the Hizb ut-Tahrir acquaint individuals who are disheartened by the current state of Islamic nations and are impassioned about ameliorating these conditions with the party's policies and principles. Subsequently, they are ushered into the initial circle of the party, facilitating engagement in party and organizational activities. Those introduced to this inner circle commence their journey by studying the book '*The Islamic State*,' authored by Taqiuddin Nabhani, under the guidance of a mentor alongside several others who also seek membership.

Individuals whose sole source of knowledge comprises the writings of Nabhani and other authors affiliated with the Hizb ut-Tahrir often perceive no alternative and reject other viewpoints. They regard all others as misguided maintaining that adherence to their ideology represents the sole means to safeguard Muslims.

They send representatives to invite politicians, influential individuals, and societal elites and encourage them in to participate in the Hizb ut-Tahrir movement. Employing propaganda tactics, the Hizb ut-Tahrir endeavours to enhance its visibility and, by presenting itself as an Islamic movement, seeks to elicit sympathy and support from others.

4.3.8 Common Ground between Jamiat Eslah and Hizb ut-Tahrir in Afghanistan

Common ground between Jamiat Islah and Hizb ut-Tahrir in Afghanistan exists primarily in their shared status as politico-religio entities pursuing similar objectives. Both parties engage in activities centred on preaching, advocacy, regular educational initiatives based on their respective curricula, and consistent dissemination of materials across various mediums such as print, audio, video, and the Internet. Notably, both groups exert a significant and systematic intellectual influence on society, yet refrain from incorporating armed actions into their agendas. This observation bears crucial implications for understanding the trajectory of extremism in Afghanistan, as these politico-religio currents serve as breeding grounds for the proliferation of violent extremism. Such violence may be perpetrated by groups such as Taliban, al-Qaeda, ISKP, and other extremist Islamist factions, all of which operate concurrently. Consequently, mitigating extremism within Afghanistan society poses considerable challenges.

4.4 Support Base of Islamic Extremism among Afghanistan's Political Elites

As noted above, numerous factors have contributed to the proliferation of religious extremism in Afghanistan. Along with geographical and political determinants, the manipulation of religious extremism by political elites stands out as a significant catalyst, employed to consolidate and perpetuate political authority. Notably, Pashtun political elites have been particularly adept at leveraging religious extremism for their strategic ends. For instance, during the Soviet invasion of Afghanistan, the predominant leadership of the various jihadi factions, with the exception of Shia parties, was exclusively Pashtun; only one of them was Tajik (Burhanuddin Rabbani).[5] These elites historically instrumentalized religious extremism as a means to secure and reinforce their hold on power. Moreover, Taliban 1.0, predominantly comprised Pashtun fighters and leaders, further underscoring the entwinement of Pashtun political elites with religious extremism in Afghanistan's socio-politico landscape.

Following the events of 2001, Pashtun technocrats such as Hamid Karzai and Ashraf Ghani Ahmadzai assumed positions of political authority in Afghanistan. Contrary to expectations, these leaders not only refrained from quelling Islamic extremism but also demonstrated a degree of sympathy towards extremist factions, notably in Taliban 2.0. Karzai, for instance, adopted conciliatory rhetoric towards the Taliban, referring to them as 'brothers,' while Ashraf Ghani Ahmadzai signed an order to release 5,000 Taliban prisoners in March 2020. This serves as a stark illustration of their sympathetic disposition.

(Etilaatroz, 2020) Such actions underscore the complexities of their approach to managing Islamic extremism within the country.

The manifesto of Pashtun political elites after 2001 was based on 'Afghanism' and 'Islamism'. 'Afghanism' denotes the assertion of superiority and centrality by Afghans (Pashtuns) over other ethnic groups in Afghanistan. It embodies the notion of ethnic domination by Pashtuns, perceived as their rightful prerogative. Similarly, 'Islamism' represents the supremacy and centrality of the religion over all aspects of life, advocating that all actions should align with Islamic principles as it is considered a comprehensive faith. When these two elements, rooted in ethnic and religious ideologies, converge, Afghanistan has historically witnessed outcomes akin to those experienced over the past two centuries. (Bashar 2022) The Taliban fundamentalist group serves as a contemporary and explicit manifestation of this blend of religious and ethnic amalgamation.

The relationship between ethnic identity (*Afghanism*) and religious identity (*Islamism*) exhibits a robust and enduring connection. While one may occasionally take precedence over the other, they generally work in tandem, mutually reinforcing and complementing each other. For instance, Taliban 2.0 places primacy on 'Islamism', framing and justifying their policies within a religious framework, followed by considerations of 'Afghanism'. Conversely, Pashtun technocrats such as Hamid Karzai and Ashraf prioritized ethnicity (*Afghanism*) before religion (*Islamism*). The guiding principle behind the policy agendas of both factions of Pashtuns—be it Islamist extremists or secular technocrats—is based on the maintaining of political power calculations.

4.5 External Influence over and Linkages with Islamist Extremism: Pakistan, Iran, Saudi Arabia and the USA

There is no doubt that Afghanistan possesses the social capacity to foster and propagate Islamic extremism. However, sovereign actors have played a pivotal role in both the proliferation and direction of Islamist extremism within Afghanistan. Two illustrative cases substantiate the connection between active Islamic extremist groups in Afghanistan and sovereign actors. Firstly, many of these groups have been strategically formed based on regional calculations by both regional and extra-regional powers. The Taliban serves as a prominent example, demonstrating Pakistan's utilization of them as an effective instrument to further its regional strategy since the inception of the group. The intricacies behind Pakistan's motivations for this have been thoroughly examined in the fourth chapter.

Secondly, numerous spontaneous extremist groups emerged in Afghanistan, albeit many of them eventually became directly or indirectly reliant on external powers according to their exigencies. This symbiotic relationship entailed mutual dependence, albeit with nuanced distinctions. Notably, the extremist groups operating in Afghanistan exhibited greater financial and logistical dependency, whereas external powers harboured more strategic dependency, aiming to target and curtail the influence of their adversaries beyond their borders. This strategic manoeuvre aimed to mitigate the financial and human costs associated with direct warfare. A prominent instance of this dynamic is evidenced by the substantial financial backing provided to the mujahideen by the USA and Saudi Arabia, in direct collaboration with Pakistan. This support was orchestrated to thwart Soviet military advancements in the region. (*The Young Turks* 2021).

After 2001, Iran not only extended political and financial backing to Shia jihadist factions but also established direct ties with the Taliban. Despite ideological disparities with the Taliban, Iran supplied them with financial aid and weaponry in the western part of Afghanistan. Iran's objective was to get the USA pinned down in Afghanistan. Concurrently, whenever the USA imposed fresh sanctions on Iran, the number of suicide and frontal attacks by the Taliban escalated.

4.5.1 The Future of Islamic Extremism in Afghanistan: A Comparative Analysis

Afghanistan serves as a battleground for competing independent actors. Regional and extra-regional powers engage in indirect conflict beyond their borders, driven by strategic competition. The absence of a strong central government rendered Afghanistan a fertile ground for these rivalries. Islamic extremist groups, such as the Taliban, al-Qaeda, and ISKP, are pivotal tools of warfare employed by these powers. However, the central question remains: what trajectory will Islamic extremism follow in Afghanistan's future?

Abdullah Anas, one of the leaders of the *Afghan Arabs*, who has been in Afghanistan for more than a decade during the jihad period, posits that the prospect of extremism in Afghanistan is inherently limited, driven by two pivotal factors. Firstly, the protracted and exhaustive nature of Afghanistan's four-decade-long conflict has engendered widespread fatigue among its populace, leading to a prevalent aversion towards Islamist extremism characterized by violence and strife. Secondly, a predominant adherence to the Hanafi School of jurisprudence among the Afghanistan population underscores a tradition of moderation and tolerance within the religious framework. Consequently, the convergence of these factors delineates a trajectory wherein terrorism and extremism are increasingly marginalized within Afghanistan's societal fabric. However, Anas underscores the indispensable acknowledgment of the role played by regional and extra-regional intelligence apparatuses in the propagation and perpetuation of extremist ideologies, a factor not to be disregarded. (Anas 2024)[6]

He also acknowledges that the instrumental use of Islamist extremism by foreign intelligence agencies transcends the confines of Afghanistan, manifesting as proxy groups utilized by foreign intelligence in countries such as Iraq, Yemen, Syria, Libya, and various other nations. (Anas 2024) This strategic utilization underscores a pervasive pattern wherein extremist entities are leveraged to serve the interests of foreign intelligence agendas on a global scale.

Considering historical evidence, indigenous elements and capacities, Islamic extremism in Afghanistan will have a long life. Islamic extremist groups emerge and after some time are destroyed or dissolved in society. The life of any Islamic extremist group depends on regional economic and security calculations and independent actors. For example, the Afghanistani Mujahideen, who were a spontaneous Islamic extremist force, were supported by America and its regional allies based on the rivalry between imperialism and communism. The Mujahideen period (1979-1994) was the stage of the emergence and growth of Islamist extremism in Afghanistan. After the fall of the Soviet Union, the phase of dissolution of the mujahideen in Afghanistan began with the emergence of Taliban 1.0.

Since 1996, Taliban 1.0 has been an active and disruptive actor in Afghanistan politics and regional dynamics for more than two decades. It is undeniable that Pakistan, the USA and the United Kingdom played significant roles in the creation and formation of Taliban 1.0, underscoring the influence and connections of sovereign actors with Islamist extremism in Afghanistan.

There are indications that Taliban 2.0 will continue to wield significant influence in Afghanistan politics for several more years, possibly until 2028. However, their rise to power in August 2021 may also signal their eventual downfall and dissolution.

This assertion is founded on the analogy drawn between the mujahideen and the Taliban, elucidating the ways in which regional and major powers engage with Islamic extremism. Nonetheless, a distinction exists between the mujahideen and Taliban 2.0. Notably, unlike the mujahideen, the Taliban, even after assuming power, was supported by several sovereign actors, including the USA.

Documents reveal that following August 2021, a sum of $ 2.9 billion in cash, under the guise of humanitarian aid, has entered Afghanistan through the UN. (SIGAR 2024:6) These donor countries lack direct control and oversight over these funds, raising concerns about whether they have truly been allocated to assist those in need or if the Taliban have used it for political and military purposes.

Presently, the Islamic State of Khorasan Province (ISKP) stands poised to assume an active role in Afghanistan as an exceptionally radical Islamic reserve force. Now, the ISKP predominantly operates in the south-eastern region of Afghanistan. Western and regional media outlets are increasingly spotlighting this group, thereby priming public opinion to acknowledge its emergence. With the elimination or dissolution of Taliban 2.0, the ISKP assumes a direct and prominent role in the scenario. This trend of fostering Islamist extremist groups is likely to persist in Afghanistan, potentially paving the way for the incorporation of another Islamic extremist group, X, into the equation following ISKP.

This comparative analysis illustrates the cyclical nature of extremism in Afghanistan and suggests that Islamic extremism is entrenched, indicating its enduring presence in the country. Consequently, the prospect of attaining sustainable peace in the near future appears bleak. Not only does Islamist extremism benefit from external influence and foreign connections, but Afghanistan society itself is fragmented, hindering its ability to cohesively confront this shared challenge.

4.6 Manifestations and Influence over Policymaking

In order to gain a comprehensive understanding of the impact of religious extremism on policy-making within the Afghanistan government, this section is divided into two parts. The initial part provides an overview of policy-making institutions and their operational mechanisms, with particular emphasis on security institutions. Subsequently, the second part delves into how these institutions are affected by Islamist extremism.

4.6.1 Policy-Making Institutions

As mentioned in the previous chapters, the political system of Afghanistan is a presidential and centralized system. According to Article 64 of the Constitution of Afghanistan, the President of Afghanistan has extraordinary powers in all areas of governance. Among all, the Afghanistan National Security Council (ANSC) was one of the most important policy-making institutions and was indirectly considered a part of the President's office. The NSC is an authority that operated in order to make better decisions in line with national interests and protect national values, territorial integrity and national sovereignty of the country under the chairmanship of the president who was Commander-in-Chief of the Afghanistan Armed Forces. In addition to the vice presidents, the members of the National Security Council include the ministers of the defence and security forces, foreign affairs, finance and the national security adviser. The administrative affairs of the National Security Council were carried out by a separate office under the title 'Office of the National Security Council of Afghanistan 'and under the direct supervision of the National Security Advisor.

The aim of this concise introduction is to examine the policy-making framework governing peace and conflict dynamics within the Afghanistan government, particularly concerning its engagements with extremist Islamist factions. An area warranting further scrutiny pertains to the Afghanistan National Security Council's personnel and their contributions to policymaking endeavours aimed at combating armed extremism.[7] Given Afghanistan's multi-ethnic makeup, the appointment of high-ranking governmental officials has historically been influenced by ethnic considerations. Post-2014, under the leadership of Ashraf Ghani Ahmadzai, a Pashtun technocrat, there was a notable trend of key governmental positions being allocated to Pashtun individuals.

This included pivotal roles such as advisory positions within the National Security Council. Concurrently, Ghani instituted measures to curtail the military, administrative, and policymaking authorities traditionally held by the ministries of defence, interior affairs, and the National Directorate of Security. Furthermore, it is evident that appointments were not solely driven by merit and expertise but were instead influenced by ethnic and linguistic affiliations. A case in point is Ashraf Ghani's appointment of Hamdullah Mohib as the national security adviser. Mohib, a software engineer by profession, lacked the requisite expertise in matters of warfare. Despite this, he was entrusted with significant authority and oversight in military operations in the Afghanistan government.

This issue holds significance on two fronts. Firstly, it underscores the centrality of political power and its preservation in Afghanistan. Secondly, it highlights the pervasive lack of socio-political trust among the country's diverse ethnic groups, each harbouring apprehensions about the intentions of the others. Such socio-political apprehension is deeply entrenched in perceptions surrounding the acquisition and exercise of political power, as well as the prevailing political system. Each ethnic group perceives control of the presidency as essential for ensuring the survival and prosperity of their own community. Conversely, the absence of their ethnic group at the helm of power is often interpreted as a harbinger of their community's downfall. This belief is particularly ingrained within the Pashtun *'Afghan'* community and is regarded as a fundamental principle guiding their political outlook.

Consequently, appointments to high-ranking government positions, such as those in the National Security Council, were not primarily driven by merit or necessity, but rather by considerations of ethnicity and the perpetuation of political dominance. Individuals demonstrating ethnic allegiance were often favoured over qualified experts. This approach resulted in the dysfunction of policy-making institutions, leading to the formulation of impractical, flawed, and ineffectual policies.

4.6.2 Influence Over Policy Implementation

Influencing policy-making institutions involves strategic engagement and advocacy aimed at shaping the direction and content of governmental policies. Since 2009, the Afghanistan government has primarily pursued two overarching approaches towards armed Islamist extremist groups. The first involved a militaristic approach, empowering Afghanistan security forces and international counterparts to combat and dismantle these groups. This war policy was characterized by a clear stance from the government, presenting armed opponents with two choices: either to disarm and integrate into society by embracing democratic principles, or to face destruction through military confrontation. While the government's war policy exhibited some effectiveness, it was not without its flaws and operational challenges, including shortcomings in implementation and oversight by the authorities, notably the presidents. The second approach entailed a policy of peace and reconciliation, marked by the establishment of the 'High Peace Council (HPC)' by the Afghanistan government, aimed at fostering dialogue and negotiation with extremist factions for the purpose of achieving lasting peace.

However, the implementation of these two policies encountered several challenges. Firstly, both policies were executed concurrently, resulting in a simultaneous pursuit of military action and peace negotiations. This parallel implementation sometimes led to conflicts between the two approaches, as the weaker party in the conflict often found itself at a disadvantage during peace talks due to its weakened position in the ongoing warfare. Consequently, progress in peace negotiations often stagnated. Secondly, the existence of the High Peace Council of Afghanistan facilitated indirect communication between extremist Islamist groups, such as the Taliban, and key governmental bodies like the National Security Council and the Afghanistan presidency. Over time, this channel of communication evolved into a nexus of political and military alignment and created sympathy between the Taliban, the presidency, and the National Security Council. It is important to note that the presence of the High Peace Council itself was not inherently problematic; rather, both sides misused or capitalized on the opportunities and mechanisms provided by the other, leading to failure of the government.

For instance, President Karzai adopted a hybrid approach that intertwined both peace and war policies. However, starting from 2009, he failed to provide a coherent and unambiguous delineation between friends and foes of the Afghanistan government. Despite the Taliban's active hostility towards the government, Karzai referred to them as 'brothers'. Concurrently, he took two significant measures as well: firstly, ceasing aerial bombardments against the

Taliban; and secondly, restraining efforts to locate and target the residences of Taliban and other terrorist groups. These decisions had detrimental repercussions on the morale and efficacy of Afghanistan's defence and security forces, severely undermining their combat readiness. (Nikbeen 2024)[8]

Thirdly, after 2014, President Ghani initiated a direct engagement with the Taliban through the National Security Council as a means to consolidate his hold on power, leveraging this relationship as a tool to exert pressure on his democratic political adversaries. The abrupt departure of Ashraf Ghani on 15 August 2021, serves as compelling evidence supporting this assertion. Conversely, the Taliban capitalized on similar opportunities, resorting to peace negotiations whenever they found themselves at a disadvantage on the battlefield.

Fourth, it is a direct result of the third case. President Ghani entrusted the management of the war to the National Security Advisor, and due to the direct and unofficial relationship he had with the Taliban, most of the government's war policies were suspended or did not provide effective and useful policies. On the other hand, what is extremely important to mention is that President Ghani gave his national security adviser, Hamdullah Mohib, extraordinary powers, even higher than the ministers of defence and interior. His hierarchical constraint on ministries tasked with defence and war efforts rendered them ineffectual and ensnared them in a stifling bureaucratic quagmire.

Documents reveal that between December 2014 and January 2019, a staggering number of 45,000 Afghanistan security forces lost their lives. (Etilaatroz 2019) Furthermore, a report published by UNAMA on 26 July 2021 disclosed that during the first half of 2021 alone, 5,183 civilians had been killed or wounded. (UNAMA 2021) It is imperative to note that these UNAMA statistics only account for registered casualties, implying that the actual toll of unregistered fatalities and injuries is likely to be higher. These figures underscore two critical points. Firstly, they highlight the ineffectiveness of both the Afghanistan government's strategies in combating or reconciling with extremist Islamist groups. Secondly, they shed light on the deficiency in expertise, commitment, and integrity among high-ranking officials, notably individuals like the National Security Advisor, Hamadullah Mohib, tasked with executing these policies. However, it is worth noting that the level of commitment and honesty among the defence forces and soldiers was much higher than that of the officials.

The undue and unwarranted interference of Ashraf Ghani's National Security Advisor in the operational and strategic affairs of the ministries of Defence and Interior resulted in conflict and tension between the policy-making apparatus and the combat forces of the Afghanistan government. This interference often led to a decline in troop morale, with instances where the morale of the troops was severely compromised. For instance, during operations against the Taliban, upon the capture of Taliban forces, the National Security Council office would promptly contact the Afghanistan army and issue orders to release the Taliban fighters after providing them with hospitable treatment, bypassing any judicial process. Such directives inflicted significant harm on the combat readiness and morale of the Afghanistan defence and security forces.

As a result, Islamist extremist groups exerted greater influence and capitalized on more opportunities in the Afghanistan policy-making apparatus. The underlying cause of this influence can be traced to the ethnic tensions prevalent in Afghanistan. Additionally, the role and impact of US and NATO forces in shaping both war policies and peace negotiations cannot be overlooked. Given the diverse support bases of Islamic extremism in Afghanistan, its influence and effectiveness have been greater.

4.7 Resistance in Afghanistan

In examining the resistance against Islamist extremism, it is evident that every intellectual, political, and religious movement naturally garners both supporters and opponents within societies. As previously discussed, Islamist extremism in Afghanistan draws upon various support bases. This section delves into four key categories of movements and forces that oppose Islamist extremism.

4.7.1 Urban Generation after 2001

An examination of the post-2001 generation of Afghanistan is important because they have witnessed the repetition of history in Afghanistan. When Taliban 1.0 (1994-2001) controlled large parts of Afghanistan, this generation was in its infancy. They witnessed many of the Taliban's actions and policies towards the people. And when Taliban 2.0 came to power, a large number of this generation who lived in cities had experienced the nascent period of democracy and most of them had graduated from universities. At least this generation of urban dwellers experienced social and political diversity and largely believed in a democratic society, regardless of small ethnic and local ties. Therefore, the first force against Islamist extremism was the urban youth that had experienced democracy and individual freedoms for 20 years.[9]

For this generation, certain values have been transformed into social and political priorities, including access to higher education, freedom of speech, and the right to participate in elections. These values held significant importance for them, and they have demonstrated a willingness to protest against government policies that contradict their beliefs. Having grown up amidst the principles of democracy and individual freedoms, and having experienced these principles firsthand, this generation finds it challenging to accept the narrow-minded and dogmatic ideologies of extremist groups that reject social pluralism. As a result, the post-2001 urban generation emerged as the first spontaneous social resistance force against Islamist extremism. However, due to a lack of organizational cohesion and unified leadership, they have had less influence on the policymaking process of the Afghanistan government.

4.7.2 Women Movements

Following the advent of democracy in 2001, women in Afghanistan experienced significant advancements, notably in the realms of education and employment opportunities. Key achievements include the inclusion of women in government cabinets, their representation in the Afghanistan parliament, and their participation in civil protests. Furthermore, the involvement of women in peace negotiations with the Taliban stands out as a notable achievement. These advancements underscored the progress made by women in Afghanistan since 2001, reflecting a broader movement towards gender equality and female empowerment.

Indeed, the women of Afghanistan have emerged as a second powerful force of spontaneous social resistance against Islamist extremism, primarily because they are often the primary targets and victims of such extremism. Extremist groups have systematically curtailed women's basic human freedoms by imposing draconian restrictions, denying them the right to work, study, and participate in political life. These groups propagate regressive ideologies that view women as mere objects to be confined to the home, devoid of autonomy or agency. For them, a woman's sole purpose is to bear children, tend to household duties, and obediently adhere to her husband's directives. The Taliban's treatment of women, in particular, has been characterized by extreme oppression and brutality. It is important to acknowledge that Afghanistan's traditional social norms and structures have also played a pivotal role in facilitating the oppression of women by Islamist extremists. These entrenched societal configurations have provided a fertile ground for extremists to perpetuate their agenda of denying Afghanistani women their fundamental rights and individual freedoms.

Although Afghanistani women never succeeded in forming a party or inclusive women's movement, despite the support of the international community and the Afghanistan government, they worked as a powerful force in Afghanistan's political equations as much as they could and showed more effectiveness. They were able to raise their voice of protest in many cases. If the women of Afghanistan wanted, they had and still have many opportunities to make an important and effective movement.

4.7.3 Political Parties

The third group opposing Islamic extremism in Afghanistan comprises the jihadi political parties and other parties established after 2001. While these jihadi parties were once themselves aligned with extremist ideologies, they have since integrated into society and embraced democratic principles such as elections, freedom of speech, and political participation. Many of these parties participated in the post-2001 government of Afghanistan and have consistently voiced their opposition to extremist groups like the Taliban, either directly or through the government. However, there has been a lack of cohesion and unity among these parties, hindering their ability to prevent Afghanistan from succumbing to Islamist extremism. These parties typically aligned themselves with the policies of the Afghanistan government, often in line with those of the USA and the international community. While they served as a barrier against extremist groups, they did not offer alternative plans to navigate Afghanistan through challenging circumstances.

4.7.4 Armed Opponents of Extremism

Armed opponents of extremists are groups that actually had weapons or had the capacity to acquire weapons and ammunition to fight against Islamic extremists such as the Taliban or ISIS. This force was active outside the Afghanistan government (that is, it did not include government structures). The leader of this movement is Ahmad Masoud, the son of Ahmad Shah Masoud. Ahmad Shah Masoud led the 'First Resistance' between 1994 and 2001 against the Taliban and al-Qaeda in Afghanistan and was finally assassinated by al-Qaeda two days before 9/11.

After 2014, Ahmad Masoud actively mobilized people against the Taliban and other extremist groups with increasing frequency. Recognizing the potential resurgence of the Taliban and other extremist factions, Ahmad Masoud, understanding the regional and global dynamics at play, foresaw the threat to Afghanistan freedoms. In response, he organized and led a movement known as the 'Second Resistance' rallying people to safeguard their freedoms and resist the return of extremist rule. Unlike political parties, Ahmad Masoud offered a tangible alternative plan for Afghanistan in challenging circumstances, positioning himself as a genuine threat to the Taliban and other extremist groups.

Ahmad Masoud and the 'Second Resistance' encountered three significant obstacles in their efforts to resist terrorism and extremism in Afghanistan. Firstly, the international community, led by the USA, engaged in direct negotiations with the Taliban under the guise of peace talks, known as the Doha talks. This engagement meant that the West will not support the 'Second Resistance' in the fight against terrorism and extremism in Afghanistan. Moreover, regional actors, motivated by political considerations, were uninterested in supporting the 'Second Resistance'. In fact, countries such as Pakistan, Iran, and China held positions contrary to the goals of the 'Second Resistance'.

Secondly, the Afghanistan government's policies did not capitalize on the 'Second Resistance' as a potent force alongside Afghanistan defence and security forces in emergency situations. President Ashraf Ghani, a Pashtun technocrat, perceived support for the 'Second Resistance' as a threat to Pashtun ethnic dominance. Consequently, there was a lack of desire to bolster this movement from within the government. These obstacles posed significant challenges to

Ahmad Masoud and the 'Second Resistance', impeding their efforts to combat terrorism and extremism effectively.

The third issue pertaining to the 'Second Resistance' lies in the inclusion of individuals accused of corruption in the leadership ranks of the Afghanistan government following the events of 2001. Despite Ahmad Masoud's personal popularity and the broad support the 'Second Resistance' enjoyed from the Afghanistan populace, these factors posed significant challenges to the efficacy of the popular armed struggle against the Taliban.

4.8 CONCLUSION

In summary, while Islamist extremism shares inherent characteristics across different groups, their operational dynamics vary based on geographical contexts. In Afghanistan, these dynamics stem from factors such as the interplay between ethnicity and political power, low literacy rates, predominantly rural demographics, and the influence of parties and organizations propagating extremist ideologies. Consequently, it is evident that some part of Afghanistan society possesses an inherent susceptibility to the growth of Islamist extremism. Furthermore, the involvement of regional and extra-regional powers in the trajectory of extremist groups cannot be overlooked.

Additionally, opposing forces stand in opposition to the support bases of Islamist extremism in Afghanistan. These oppositional elements comprise the post-2001 urban generation, women, political parties, and non-governmental armed factions. A notable disparity between the supporters and detractors of Islamist extremism in Afghanistan lies in the organizational structure and strategic coherence. While supporters often operate under a relatively unified leadership with a predetermined strategy, opposing forces have struggled with a lack of singular leadership and cohesive perspective. Consequently, these oppositional factions have failed to forge a social consensus between themselves.

NOTES

1. According to data available on the CIA website, there are currently three types of Islamist extremist groups. First, there are large or international groups such as al-Qaeda and ISIS, which operate across multiple countries. Second, there are medium (regional) terrorist groups that operate within specific regions or across several countries, such as al-Shabaab (AS) in Somalia, Kenya, and Ethiopia; Ansar al-Islam (AAI) in Syria and Iraq; Army of Islam (AOI) in Egypt, Gaza, and Israel; and the Islamic Movement of Uzbekistan (IMU), which is active

in Afghanistan, Pakistan, Syria, Turkey, and Central Asia. The third category comprises small terrorist groups that operate within specific countries, such as the Taliban and the Haqqani network in Afghanistan; Ansar al-Dine (AAD) in Mali; and Lashkar i Jhangvi (LJ) in Pakistan. For more details see the CIA official websites available at https://www.cia.gov/the-world-factbook/references/terrorist-organizations/ accessed 10 May 2024.

The prevailing belief is that global jihad is solely the agenda of large and international Islamic extremist groups like al-Qaeda and ISIS. It is often assumed that other Islamic extremist groups operating in specific geographic areas do not prioritize global jihad. However, the reality is that all terrorist groups, whether active in a particular region or globally, have global jihad in their agenda. The distinction lies in their prioritization, operational methods, and resources.

The Taliban, who have been active in Afghanistan for more than two decades, have global jihad in their agenda. However, they have prioritized their efforts within Afghanistan. Several reasons underline the Taliban's endorsement of global jihad. Firstly, the presence of foreign fighters such as members of the Islamic Movement of Uzbekistan (IMU) and TTP is based on a mutual understanding. These understanding dictates that they will collectively combat to liberate Afghanistan first, followed by Pakistan, other Central Asian countries, and beyond. Secondly, even amidst recent escalation in the conflict between Israel and Palestine, Amir Khan Muttaqi, the Acting Minister of Foreign Affairs of the Taliban, conveyed sympathy for the loss of children during a telephone conversation with Ismail Haniyeh, the head of Hamas' political bureau, on 14 April 2024. There may be additional documents and reasons underlying the Taliban's embrace of the concept of global jihad. For more details visit the website of Ministry of Foreign Affairs of Emirate Islami Afghanistan, available at https://mfa.gov.af/en/16665 accessed 10 May 2024.

2. Jamiat Eslah, as a religious movement, has been operating in Afghanistan for the past two decades, predominantly emphasizing religious teachings in a peaceful and subdued manner. However, it is argued by some that despite its outwardly peaceful demeanour, this movement has played a role in psychologically conditioning society to embrace Islamic extremism, thereby laying the groundwork for the emergence and acceptance of armed extremism within Afghanistan. For more details see https://eslahonline.net/english/
3. Dar al-Hefaz is a madarsa that prioritizes the memorization of the Quran.
4. The activities of Hizb ut-Tahrir in Afghanistan are clandestine. Owing to security restrictions, despite numerous attempts, definitive confirmation or refutation of this assertion remains unattainable.
5. The Jihadist Pushtun leaders were Gulbuddin Hekmatyar, Abdul Rab Rasol Sayaf, Peer Said Ahmad Geelani, Mawlavi Jalaluddin Haqqani, and Mawlavi Mohammad Yunus Khales.
6. Mr. Boudjema Bounoua - known under the nom de guerre 'Abdullah Anas' - is an Algerian scholar, politician in exile, and former Mujahid. In 1984 he joined the fight against Soviet occupation in Afghanistan under the command of Ahmed Shah Masoud. He was then appointed director of the Office of Services for Mujahideen. He married the daughter of Abdullah Azzam, known as 'the father of global Jihad', and was a contemporary of Osama bin Laden. After the fall of communism, Anas left Afghanistan in 1992 and pursued a career in media and peace-building. He became an advisor to former Afghan President Burhanuddin Rabbani, when he was head of Afghanistan's High Peace Council, formed in 2010 to initiate talks with the Taliban.

Anas is currently director of a pan Arab news satellite channel, is a member of the International Union of Muslim Scholars and is the author of '*To the Mountains – My life in Jihad, from Algeria to Afghanistan*'. For more details, visit Why Did It All Go So Wrong? An Arab Veteran of the Anti-Soviet Jihad Speaks (warontherocks.com)
From Armed Struggle to Peaceful Protest, a Road Still to Travel - The New York Times (nytimes.com)andhttps://www.cat-int.org/index.php/pdfviewer/to-the-mountains-my-life-in-jihad-from-algeria-to-afghanistan-abdullah-anas-tam-hussein-2019/

7. Although the Ministries of Education, Higher Education, and Hajj and Islamic Affairs undoubtedly contribute significantly to shaping policies aimed at mitigating Islamic extremism, it is the National Security Council that holds direct authority in making decisions regarding war and peace. Consequently, the outcomes of the Security Council's endeavours are often promptly discernible. Conversely, the impacts of initiatives undertaken by the Ministries of Education, Higher Education, and Hajj and Islamic Affairs tend to manifest gradually. Regrettably, none of these institutions managed to formulate an effective policy spanning the period from 2001 to 2021 aimed at curtailing Islamic extremism.
8. Major General Mohammad Sadeq Nikbeen is a highly accomplished military leader with extensive experience in strategic planning and operational command within the Afghan National Defence and Security Forces (ANDSF). He served as Chief of Staff at the Kabul Military Training Centre (KMTC) from 2006 to 2009 before commanding the 203 Thunder Corps' 4th Combat Brigade in Logar and Wardak provinces (2009-2010) and the 201 Selab Corps' 1st Combat Brigade in Laghman and Nangarhar provinces (2011-2012). He later assumed key roles in planning and training within the Ministry of defence, culminating in his appointment as Chief of Training and Education for the General Staff and Doctrine (2016-2019). Major General Nikbeen's leadership has been instrumental in enhancing military capabilities and fostering stability in Afghanistan.
9. The difference between the urban and rural youth of the post-2001 generation lies in the divergent opportunities which were available to them. Urban dwellers typically had greater access to education, employment, and exposure to democratic principles, fostering a familiarity with the tenets of democracy. Conversely, rural youth often faced geographic deterrence, with fewer opportunities for advancement. Moreover, rural areas were more susceptible to the influence of extremist Islamist groups, who were predominantly active in these regions. Consequently, there was a higher likelihood of Islamist extremist groups attracting rural youth compared to their urban counterparts, leading to a propensity for extremism among rural youth. The prevailing belief suggests that if rural youth were afforded the same opportunities as their urban counterparts, they would align with the democratic values embraced by urban youth. However, the reality has been quite the opposite, with rural youth exhibiting a greater acceptance of extremism despite the potential for alignment with urban youth.

Chapter 5
Conclusion

5.1 INTRODUCTION

In the previous chapter, Islamist extremism and its internal and external relations in Afghanistan were examined. Islamist extremism generally possesses inherent characteristics that create common ground among extremist groups worldwide. However, their functional characteristics vary, depending on the operating conditions and environments. In Afghanistan, Islamist extremism can be characterized by a well-organized leadership and a suitable operating environment. In contrast, the forces opposing extremism in Afghanistan, despite having greater capacities and resources, lacked unity and an orderly and organizational leadership. In this final chapter, the key findings from the previous chapters are discussed to elucidate the relationship between Islamist extremism and the repeated failures of the states in Afghanistan to contain the same. Additionally, the role of sovereign regional actors who have leveraged Islamist extremism to advance and expand their goals in the country and beyond has also been examined

5.2 KEY FINDINGS

Following the introductory section, the first chapter focused on the differences between Islam as a religion and political Islam, which is the political use of religion by various actors. In this chapter, we thoroughly examined Islam as both a religion and a religio-politico approach. We critically evaluated two viewpoints: the Western perspective and the perspective of Islamic thinkers. The Western perspective, based on the separation of religion and politics, asserts that any Islamic group with political goals falls under the category of political Islam. In contrast, Islamic thinkers firmly argue that religion and politics are inseparable, seeing Islam inherently as both a religion and a political entity. Consequently, they assert that extremism is a fundamental component of political Islam.

The findings show that Islamist extremism has its basis in the methods used by Islamic jurisprudence schools for deriving Sharia rulings from the primary Islamic sources, the Qur'an and Sunnah. These schools can be divided into two categories: rationalistic and textualist (anti-rationalistic). Rationalistic schools use additional sources such as *Ijma* (consensus), *Qiyas* (analogical reasoning), and *Ijtihad* (independent reasoning) alongside the primary Islamic sources. Textualist schools, on the other hand, rely solely on a literal interpretation of the Qur'an and Sunnah, rejecting any form of interpretation based on reason. The research indicates that contemporary Islamic extremism is rooted in these anti-rationalistic schools. Additionally, the findings suggest that Shia Islam has traditionally been more rationalistic, and in Sunni jurisprudence, the Hanafi School has also demonstrated a rationalistic approach in deriving religious rulings.

Figure 4: Islamic Extremism

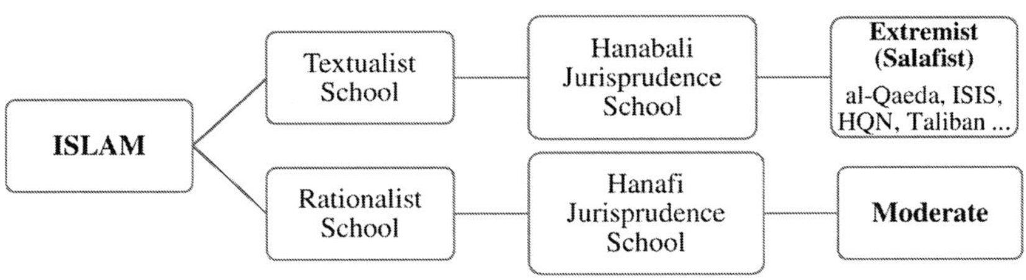

Source: Author 2024

In the second chapter, we explored the theoretical framework of this study, identifying structuralist realism as the most suitable theory of international relations for understanding issues related to Afghanistan. While the constructivist theory is useful for explaining matters pertaining to ideology, identity, and culture, we favoured structural realism for its foundational principles and explanatory power. Structural realism emphasizes three key principles. First, it asserts that states are the primary actors in international politics. Second, it posits that the main goal of states in the international system is to ensure their own survival. Lastly, structural realism underscores the anarchic nature of the international system, where the absence of a central authority requires states to rely on self-help mechanisms for their security and preservation in the international system.

The analysis of Afghanistan in the framework of structural realism theory can be broken down to three levels. At the state level, Afghanistan is considered fragile, and due to numerous factors in its history, it has never truly formed a nation-state. The internal situation in Afghanistan reflects the views of Thucydides and Morgenthau, and objectively demonstrates the harsh nature of humans as described by Thomas Hobbes ("man is a wolf to man"). According to Waltz's definition of power as the ability of states, Afghanistan lacked the power to survive in the international system.

At the regional level, two main factors contribute to Afghanistan's struggles. Firstly, its geopolitical location acts as a magnet for sovereign actors, resulting in complex political, military, and economic interactions with neighbouring countries. These interactions trigger reactions from other sovereign actors, in line with the assumption of structural realism that states cannot be certain about the intentions of others. The second reason is Afghanistan's diplomatic weaknesses, which have hindered its ability to convey to sovereign actors that engagement with one country does not equate with hostility towards others. Afghanistan's diplomatic apparatus has failed to effectively communicate its intentions and foster mutual understanding among regional actors.

At the international level, Afghanistan gained significant attention from the USA following the events of 9/11, primarily due to its strategic geopolitical position. The US intervention in Afghanistan aimed to combat terrorism and eradicate al-Qaeda, but in practice, it served broader geopolitical interests, including the containment of China, Russia, and Iran. From 2001 to 2021, the USA exerted considerable influence over the political landscape and developmental trajectory of both Central and South Asia through its presence in Afghanistan. As a result, regional powers such as China and Russia sought to establish a balance of power in Asia, leading to the formation of regional security organizations like the Shanghai Cooperation Organization, underpinned by realist principles. The international community engaged with Afghanistan in various ways in the realm of international politics, perceiving it as a buffer zone between great powers, a battleground for proxy wars, a crucial transit corridor, a source of military strategic depth, and a source of instability posing a burden on the international community.

In the third chapter, the challenges of state-building in Afghanistan were examined from both internal and external perspectives. The main findings of this chapter suggest that Afghanistan has not yet completed its nation and state-building process. Internally, obstacles such as ethnic divisions, identity crises, deep-rooted violence stemming from the national identity crisis, ethnocentrism, political oppression, issues with the constitution, the national anthem, the name of Afghanistan itself, cultural poverty, and extreme traditionalism of society are significant barriers to state-building in Afghanistan. Additionally, there are two additional indigenous views:

1. Pashtun-Oriented View: This perspective argues that the presence and intervention of foreign forces (American and NATO) in Afghanistan have disrupted the state-building process.
2. Non-Pashtun-Oriented View: Proponents of this view believe that even without foreign forces, Afghan politicians, mainly from the Pashtun ethnic group, have been unable to establish a comprehensive and inclusive national government since 1747. Rather than forming a national government, they have sought to create an ethnic government, promoting ethnic hegemony.

The Non-Pashtun-oriented view suggests that Afghanistani politicians, mainly from the Pashtun ethnic group, have failed to establish an inclusive national government since 1747. Instead, they have attempted to create an ethnic government, emphasizing the dominance of ethnicity. After the Bonn Conference in 2001, the international community, along with the US and Afghanistani stakeholders, began the process of state-building in Afghanistan. The decisions made at the conference led to the adoption of the top-down state-building model, also known as the American model. However, this approach was not suitable for Afghanistan because of its internal divisions and lack of a unified national identity. The more appropriate model for Afghanistan would have been the European model, which prioritizes nationbuilding before state-building. Afghanistan needs to define its national identity and promote collaboration among its ethnic groups for successful state-building and maintenance of state institutions.

The fourth chapter thoroughly analyzes Islamist extremism in the specific context of Afghanistan. Its findings reveal that Islamist extremism generally exhibits two distinct sets of features. Firstly, there are inherent characteristics that create a common thread among extremist groups worldwide. Secondly, their operational characteristics are influenced by the social, political, and geographical conditions in which they operate. In Afghanistan, these groups find support and strength rooted in various factors such as poverty, low literacy rates, ethnic tensions, nature of the political regime, foreign relations, and the geographical landscape. Typically, these support bases are overseen by single or multiple leadership figures acting in coordination. Conversely, there are opposing forces to Islamist extremism in Afghanistan, including the post-2001 urban generation, women, political parties, and non-extremist armed forces. However, these opposing forces lack unified leadership and coordination. Additionally, Afghanistan's political regime, characterized by a presidential and centralized system, concentrated all power in the hands of the president. Presidents of Afghanistan from 2001 to 2021 failed to perceive Islamist extremism as a significant threat to national security. Instead, they prioritized ethnic and linguistic ties over addressing extremist threats.

Furthermore, the findings suggest that the longevity of Islamist extremists in Afghanistan is probable, given the lack of a unified nation that makes the prompt establishment of a strong government unlikely, hindering the nation's ability to effectively address internal challenges and foreign interventions. Islamist extremism serves as a potent instrument wielded by independent actors who use it as a proxy group within Afghanistan. The emergence and ongoing evolution of ISKP in Afghanistan signal the potential for continued Islamist extremism, both as a foreign influence and a proxy force.

5.3 How Have Political Regimes Dealt with Islamist Groups in Afghanistan?

In the second chapter, we discussed the importance of examining historical contexts and evaluating various political regimes to find an accurate answer to our questions. The first political regime in Afghanistan to extensively use Islamic extremism for its survival was during the rule of Abdul Rahman Khan, who ruled from 1880 to 1901. He severely suppressed the Hazaras by employing religious extremism, leaving a bitter and shocking mark on Afghanistan's history. Following his reign, Amanullah Khan attempted extensive reforms. Shortly after coming to power, he implemented changes that were ahead of his time, but they were met with resistance from Afghanistan society. The deeply rooted rural and tribal culture, which had strong religious and traditional values, resisted his modernization efforts. Religious scholars (Ulama) were among Amanullah's most powerful opponents, as they opposed reforms that contradicted Sharia, customs, and traditions. They were also dissatisfied with their diminishing role in the administration. Consequently, the first political regime after Afghanistan gained independence fell due to religious extremism.

After a period of relative peace, in 1979, Islamist extremist forces re-emerged in response to the communist government's policies in Afghanistan. By 1992, the communist regime fell to the mujahideen. From 1992 to 2001, Afghanistan was governed by Islamist groups, including the mujahideen and the Taliban. In 2001, the Taliban's extremist regime was dismantled by a coalition of indigenous resistance forces, American forces, and the international community following the 9/11 attacks. This period was a window of hope for the people of Afghanistan and marked a turning point for contemporary governance in Afghanistan. However, from 2001 to 2021, the Afghanistan government failed to formulate and implement effective policies to curb Islamic extremism. Evidence indicates that the post-2001 Afghanistan government did not perceive Islamist extremist forces as a genuine threat to national security. Consequently, the government was overthrown by Islamist extremists once again.

The fall of the Afghanistan government in 2021 can be attributed to two main reasons. Firstly, the close linguistic and ethnic connections between extremist Islamist forces like the Taliban, and key figures within the Afghanistan government, including the president, national security adviser, and ministers who played a significant role. Secondly, the centralized political regime of Afghanistan created a power struggle, as different groups vied for control. The perspectives of Afghanistan's ethnic groups on political power, along with the activities of extremist Islamist groups, were crucial factors in the government's collapse.

Regarding the interaction of political regimes in Afghanistan with Islamist extremism, three main approaches can be identified. Some regimes, such as the reign of Abdul Rahman Khan between 1880 and 1901, and the presidencies of Hamid Karzai and Ashraf Ghani Ahmadzai between 2001 and 2021, took an instrumental and supportive approach with extremist Islamist groups, using them to suppress internal political rivals. Others, such as the communist regime, adopted a hostile attitude towards Islamist extremist groups and actively opposed and combated Islamist extremism. Lastly, Islamist regimes like those of the mujahideen and the Taliban not only did not hinder the growth of Islamist extremism, they supported it, resulting in the emergence of many extremist groups beyond Afghanistan's borders.

5.4 WHAT IS THE EXTENT TO WHICH HAVE THEY SUCCEEDED OR FAILED IN THEIR APPROACH?

The question at hand can be approached from two perspectives. First, it is important to consider the intentions, goals, and chosen approaches of the political regimes in Afghanistan. Specifically, we should examine the approach chosen by these regimes and their intentions. Second, it is essential to analyse the consequences of the interaction between these regimes and Islamist groups for the general population of Afghanistan.

First, several regimes that adopted an instrumental, friendly, and supportive approach to Islamist extremism found success in their strategies. For instance, Abdul Rahman Khan effectively used Islamists to suppress local political rivals who threatened his kingdom. He had the support of Islamist clerics (Ulama) and circulated fatwas among his soldiers to boost their fighting spirit, as evidenced by the Hazara massacre between 1891 and 1894. Abdul Rahman Khan's instrumental approach to Islamic extremism helped him maintain his political power and was highly successful.

Second, regimes that adopted a hostile approach to Islamist extremism, such as the communist regime of Afghanistan, failed in their strategy. The communist regime aimed to remove Islam from government and social affairs, but this approach did not succeed due to the deep-rooted nature of Islam in Afghanistan society. The historical strength of Islam in Afghanistan led to strong opposition to alternative ideologies, such as communism or liberal democracy. Consequently, the communist regime, despite its power and resources, failed in Afghanistan.

Third, post-2001 governments in Afghanistan adopted a supportive approach to Islamist extremism. This approach was influenced by ethnic and linguistic ties, as well as the centralized political regime. Most Islamist extremists, particularly the Taliban, were predominantly Pashtuns, as were the presidents between 2001 and 2021. The details of this matter have been discussed in previous chapters and will not be repeated here. However, the supportive approach was chosen to maintain political power and ethnic dominance after 2001. The recent events, such as the escape of President Ashraf Ghani Ahmadzai on 15 August 2021, and the unopposed dominance of the Taliban, illustrate this approach.

The consequences of these interactions on the people of Afghanistan must also be examined. The type of interaction each regime chose with Islamist extremism was influenced by political, social, and economic conditions. Unfortunately, the result of these interactions has been a catastrophic and prolonged period of war and destruction for the people of Afghanistan. After more than four decades of continuous conflict, the hope for a peaceful and prosperous future for the people of Afghanistan remains uncertain.

5.5 WHAT ROLE HAVE EXTERNAL SOVEREIGN ACTORS PLAYED VIS-A-VIS ISLAMIST EXTREMISM?

Afghanistan holds a crucial geopolitical position, but it is a weak and vulnerable country. Many global and regional powers understand that Afghanistan does not pose a direct threat to them due to its limited military and economic power. However, their main concern is that other countries might exploit Afghanistan's strategic location to their advantage. This concern is rooted in the principles of realism, which states that all states aim to maximize their power and gain in an anarchic international system.

As a result of these concerns and Afghanistan's weak government, several countries such as Pakistan, Iran, Qatar, Saudi Arabia, Russia, China, and the USA have established either a direct or an indirect presence in Afghanistan. These countries have created proxy groups to counteract the influence of their rivals and to gain advantages in line with their interests. One of these proxy groups is Islamist extremists. Some of the mentioned countries, particularly the USA, Saudi Arabia, Pakistan, and, more recently, Qatar, have benefitted significantly from their ties with these extremist groups in Afghanistan. The relationship between these sovereign actors and the extremists is mutually beneficial, with the former providing financial support, military aid, and safe havens for the extremists to gain power in Afghanistan. Meanwhile, the extremists further the interests of these countries at the governmental level.

5.6 How Has the Failure to Deal with Islamist Extremism Affected State-Building in Afghanistan and Perpetuated Conflict?

The failure to address Islamist extremism has had significant effects on the state-building process in Afghanistan and has contributed to the continuation of the war. The first effect was the weakening of governmental authority in Afghanistan. Islamist extremist groups established their own rules and principles for managing affairs in the areas under their influence. Furthermore, in some areas ostensibly under government control, power was effectively wielded by commanders, leaders of jihadi parties, or other influential figures. The situation with extremist groups like the Taliban is distinct, as their primary goal was to overthrow the government.

The islands of power that existed under the shadow of the government often prevented the implementation of government programs. The Afghanistan government, acting alone and without the support of these influential figures, was frequently unable to implement its programs or maintain its institutions. Consequently, the primary effect of extremism, or the efforts to combat it, was a continuous state of war that empowered individuals rather than the government.

The second effect is the destruction of patriotism among many high-ranking officials of the Afghanistan government, which has promoted corruption and governance challenges. Corruption is particularly significant because many individuals employed in Afghanistan governments after 2001 did not believe in the creation of a nation-state. These individuals viewed their positions as opportunities to accumulate wealth, convinced that the government would fall sooner or later. They lacked any sense of patriotism, prioritizing their own interests and those of their families over the welfare of the people or the government. From the outset, they believed in an alternative government, demonstrating their lack of commitment to the people of Afghanistan.

Despite the good intentions of the international community and the USA regarding state-building in Afghanistan, the presence of such individuals and widespread corruption severely undermined the process. The root of this issue lies in the fact that for over three decades, at least three governments—the communist government in 1992, the mujahideen government in 1996, and the republic in 2021—were overthrown by Islamist extremists in Afghanistan.

The rapid succession of regime changes cast doubts on every sincere and constructive effort to build a stable state in Afghanistan.

Third, the failure to address Islamist extremism has also affected international support for Afghanistan. Concerned about the risks of continued violence and instability, many international actors have been reluctant to fully commit resources to long-term state-building projects. Additionally, the presence of extremist groups has complicated the efforts of international organizations to provide aid and implement development programs.

Finally, the successive failure to address Islamist extremism has significantly contributed to the continuation of the war in Afghanistan. In a war situation, it is natural for hatred and enmity to arise between the parties involved, perpetuating the conflict. The ongoing conflicts fuelled by extremist groups have led to widespread displacement within Afghanistan, causing a significant humanitarian crisis. Displacement disrupts community structures, reduces agricultural productivity, and strains the limited resources of the government and international aid organizations, undermining efforts to build a stable and cohesive society necessary for successful state-building.

References

Abraham, R. (2013). "Politics of ethnicity in Afghanistan: Understanding the Pashtuns and the minor ethnic groups", *Defence and Diplomacy Journal*, 2(2), 69-81.

Adami, Ali & Hameed Reza, A. (2013). "The Shanghai Cooperation Organization and the Common Security Threats in Central Asia", [in Persian], *ntral Asia and the Caucasus Journal*, 19(81), 1-28.

Afghanistan Information Network (2020) "Religious Structure in Afghanistan ", [in Persian], [Online: web], Accessed 17 February 2020, URL: https:// www.Afghanpaper.com /inf o/etelaat%20omomi/mazhabeafghanestan.htm

Afridi, M. K. et al. (2014). "Pak-China-US Triangle vis-à-vis Soviet Union in Afghan War", *Mediterranean Journal of Social Sciences*, 5(20), 2192-2198.

Ahmed, H. & Stuart, H. (2009). *Hizb ut-Tahrir: Ideology and Strategy*, London: The Centre of Social Cohesion.

Akhlaq, S.H. (2015). "The Crisis of National and Religious Identity in Afghanistan Today", *Open Democracy*, [Online: web], accessed 7 April 2021, URL: https:/ /www.opendem ocracy.net/en/crisis-of-national-and-religious-identity-in-afghan istan-today/

Akhwan Kazemi, M. (2006). "Shanghai Cooperation Organization; Geostrategic Importance", [in Persian], *Journal of Central Asia and Caucasus Study*, 55 (4): 93-128.

Alipour, A. et al. (2017). "The impact of Ibn Taymiyyah's Thoughts on the Ideological and Policy lines of Salafi-Takfiri Groups", *Quarterly Journal of Political Thought in Islam*, [in Persian], [Online: web], accessed 21 March 2021, URL: https://civilica.com/ doc/752898

Alizadeh Mousavi, S. M. (2019). "Salafism and Wahhabism; Essence, beliefs, and types", *Rah Toosheh Quarterly*, [in Persian], 1441 (Special Issue on Shared Areas), 93-116. https: //doi.org/10.22081/rt.2019.67456

Almasi, M. & Ezati, Ezatullah. (2007). "Caucasus, Interaction or Confrontation", [in Persian], *Journal of Human Geography Research*, 3 (1): 31-44.

Aman, Soheila. (2014). *Deoband School and Fundamentalism in Afghanistan and Pakistan*, (in Persian). Kabul: Ministry of Foreign Affairs of Afghanistan, Strategic Studies Centre.

Amiri, Ali. (2013). *The Rise and Fall of Rationality in the Islamic World*, [in Persian], Kabul: Amiri Publications.

Amirkhani, A. (2024). "Imam Abul A'la Maududi and the neo-Salafism movement", *Theological Knowledge Quarterly*, 1(3). [in Persian], [Online: web], accessed 10 January 2024, URL:https://www.islahweb.org/fa/post/%D8%A7%D8%A8%D9%88%D8%A7%D9%84%D8% A7%D8%B9%D9%84%DB%8C-%D9%85%D9%88%D8%AF%D9%88%D8%AF%DB%8C-%D9%88-%D8% AC%D8%B1%DB%8C%D8%A7%D9%86-%D9%86%D9%88%D8%B3%D9 %84%D9%81%DB%8C-%DA%AF%D8%B1%DB%8C

Amirzadeh, H. (2013). "Has the World's Thinker Sunk in the Quagmire of Tribal Thinking?" Afghanistan Information Network, [in Persian], [Online: web], accessed 17 February 2020, URL: https://www.afghanpaper.com/nbody.php?id=65 653

Angstrom, J. (2008). "Inviting the Leviathan: External Forces, War, and State-building in Afghanistan", *Small Wars & Insurgencies*, 19(3), 374-396.

Ansari, N. (2015). "An Unstable Afghanistan: The Potential Impact of NATO's Departure on Pakistan", *Journal of European Studies* (JES), 31(2), 114-133.

Arianfar, A. (2016). *The Roots of the Failure of Nation-Building and State-Building Projects in Afghanistan*, [in Persian], Kabul: Kawa Publication.

Aristotle, U. (1944). *Politics*, translated by H. Rackham, Aristotle in 23 volumes, vol. 21 Cambridge, MA, Harvard University Press; London, William Heinemann Ltd. 1944. P3-1252a. [Online: web], accessed 29 November 2022, URL: https: //www .perseus.Tufts.edu/hopper/text?doc=urn:cts:greek Lit:tlg0086.tlg035.perseus-eng 1:1.1252a

Baldwin, D. A. (1993). *Neorealism and Neoliberalism: The Contemporary Debate*, New York: Columbia University Press.

Balkhi, M. (2020). *American Nation-Building: A Comparative Study of Iraq and Afghanistan,* [in Persian], Kabul: Afghanistan Institute of Higher Education and Amiri Publication.

Balkhi, Mirwais. (2012). *Saudi Arabia's Policy towards Afghanistan from 1991 to 2001,* [in Persian], Kabul: Gohar-e-Khorasan Research and Publishing Institute.

Baloch, Q. B. & Niazi, A. H. K. (2008). "Indian encroachment in Afghanistan: A new imperialism in the making", *The Dialogue*, 3(1), 16-33.

Bashar, M. (2022). "Afghanism and Islamism", [in Persian], [Online: web], accessed 9 February, 2022, URL: https: //virgool.io/@Mo.bashar/%D8%A7% D9%81%D8%BA%D8%A7%D9%86%DB%8C%D8%AA-%D9%88-%D8%A7%D8%B3%D9%84%D8%A7%D9%85%DB%8C%D8%AA-vue95glsevyz

BBC News (Persian). (2009). "The growth of Shi'ism in Afghanistan and the role of Iran", [Online: web], accessed 24 December 2019, URL: https://www.Bbc.com/persian/afghanistan/2009/01/090106_ba-wpost-shiite-afghanist an 06 Jan 2009

Bearden, M. (2001). "Afghanistan, Graveyard of Empires", *Foreign Affairs*, 80(6), 17–30. https://doi.org/10.2307/20050325

Beck, C. J. (2008). "The Contribution of Social Movement Theory to Understanding Terrorism." *Sociology Compass*, 2(5), 1565-1581. DIO:10.1111/j.1751-9020.2008.00148.x

Behrozlak, G. R. (2021). "Political Islam and Contemporary Islamism", [in Persian], [Online: web] aAccessed 13 March 2021, URL: https: //www.sid.ir/paper/50162 6/fa

Bergen, P. L. (2002). *Holy war, inc.: Inside the Secret World of Osama bin Laden*, New York: Simon and Schuster.

Berman, S. (2010), "From the Sun King to Karzai: Lessons for State Building in Afghanistan", *Foreign Affairs*, 89, 2.

Borárosová, Ingrid et al. (2018). *Global Jihad: Case Studies in Terrorist Organization,* (Monograph), Polska, Poland: Research Institute for European Policy.

Borthakur, A. & Kotokey, A. (2020). "Ethnicity or religion? The genesis of the Taliban movement in Afghanistan", *Asian Affairs*, 51(4), 817-837.

Borum, R. (2011). "Radicalization into Violent Extremism II: A Review of Conceptual Models and Empirical Research", *Journal of Strategic Security*, 4(4), 37–62. DIO: http://dx.Do i.org /10.5038/1944-0472.4.4.2.

Bukhari, S. W. H. & Bakht, N. (2013). "Central Asia-Afghanistan Relations under the Shadows of Great Powers Politics", *Journal of Humanities and Social Science*, 11(1), 9-17.

Butterfield, H. (1951). "*History and Human Relations",* London: Collins, [Online: web], accessed 4 April 2022, URL: https://archive.org/details/HistoryAndHumanRelation/page/n163/mo de/2up

Carati, A. (2015). "No Easy Way Out: Origins of NATO's Difficulties in Afghanistan", *Contemporary Security Policy*, 36(2), 200-218.

Carr, E. H. (1964). *The Twenty-Year Crisis, 1919-1939: An Introduction to the Study of International Relations,* London and New York: Harper Torchbooks.

Chinoy, S. (2022). "India-China Boundary Issues: A Primer", New Delhi: Parliament Library and Reference, Research, Documentation, and Information Service (LRRDIS).

CIA. The World Factbook, Terrorist Organizations, [Online: web], accessed 19 April, 2024 URL: https://www.cia.gov/the-world-factbook/references/terrorist-organiz actions/

Coll, Steve. (2018). *Directorate S: The C.I.A. and America's Secret Wars in Afghanistan and Pakistan, 2001-2016*, New Delhi: Penguin Random House UK & Thomson Press India Ltd.

Counter Terrorism. (2022). "Haqqani Network (HQN)", [Online: web] Accessed 19 April 2024. URL: https://www.dni.gov/nctc/ftos/hqn_fto.html

Dallgaard-Neilsen, A. (2008). "Studying Violent Radicalization in Europe I: The Potential Contribution of Social Movement Theory". Danish Institute for International Studies, DIIS Working Paper no 2008/2.

Dobbins, J. (2008). *After the Taliban: Nation-building in Afghanistan*, Virginia: Potomac Books, Inc.

Donelan, M. (1992), *Elements of International Political Theory*, USA: Oxford University Press.

Dunne, T. et al. (eds.). (2021). *International Relations Theories: Discipline and Diversity*, 3rd edition, USA: Oxford University Press.

Dunning, S. (2021). "China is Protecting its Thin Corridor to the Afghan Heartland", *Foreign Policy*, [Online: web], accessed 23 September 2022, URL: https://foreignpoli cy.com/2021/08/14/china-afghanistan-wakhan-corridor-imperial-ambitions/

Edwards, L. M. (2010). "State-building in Afghanistan: a case showing the limits?" *International Review of the Red Cross,* 92 (880), 967-991.

Emadi, H. (1997). "The Hazaras and their role in the process of political transformation in Afghanistan", *Central Asian Survey*, 16(3), 363-387.

Esposito, J. L. (ed.). (1999). *The Oxford History of Islam*, Oxford University Press.

Etilaatroz. (2019). "Ashraf Ghani: More Than 45 Thousand Afghan Security Forces Have Been Killed in the Last Four Years", [in Persian], [Online: web] aAccessed 19 April 2024, URL: https://www.etilaatroz.com/71728/more-than-45000-afghan-forces-have-been-killed-in-the-past-four-years/

Etilaatroz. (2020). "Ashraf Ghani signed an Order to Release 5000 Taliban Prisoners". [in Persian], [Online: web], accessed 23 March 2024, URL: https://www.etila atroz.com/94533/ashraf-ghani-signed-decree-on-release-of-5000-taliban-prison ers/

European Bank for Reconstruction and Development. (2022). "Belt and Road Initiative", [Online: web], accessed 30 July 2022. https://www.ebrd.com/what-we-do/belt-and-road/overview. html

Faghihi, A. A. (1998). *Wahhabis: An investigative study of the beliefs and history of the Wahhabi sect*, [in Persian], Tehran: Saba.

Farrall, L. (2017). "Revisiting Al-Qaida's Foundation and Early History", *Perspectives on Terrorism*, 11(6), 17-37.

Filkins, D. and Rubin, A. J. (2010). "Afghan Leader Admits His Office Gets Cash from Iran", *The New York Times*, [Online: web], accessed 12 October 2022, URL: https://www.nytim es.com/ 2010/10/26/world/asia/26afghan.html

Fredholm, M. (2011). "Kashmir, Afghanistan, India and Beyond: A Taxonomy of Islamic Extremism and Terrorism in Pakistan", *Himalayan and Central Asian Studies*, 15(3), 24.

Freeman, C. (2007). "Introduction: Security, governance and state building in Afghanistan", *International Peacekeeping*, 14(1), 1-7.

Freeman, C. (2007). "Introduction: Security, governance and state building in Afghanistan", *International Peacekeeping*, 14(1), 1-7.

Fukuyaman, F. (ed.). (2006). *Nation-Building: Beyond Afghanistan and Iraq*, Baltimore, MD: The John Hopkins University Press.

Gates, R. M. (1996) *From the Shadows: The Ultimate Insider's Story of Five Presidents and How They Won the Cold War*, New York: Simon and Schuster.

Giddens, A. (1990). *The Consequences of Modernity*, USA: Stanford University Press. California.

Giustozzi, A. (2019). *The Taliban at War: 2001-2021*, UK: Oxford University Press.

Goldstein, J. S. & Pevehouse, J. C. (2013-14). *International Relations*, 10th edn., New York: Pearson.

Goodhand, J. (2004). "From war economy to peace economy? Reconstruction and state building in Afghanistan", *Journal of International Affairs*, 58(1), 155-174.

Goodson, L. P. (2001). *Afghanistan's endless war: State failure, regional politics, and the rise of the Taliban*. University of Washington Press.

Grieco, J. M. (1997). "Realist International Theory and The Study of World Politics", *New Thinking in International Relations Theory*, 167-201.

Griffiths, M. (2021) *Realism, Idealism and International Politics*, New York and London: Routledge.

Gunaratna, R. (2005), "Al Qaeda's ideology. *Current Trends in Islamist Ideology"*, 1, 59-68.

Haghnavaz, J. (2013). "A brief history of Islam: The Spread of Islam", *International Journal of Business and Social Science*, 4(17).

Hanauer, L. & Chalk, P. (2012). "India's and Pakistan's Strategies in Afghanistan: Implications for the United States and the Region," RAND Corporation. [Online: web], óaccessed 12 December 2023 URL: http://www.jstor.org/stable/10.7249/j.ctt1q6105

Hawza News Agency. (2011). "Geopolitical Analysis of Afghanistan", [in Persian], [Online: web], accessed 9 March 2021, URL: https://noo.rs/OJLfK

Hazara Research Collective—Written Evidence (AFG0008), (2020). *"International Relations and Defence Committee: The UK and Afghanistan, Call for Evidence"*, Published by UK Parliament. [Online: web], óaccessed 12 December 2023, URL: https://committees.parliament.uk/writtenevidence/11165/pdf/

Henzel, C. (2005). "The origins of al-Qaeda's ideology: Implications for US strategy", *The US Army War College Quarterly: Parameters* 35(1), 8.

Hippler, J. (2005). *Nation-Building: A Key Concept for Peaceful Conflict Transformation,* London: Pluto Press.

Hizb ut-Tahrir—Afghanistan Province. (2024). "Introduction to Hizb ut-Tahrir", official website, [Online: web], accessed 4 April 2024, URL: http://hizb-afghanistan.o rg/to pic/aboutus.a spx?lang=dari

Hobsbawm, E. (1996). "Language, Culture, and National Identity", *Social Research*, 63(4), 1065–1080, [Online: web], accessed 23 November 2022, URL: http://www.jstor .org/stable/ 40971324

Holmes, D. & Dixon, N. (2001). *Behind the US war on Afghanistan*, Chippendale, New South Wales: Resistance Books.

Hosseini, R. 2009. "Shiites of Afghanistan: General information about Afghanistan". *Journal of Shiism*. No. 5 [in Persian], [Online: web], accessed 23 February 2024, URL: https://noo. rs/vPouf

Hussain, A. & Alami, K. E. (2005). *Faith Guides for Higher Education: A Guide to Islam*, Subject Centre for Philosophical and Religious Studies. UK: University of Leeds, Alden Group Limited, Oxford, reprinted 2007.

Husseini, S. M. (2019). *"From Pete Khazana to Panipat,"* Afghanistan Information

Network, [in Persian], [Online: web], accessed 3 March 2020, URL: https://www.afghanp ape r.com/nbody.php?id=160821

Hybel, A. R. (2013). *The power of ideology: from the Roman Empire to Al-Qaeda*, New York: Routledge.

Hyman, A. (2002). "Nationalism in Afghanistan", *International Journal of Middle East Studies*, 34(2), 299-315.

Hynek, N. & Marton, P. (2016). *Statebuilding in Afghanistan*, New York: Routledge.

Inaç, H. & Asefi, J. (2021). "The Discussion of Political Islam and Democracy in Afghanistan", *Turkish Journal of Policy Studies*, 1(1), 1-12.

Ismailov, E. & Papava, V. (2010). "Rethinking Central Eurasia", *Central Asia-Caucasus & Silk Road Studies Program, A Joint Transatlantic Research, and Policy Centre,* Johns Hopkins University, SAIS, pp 1-116, DOI: 10.2139/ssrn.2196485

Jahanmal, Z. (2019). "Afghan Saffron Ranked Best in the World for Eighth Year", *Tolonews*, [Online: web], accessed 24 December 2022, URL: tolonews.com/business/afghan-saffron-rank ed-best-world-eighth-year. 21 December 2019.

James, P. (1995). "Structural Realism and the Causes of War", *Mershon International Studies Review*, 39(2), 181–208. https://doi.org/10.2307/222750

Kamal, M. (2020). "Afghanistan-Pakistan-India relations: A paradoxical perspective", *Journal of the Punjab University Historical Society*, 33 (02), 69-89.

Kaplan, Robert D. (2001). *Soldiers of God: With Islamic Warriors in Afghanistan and Pakistan,* New York: First Vintage Departures Edition.

Keane, C. (2016). *US Nation Building in Afghanistan*, New York: Routledge.

Keohane, R. O. (1986). *Neorealism and its Critics*, New York: Columbia University Press.

Khalilzad, Z. "How to Nation-Build: Ten Lessons from Afghanistan," *The National Interest*, no. 80 (2005): 19–27.

Koulaei, E. (2006). "Shanghai and Central Asian Security", [in Persian], *Journal of Political Science Research*, (3), 29-46.

Krause, D. (2005). "Structures and structural realism", *Logic Journal of IGPL*, 13(1), 113-126.

Kullab, S. (2022). "China eyes investment in Afghanistan's Mes Aynak mines", *The Diplomat*, [Online: web], accessed 19 December 2022, URL: https://thediplomat.com/2022/03/china-eyes-investment-in-afghanistans-mes-aynak-mines/

Ladyman, J. (1998). "What is structural realism?", *Studies in History and Philosophy of Science Part A*, 29(3), 409-424.

Lake, D. (2010), "The Practice and Theory of US State-building", *Journal of Intervention and Statebuilding*, 4(3), 257-284.

Lamb, C. J. (2010), *Unity of effort: Key to success in Afghanistan*, Collingdale, PA: Diane Publishing.

Laub, Z. (2014). "The Taliban in Afghanistan. *Council on Foreign Relations"*, 4(7), 1-9.

Mahmoodi, Z. & Shafiee, N. (2010). "Shanghai Cooperation Organization: Nascent Safe Community", [in Persian], *Journal of Central Asian and Caucasian Studies*, 7 (3):1-33.

Mahmoudian, M. (2012). "The Impact of Neo-Salafists Thoughts on the Thinking-Ideological Trend of Al-Qaida", *Research Letter of Political Science*, 7(3), 79-114.

Malejacq, R. (2020). *Warlord survival: the delusion of state building in Afghanistan*, New York: Cornell University Press.

Maley, W. (2013), "State-building in Afghanistan: Challenges and Pathologies". *Central Asian Survey*, 32(3), 255-270.

Maley, W. (2018). *Transition in Afghanistan: Hope, despair and the limits of state-building*, New York: Routledge.

Mansoor, H. et al. (2015). *The Resignation of Wisdom*, [in Persian], Kabul: Jamiatfeker.

Mansoor, H. (2018). "Black and White: Afghanistan's Constitutions Discussion", Kabul, *Tolo News*, [Online: web], accessed 12 October 2022, URL: https:// www.youube. com/watch?v =qtbpHqbZiF8&t=601s

Mapping Militant Organizations. (2017). "Haqqani Network",[Online: web], accessed 19 April 2024, URL: https://web.stanford.edu/group/ mappingmilitants/cgi-bin/groups/pri ntview/36 3

March, A. F. (2015). "Political Islam: Theory", *Annual Review of Political Science*, 18(1), 103–123. https: //doi.org/10.1146/annurev-polisci-082112-14125 0

Mearsheimer, J. J. (1994). "The False Promise of International Institutions", *International Security*, 19(3), 5–49, DOI: https://doi.org/10.2307/2539078

Mehrin, N. (2012). A study of the Democratic Republic of Afghanistan, Deutsche Welle, [in Persian], [Online: web], accessed 17 February 2020, URL: https:/ /www.dw. com /fa-af/

Milani, M. M, (2006). "Iran's policy towards Afghanistan," *The Middle East Journal*, 60(2), 235-279.

Misra, A. (2002). "The Taliban, Radical Islam and Afghanistan", *Third World Quarterly*, 23(3), 577-589.

Moinifar, H. S. & Kheiri, M. (2011). "Role and Effect of Wahhabism in Chechnya's Crisis", [in Persian], *Central Eurasia Studies*, 4(7): 151-170.

Monten, J. (2014). "Intervention and state-building: comparative lessons from Japan, Iraq, and Afghanistan", *The Annals of the American Academy of Political and Social Science*, 656(1), 173-191.

Morgenthau, H. (1948). *Politics Among Nations: The Struggle for Power and Peace*, New York: McGraw Hill.

Morgenthau, H. J. (2014). A Realist Theory of International Politics, in *The realism reader* (pp. 53-59), Routledge.

Mosaqi, S. A. (2007). *Contemporary Islamic Movements*, [in Persian], Tehran: Allameh Tabatabai University Publishing Centre, 10th edn.

Moshirzadeh, H. (2013). *Development in International Relations Theories*, [in Persian], Tehran: The Centre for Studying and Compiling University Books in Humanities (SAMT).

Mostaqeemi, B. & Ebrahimi, N. (2010). "Fundamentals and concepts of Al-Qaeda's political Islam", [in Persian], *Journal of the Faculty of Law and Political Science*, 40(3), 337-355.

Mousavi, S. M. (2011). *Typology of Islamic Movements in the 20th Century*, Tehran: Payam-e-Noor University.

Mozaffari, M. (2007). "What is Islamism? History and definition of a concept", *Totalitarian Movements and Political Religions* 8(1), 17-33.

Muhammad, M. E. (2020). "Social Contract Theories of Hobbes, Locke, and Rousseau: An Extrapolation of Point of Harmony and Tensions", *Educational Resurgence Journal.* 2(4):123-128.

Najafi, A. F. (2003). "The Ideological Foundations of Al-Qaeda and Wahhabism", *Strategy,* 11(1): 232-256, [in Persian], [Online: web], accessed 17 March 2021, URL: https://en.civilica.com/doc/1350063/

Nader, A. et al. (2014). *Iran's influence in Afghanistan: Implications for the U.S. drawdown*, RAND [Online: web], accessed 20 September, 2021, URL: https://www.rand.org/pubs/resear chreports/RR616.html#citation

Nazari, J. & Akbari, M. (2014). "How does Jamiat Islah Radicalize the Students of Afghan universities?" *Hasht-e-Subh daily,* [in Persian], [Online: web] accessed 4 April. 2020, URL: https://8am.media/fa/university-students-afghan istan-jamiate-eslah-extre mis t/

Nehru, J. (2004). *Glimpses of World History*, Penguin, UK.

Neumann, A. R. E. (2009). *The other war: winning and losing in Afghanistan*, vol. 32, Virginia: Potomac Books, Inc.

Nixon, H. (2008). *Subnational state-building in Afghanistan*, Kabul: Afghanistan Research and Evaluation Unit.

Nixon, H. & Ponzio, R. (2007), "Building democracy in Afghanistan: The state building agenda and international engagement", *International Peacekeeping*, 14(1), 26-40.

Obo, U. B. & Coker, M. A. (2014). "The Marxist Theory of the State: An Introductory Guide", *Mediterranean Journal of Social Sciences*, 5(4), 527-533.

Olesen, A. (2013). *Islam & Politics Afghanistan,* New York: Routledge.

Psillos, S. (2001), "Is structural realism possible?" *Philosophy of Science*, 68(S3), S13-S24.

Quadri, J. (2012), *Ijtihad*, Oxford Bibliographies, [Online: web] accessed 23 April 2024, URL:https://www.oxfordbibliographies.com/display/document/obo-97801 95390155/ obo-9780 195390155-0096.xml

Qutb, Sayed. (2016). *Milestones*, Translated by Mahmoud Mahmoudi, Kabul: Freelance Publications.

Rahimi, M. R. (2014). *Deconstructing the official discourse of state formation in Afghanistan*, Ph.D. thesis, Colchester: University of Essex, translated by Rahimi, M. R. (2021-22), Kabul: Amiri Publication.

Rashid, A. (2002), *Taliban: Islam, oil and the new great game in Central Asia*, London: IB Tauris.

Rashid, A. (2012). "*Descent into chaos: how the war against Islamic extremism is being lost in Pakistan, Afghanistan and Central Asia*, UK: Penguin.

Riedel, B. (2010). *The Search for al Qaeda: Its Leadership, Ideology, and Future*, Maryland: Rowman & Littlefield.

Riphenburg, C. J. (2005). "Ethnicity and civil society in contemporary Afghanistan", *The Middle East Journal*, 59(1), 31-51.

Roy, O. (1990). *Islam and resistance in Afghanistan*, vol. 8, UK: Cambridge University Press.

Roy, O. (1994). *The failure of political Islam*, Cambridge, MA: Harvard University Press.

Rubin, B. R. (1992). Political elites in Afghanistan: Rentier state building, rentier state wrecking. *International Journal of Middle East Studies*, 24(1), 77-99.

Rubin, M. (2002). "Who is responsible for the Taliban", *Middle East Review of International Affairs*, 6(1), 1-16.

Salleh, M. F. (2015). *"Introduction to Islam"*, University Selangor, [Online: web], accessed 13 March. 2021, URL: https://www.researchgate.net/publication/2835 37017_Introduction_ to_IslamDOI:10.13140/RG.2.1.1403.0801

Sandal, N. & Fox, J. (2013). *Religion in International Relations Theory: Interactions and Possibilities*, New York and London: Routledge.

Sawaqib, J. (2013). "The Process of Transformation of the School of Textualism and Principals", *Research Journal of Islamic History*. [in Persian], Tehran, Iran. pp. 35-79

Sbesta. (2020). "Profiling the World's Top Five Countries in Electricity Consumption", *NS Energy*, [Online: web], accessed 14 December 2022, URL: https://www.nsenergy business.com/features/electricity-consuming-countries/#:~:text=1.,renewable% 20sources%20in %20re cent%20years

Shahrani, N. M. (2002). "War, factionalism, and the state in Afghanistan", *American Anthropologist* 104(3), 715-722.

Shalinsky, A. C. (1982). "Islam and Ethnicity: The Northern Afghanistan Perspective", *Central Asian Survey*, 1(2-3), 71-83.

Shalizi, H. (2010). "Karzai Says his Office Gets 'Bags of Money' from Iran", *Reuters,* 25 October 2010, [Online: web], accessed 12 October 2022, URL :https://www.reuters .com/article/us-afghanistan-karzaiidUSTRE69O27Z20101025/

Shukla, A. (2011). "Pakistan's Quest for Strategic Depth: Regional Security Implications", *Himalayan and Central Asian Studies*, 15(3), 81.

Simonsen, S. G. (2004). "Ethnicising Afghanistan? inclusion and exclusion in post Bonn institution building," *Third World Quarterly*, 25(4), 707-729.

Singer, M. (2018). "Militant Islam's War Against the West", Begin-Sadat Centre for Strategic Studies, pp. 7-35.

Sinno, A. H. (2010). "The strategic use of Islam in Afghan politics", *Religion and Politics in South Asia*, 25-44.

Smith, A. D. (1998). *Nationalism and Modernism: A Critical Survey of Recent Theories of Nations and Nationalism,* London: Routledge.

Stobdan, P. (1999). "The Afghan Conflict and Regional Security", *Strategic Analysis: A Monthly Journal of the IDSA,* 23(5), [Online: web] aAccessed 14 August 2022, URL: https://ciaotest.cc.columbia.edu/olj/sa/sa_99stp02.html

Suhrke, A. (2013). "Statebuilding in Afghanistan: a contradictory engagement," *Central Asian Survey*, 32(3), 271-286.

Swenson, G. (2017). "Why US efforts to promote the rule of law in Afghanistan failed", *International Security*, 42(1), 114-151.

Tartakovsky, E. (2010). "National Identity", Chapter in *Encyclopaedia of*

Adolescence, Tel Aviv, Israel: The Bob Shapell School of Social Work, Tel Aviv University.

Taraki, R. (2010). "BBC—Pargar: Afghanistan and the National Government Project", [Online: web], accessed 23 December 2022, URL: https://www.youtube.com/watch ?v=fGGGdNG6 CqY&t= 7s

Tarzi, A. (2012). "Islam and Constitutionalism in Afghanistan", *Journal of Persianate Studies*, 5(2), 205-243.

Teschke, B. G. (1999). "*The making of the Westphalian state-system: Social property relations, geopolitics and the myth of 1648,*" UK: London School of Economics and Political Science.

Thomas, P. (1791). "*Definition of a Constitution,*" University of Michigan Library, [Online: web], accessed 12 October 2022, URL: https://quod.lib.umich.edu/e/ecco/004780 831.0001.000/1:2?rg n=div1;view=fulltext

Tibi, B. (2014)., "*Political Islam, World politics and Europe: From jihadist to institutional Islamism*, New York: Routledge.

Tibi, B. (2023). *The challenge of fundamentalism: Political Islam and the new world disorder*, vol. 9, California: University of California Press.

Tomsen, P. (2013). "*The wars of Afghanistan: Messianic terrorism, tribal conflicts, and the failures of great powers*, UK: Hachette.

Uddin, S. S. (2017). "Existence of External Forces in Afghanistan: Pakistan's Security Dilemma Since 9/11," *International Journal of Asian Social Science*, 7(4), 311-319.

USIP. (2017). "The Jihadi Threat ISIS, al-Qaeda, and Beyond", *United States Institute of Peace Wilson Centre.*

Venkatraman, A. (2007). "Religious basis for Islamic Terrorism: The Quran and its Interpretations," *Studies in Conflict & Terrorism*, 30(3), 229-248.

Votsis, I. (2005). "The upward path to structural realism", *Philosophy of Science*, 72(5), 1361-1372.

Waltz, K. (1979). "*Theory of International Politics,* London: Addison-Wesley Publishing Company.

Waltz, K. N. (2001). "*Man, the State, and War,*" New York: Columbia University Press.

Woltering, R. A. (2002). "The roots of Islamist popularity", *Third World Quarterly*, 23(6), 1133-1143.

Wu, Z. (2018). "Classical Geopolitics, Realism and the Balance of Power Theory", *Journal of Strategic Studies*, 41(6), 786-823.

Xiangyu, Z. (2011). "Afghanistan and regional security: Implications for China", *Policy Perspectives*, 65-72.

Yadav, V. & Barwa, C. (2011). "Relational control: India's grand strategy in Afghanistan and Pakistan", *India Review*, 10(2), 93-125.

Yazdanpanah, D. K. (2010). "Shanghai Cooperation Organization and US Security Reasons", [in Persian], *Journal of Human Geography Research.* 1 (2):53-61.

Zaman, R & Mohammadi, A. A. (2014). "Trends in Student Radicalization, Acors University campuses in Afghanistan," *Afghan Institute for Strategic Studies*, AISS- P-002-2014.

Primary Source

Afghanistan Constitution (2004) Chapter one, Article 4.

Agreement on Provisional Arrangements in Afghanistan Pending the Re-establishment of Permanent Government Institutions. (2001). UN Doc. S/2001/1154. United Nations Security Council.

Ahmadzai, A. G. (2013). "Interview with 1 TV, on 11 November 2013", [Online: web], accessed 13 January 2020, URL: https://www.youtube.com/watch?v=KPvNdLpfHt U

Anas, A. (2024). Personal interview. Date of interview [Zoom] 28 April 2024.

Anas, A., (2016). Personal interview, Kabul, Afghanistan, 16 October 2016.

Government of India (2009). *India and Afghanistan: A Development Partnership*, Ministry of External Affairs, New Delhi.

Government of India (2021). *India-Afghanistan—A Historic and Time-Tested Friendship*, Ministry of External Affairs, New Delhi.

Government of the United States of America (2007). *Agreement for Cooperation Between the Government of The United States of America and the Government of India: Concerning Peaceful Uses of Nuclear Energy*, "123 Agreement", US Department of State, [Online: web] aAccessed 23 November 2022, URL: https://2001-2009.state.Gov/secretary/rm/2008/10/110916.htm*and*https://2009-2017.state .gov/documents/organ ization/122068.pdf

Human Rights, Terrorism and Counter-Terrorism, (2007). Office of the United Nations High Commissioner for Human Rights, Published by the Peace and Security Section of the Department of Public Information – DPO/2439B/Rev.2.

Islamic Emirate of Afghanistan. (2024). "IEA-Foreign Minister Mawlawi Amir Khan Muttaqi held a telephonic conversation with Ismail Haniyeh, the head of the political wing of the HAMAS movement, in order to offer him condolences over the martyrdom of his children and family members", [Online: web], accessed 19 April 2024, URL: https://mfa.Gov.af/ en/16665

Jihadi and Scientific Biography of Mawlawi Jalaluddin Haqqani. (2020). *Official*

Taliban Website, Alemarah - Dari. [Online: web] accessed 19 April 2024, URL:https://www.alemarahdari.af/articles-and-views/%D8%B2%D9%86%D8 %AF%DA%AF%DB%8C%E2%80%8C%D9%86%D8%A7%D9 %85%D9%87-%D8%B4%D8%AE%D8%B5% DB%8C%D8%AA-%D8%A8%D8%B2% D8%B1%DA%AF-%D8%AC%D9%87%D8%A7%D8%AF%DB%8C-%D9%88-%D8%B9%D9 %84%D9%85%DB%8C-%D8%AC% D9%87/

Kasuri, K. M. (2015)' *Neither a Hawk nor a Dove: An Insider's Account of Pakistan's Foreign Policy*, UK: Penguin.

Nikbeen, M. S. (2024). email to author. Date of interview 26 April 2024.

Pew Research Centre (2009). *"Mapping the Global Muslim Population: A report on the size and Distribution of the World's Muslim Population"*, Pew Forum on Religion & Public Life, Washington, D.C.

Perez, F. H. (2007). "The Wandering Mujahidin: Armed and Dangerous". *United States Department of State, Bureau of Intelligence and Research*. p. 2.

Security Council, In Presidential Statement. "Reiterates Grave Concern at Afghanistan Conflict, Condemns Taliban for New Offensives (2000), UN Doc. SC/684, 20000407

Special Inspector General for Afghanistan Reconstruction. (2024), *Cash Shipments to Afghanistan: The UN Has Purchased and Transported More than $2.9 Billion to Afghanistan to Implement Humanitarian Assistance*, SIGAR 24-12 Evaluation Report.

The New Swiss Constitution, Inter-Parliamentary Union, No. 179-1st Half-year 2000/ASGP Review.

The Young Turks. (2021). "Hillary Clinton's Old Afghanistan Prediction Goes Viral", [Online: web], accessed 19 April 2024 URL: https://www.youtube.com/watc h?v= vlbZt56qv18

UN Press Release, SC/6841. (2007). Security Council, In Presidential Statement, Reiterates Grave Concern at Afghanistan Conflict, Condemns Taliban for New Offensives. [Online: web] accessed 14 March 2020, URL: https://www.un.org/pres s/en/2000/200 00407.sc6841.doc.html

UNAMA. (2021). "Civilian Casualties Set to Hit Unprecedented Highs in 2021 Unless Urgent Action to Stem Violence–UN Report", Press Release.

World Islamic Front Statement. (1998). "Jihad Against Jews and Crusaders," *Al-Quds Al-Arabi,* [Online: web], accessed 30 March 2024, URL: https://irp.fas.org/wo rld /para/d ocs/980 223-fatwa.htm

Index